A Life Well Danced

ABOUT THE AUTHOR

Jane Gall Spooner trained in classical ballet with Maria Zybina in Beckenham, Kent. Deciding against becoming a professional dancer, she earned degrees in Geology and Environmental Resources from the Universities of Manchester and Salford, and enjoyed a long career as a consultant in the minerals industry. Jane's research into Zybina's life and the lives of Zybina's teachers has been an absorbing exploration of their legacy. Jane makes her home in Toronto, Canada.

A Life Well Danced

MARIA ZYBINA'S RUSSIAN HERITAGE

Her Legacy of Classical Ballet and Character Dance Across Europe

Jane Gall Spooner

Historical Memoir, Emigration, Classical Ballet Pedagogy,
European Character Dance, Women's History.

Matador
Unit E2 Airfield Business Park
Harrison Road, Market Harborough,
Leicestershire. LE16 7UL
Tel: 0116 279 2299
Email: books@troubador.co.uk
Web: www.troubador.co.uk/matador
Twitter: @matadorbooks

ISBN 978 1 80313 482 6

British Library Cataloguing in Publication Data.
A catalogue record for this book is available from the British Library.

Printed and bound by CPI Group (UK) Ltd, Croydon, CR0 4YY
Typeset in 11pt Minion Pro by Troubador Publishing Ltd, Leicester, UK

Matador is an imprint of Troubador Publishing Ltd

In memory of Maria Zybina with love and gratitude.

TABLE OF CONTENTS

LIST OF ILLUSTRATIONS

PREFACE

This book would not even have been thought of without Katherine Mason and Christine Stripp, my friends and fellow ballet students at Maria Zybina's school. As my research into Zybina's life gathered momentum, they have given me great support and encouragement. Since Katherine's parents were close friends of Zybina and her family, her help and insight, and review of her own family documents, have been invaluable. I am indebted to Zybina's daughter, Tamara Jakasha, and her family for discussion on family history and access to documents, and for their generous hospitality at their home near Milan. I very much appreciate, also, the assistance and guidance of those who have read my drafts, in particular Jane Hill, Christopher Lattanzi, Katherine Mason, Selma Landen Odom, Anna Paliy and Christine Stripp, and my editor Elisabeth Dobson. But research and writing would not have been possible without the following who were especially helpful as each new piece of information built upon the rest, some of whom shared their own memories and photographs: Leonard Bartle, centre administrator and custodian, National Arts Education Archive; Patsy Beech, custodian of John Gregory's papers relating to the Harlequin Ballet Company; Moya Vahey Beynon, chairman of the Legat Foundation; Patricia Deane-Gray MBE, whose tape-recorded interview with Zybina provided key details; Claire Faraci; Michael Finnissy; my parents, the late Anne and David Gall, who supported my ballet training and my ambition to dance; Vida Grosl; Jill Lhotka, whose interest and encouragement over so many years has been invaluable; Linda Maybarduk, who gave early reassurance that this was an idea worth pursuing; Selma Odom, who has been endlessly helpful and encouraging; Katherine Mason's cousin, the late Donne Parsons; Cheryl

Schildknecht; Davor Schopf; my family, Amy, Rosemary and Edward Spooner; and the late Dawn Tudor. Others, too many to name, have also assisted. And although Kevin Pugh, my ballet teacher of the last twenty years and more, has not been involved in this project, his inspiring classes have allowed me to think about and appreciate Zybina's training, and her training with Nicolai Legat.

Transliteration of Russian personal and place names can be problematic. Since this is not an academic work, I have favoured the versions that are in widespread use, or were in use in England during the time when Nicolai Legat had his studio, or which were used by the individuals themselves when in England. As a result, there are instances where the spelling of siblings' or cousins' names differ. Similarly, I have not been pedantic in translating the names of all of Marius Petipa's ballets, but have used the version by which they are well known. Transliteration of Serbian and Croatian personal names may also result in a variety of spellings, with or without diacritical marks, in English sources. I have generally used the Serbian or Croatian form for ease of reference.

The Julian calendar was used in Russia until February 1918, when the western Gregorian calendar was formally adopted. Unless otherwise noted, dates in Russia are given in the Julian "old style". Dates in the Julian calendar are twelve days earlier than the Gregorian calendar in the nineteenth century, and thirteen days earlier between March 1900 and February 1918.

Zybina lived and worked in Yugoslavia before the unified federation of republics and provinces broke apart following the death of Marshal Tito in 1980. Here the term Yugoslavia is used to describe the entire country while reference is made to individual republics, as appropriate.

Every attempt has been made to ensure that inaccuracies or outright errors are as few as possible.

CHAPTER 1
BEHIND THE STORIES

Legat with delicate hand adjusts an erring movement,
directs the exercises, or accompanies them with an endless
variety of original tunes on the piano or violin.
Sir Paul Dukes, foreword to "The Story of the Russian School".

Maria Zybina was my first ballet teacher, with whom I trained for a decade until my late teens. Inspired by some chance events, my journey to understand more about her life and the lives of the people who most influenced her as a teacher of classical ballet in the Russian style has entailed much research while bringing moments of delight and great personal satisfaction. This first chapter of the resulting book gives an overview of the scope of the materials reviewed to give context for the bibliography provided at the close.

Bibliographic sources are divided into the general categories of family documents/personal archives and oral history; published memoirs; biographies and historical studies; dance journals; dance encyclopedia; specialist archives; and online material. Given the influences of Zybina's teachers and the circumstances of her life, these relate broadly to classical ballet in St Petersburg, Russia, in the second half of the nineteenth century and into the early 1920s, to the development of ballet in Yugoslavia, and to material relating to Zybina's school in the London suburb of Beckenham in Kent. Since a number of her close friends worked in intelligence during the Second World War, material relating to the activities of the British Special Operations Executive in Yugoslavia has also been consulted.

Zybina's teachers all came from the Russian classical system of the second half of the nineteenth century so it has been of particular interest to locate first-hand accounts of how ballet masters like Christian Johansson and Nicolai Legat taught their classes in order to identify any similarities with Zybina's own. Although she was already dancing professionally by the time she studied with Legat in London, he was an important influence on her as a teacher. In the same way, since preservation of the heritage of character dance (in this context, Russian and European national dance) was so important to her, material which references teaching and performance of character dance has been sought.

An interview with Zybina was tape-recorded around 1980 by Patricia Deane-Gray MBE during the course of Deane-Gray's research for a biography on the Croatian ballerina and teacher Ana Roje. Deane-Gray's interview has provided the framework for much of this book and is the source of many of the quotes. Despite shortcomings of poor audio quality, Zybina describes how her family left Russia at the end of 1918; her early ballet training with Evgenia Eduardova in Berlin; her first marriage to Hugh Pearse; her advanced training in Belgrade with Elena Poliakova; her first meeting with Ana Roje; and how both she and Roje came to London to study with Legat. The interview also provided the starting point for the gathering of my own memories of my time at Zybina's school and has guided much of my research.

The interview is complemented by documents provided by Zybina's daughter, Tamara Jakasha, and oral history relating to the Zybina and Jakasha families. Tamara allowed review of photographs, passports and identification papers, and provided information on portions of a diary written by Zybina between August 1926 and March 1927. My fellow classmates at Zybina's school in Beckenham, Katherine Mason, Cheryl Schildknecht and Christine Stripp, supplemented my collection of photographs and news clippings with their own photographs and programmes. Our memories, spanning approximately ten years between the second half of the 1950s and the late 1960s, were added to by Tamara and by Claire Faraci, who trained with Zybina a few years before us. Claire also passed on memories of her time at the school run by Ana Roje and her partner and husband Oskar Harmoš at Kaštel Kambelovac, Croatia, in the early 1950s. Jill Lhotka attended the Legat School led by Legat's widow, Nadine Nicolaeva-Legat, as well as the school at Kaštel Kambelovac. While she describes those times in her memoir, "Dance to the Challenge" (2013), she shared many insights with me both before and after its publication. Zybina wrote a series of articles on character dance in the *Dancing Times* in 1963 and 1964. These convey her depth of knowledge and served as useful *aides-memoires* for dances that she taught her students and which were performed over a period of some twenty-five years between the early 1950s and late 1970s. Katherine Mason's parents were friends of Zybina in Belgrade before the war, and remained so when both they and Zybina moved to Beckenham in the late 1940s. She has shared family material relating to their time in Belgrade and also given important insight regarding my research into the Special Operations Executive.

Memoirs have been of particular interest because they provide first-hand and often moving accounts of the lives of ballet dancers, students, teachers and choreographers in Russia from around 1875 into the early 1920s. Unmistakable for its wit and humour, captured in Sir Paul Dukes's translation of the manuscript, Legat's own voice is heard through his memoir, "The Story of the Russian School" (1932), later expanded and republished after his death as "Ballet Russe" (1939), and his articles for the *Dancing Times* in England in the 1920s and 1930s on aspects of ballet technique, as well as three on character dances. Equally witty and humorous are the caricatures drawn by Legat with his younger brother, Sergei, and published in St Petersburg between 1902 and 1905 as "Русскій балетъ въ каррикатурахъ", "The Russian Ballet in Caricatures". Finely observed, they provide a unique perspective on the leading dancers of the day, including Zybina's earlier teachers, Evgenia Eduardova, Elena Poliakova and Olga Preobrazhenskaya, and her fellow examiners in the Federation of Russian Classical Ballet, Tamara Karsavina and Mathilde Kschessinskaya. Published in 2021, the memoir of Nadine Nicolaeva-Legat, "The Legat Story", brings to light some details not contained in her books and articles.

Certain sources have been constant companions throughout the writing and researching of this book. John Gregory danced with the Anglo-Polish Ballet and with Ballets Jooss but his life's work became the fostering of the teaching of ballet in the Russian classical style that was exemplified by Legat. Among the results were his biography, "The Legat Saga" (1992), and the writing of a number of articles in both the *Dancing Times* and *Dance and Dancers*. "The Legat Saga" has a wealth of detail on Legat's family background and his career as a dancer, choreographer and teacher. Gregory draws on Russian sources as well as on Legat's unpublished notes for this work. Gregory was the co-author of "Heritage of a Ballet Master: Nicolas Legat" (1978) with André Eglevsky, who studied with Legat in London and was a soloist with the Ballet Russe de Monte Carlo, and later with both American Ballet Theatre and New York City Ballet. The biography, "Ana Roje" (2009), by Davor Schopf and Mladen Mordej Vučković, has provided invaluable information on her life and that of Oskar Harmoš. Schopf has kindly provided further details on Harmoš's life and work.

In addition to Legat's "The Story of the Russian School", are a number of key memoirs which also provide first-hand insight into the ballet company of the Mariinsky Theatre and the Imperial Theatre School in pre-revolutionary St Petersburg. Karsavina's "Theatre Street" (1930) is well known and well loved, but "Early Memoirs" (1981) by her slightly younger contemporary, Bronislava Nijinska, sister of Vaslav Nijinsky and choreographer for Serge Diaghilev's Ballets Russes, is even more detailed. Mathilde Kschessinskaya (the Princess Romanovsky-Krassinsky) in "Dancing in Petersburg" (1960), and Lydia Kyasht in "Romantic Recollections" (1929), write more of themselves than do Karsavina and Nijinska, but their stories are integral to Legat's. In "A Century of Russian Ballet, Documents and Eyewitness Accounts, 1810–1910" (1990), John Roland Wiley provides observations from a number of Legat's contemporaries and colleagues.

In his "Reminiscences of the Russian Ballet" (1941) Alexandre Benois describes the inspiration for and inception of the abandoned production of "Sylvia", which Legat and his brother Sergei were to have choreographed, and "The Fairy Doll", which was successfully choreographed by them. The choreographer and ballet master Michel (Mikhail) Fokine saw Legat as old-fashioned and reactionary, but his comments in "Fokine, Memoirs of a Ballet Master" (1961), add perspective on Legat's teaching, and on others in the theatre and the school. Important, too, have been the memoirs of Marius Petipa, the choreographer of "La Bayadère", "The Sleeping Beauty" and "Swan Lake", and of the Italian ballet master, Enrico Cecchetti.

Among the biographies, Gennady Albert's work on the twentieth-century Russian teacher Alexander Pushkin, "Alexander Pushkin: Master Teacher of Dance" (2001), has an important chapter on Legat's position as the link between Christian Johansson in the nineteenth century and Pushkin and Agrippina Vaganova in the twentieth. Anatole Bourman's thoughtful biography of his classmate, "The Tragedy of Nijinsky" (1936), provides insight into Legat's relationship with the young Vaslav Nijinsky. Elvira Roné's "Olga Preobrazhenskaya" (1978) draws on her own knowledge of that ballerina's life as a dancer and teacher. Coryne Hall's biography of Kschessinskaya, "Imperial Dancer", provides detail on this major figure in the Mariinsky Theatre that is complementary to Kschessinskaya's own memoir. "Alexander Shiryaev: Master of Movement" (2009), edited by Birgit Beumers, Victor Bocharov and David Robinson, is biographical and contains much information on the people who surrounded him, as well as Shiryaev's previously unpublished memoir; related is Bocharov's documentary film, "A Belated Premiere" (2003), on Shiryaev's stop-motion films.

There is nothing of comparable detail relating to Zybina's teachers, Eduardova in Berlin and Poliakova in Belgrade. The story of Eduardova's life after she left Russia is described by Marion Kant in "Joseph Lewitan and the Nazification of Dance in Germany" in "The Art of Being Jewish in Modern Times" (2008), and in Kant's work with Lilian Karina, "Hitler's Dancers: German Modern Dance and the Third Reich" (2003). Johanna Laakkonen's "Canon and Beyond. Edvard Fazer and the Imperial Russian Ballet 1908–1910" (2009) is an invaluable record of the tours organised by Fazer in 1908–1910 of the company known as the Imperial Russian Ballet. Drawing on contemporary material published in the cities visited on those tours, Laakkonen presents accounts of performances by the dancers including Eduardova.

Material on Poliakova is sparse. A contemporary of Karsavina at the Imperial Theatre School and a principal dancer with Diaghilev's Ballets Russes, she is referenced in Karsavina's "Theatre Street", in Andrew R. Foster's "Tamara Karsavina: Diaghilev's Ballerina" (2010) and "The Dictionary of Women Worldwide: 25,000 Women Through the Ages" (2006) and is mentioned in the archives of the Belgrade National Theatre. A short obituary appeared in the *Dancing Times* of February 1973. Details of performances of Poliakova, and of Margarita and Maximilian Froman (Frohman) with Diaghilev's Ballets Russes, are given by Fokine in his memoir; by Sergei Grigoriev in "The Diaghilev Ballet, 1909–1929" (1953); by Lynn Garafola in "Diaghilev's Ballets Russes" (1989) and "Legacies of Twentieth-Century Dance" (2005); by Garafola and Nancy Van Norman Baer in "The Ballets Russes and Its World" (1999); and by Nesta Macdonald in "Diaghilev Observed by Critics in England and the United States 1911–1929" (1975). Viktor I. Kosik's review, "Russian Masters of Ballet on the Belgrade Scene in the XX and Early XXI Centuries" (2017), and Melita Milin's "The Russian Musical Emigration in Yugoslavia after 1917" (2002), together with Nadežda Mosusova's "The Heritage of the Ballet Russe in Yugoslavia Between the Two World Wars" (1988) and "Are Folkloric Ballets an Anachronism Today?" (2002), have provided useful biographic details on Russian *émigrés* to Yugoslavia, their contribution to the development of dance in Yugoslavia, and the choreography of ballets based on folk themes.

Joan Lawson's 1986 translation of "Osnovy kharakternogo tantsa" ("The Fundamentals of Character Dance") (1939) by Andrei Lopoukhov, Alexander Shiryaev and Alexander Bocharov, as "Character Dance", and Jürgen Pagel's "Character Dance" (1984), have been welcome references on Russian and European national dances. Both give *barre* and centre exercises that are very similar to the ones taught by Zybina.

A wealth of information has been published by the *Dancing Times* in London from the time of the First World War, when Legat first came to England, to the late 1970s when Zybina retired from teaching at her school. Advertisements for ballet studios and news items have helped to confirm when and where teachers were active, as have notes on dancers and performances written by "Sitter Out" (P.J.S. Richardson OBE, editor of the *Dancing Times* for nearly fifty years). Detailed articles by Karsavina on the dancers and teachers of the Mariinsky, and on her later tours, extend the scope of "Theatre Street". The magazine *Dance and Dancers* was also reviewed but, because of its editorial focus, it is the source of relatively few, albeit important, relevant articles. Nadine Nicolaeva-Legat gives significant information in her articles for the magazine *Ballet* on "How I Came to England" in January–February and March 1951. The *Journal of the Society for Dance Research* yielded an article on Pietro Coronelli, an early ballet master in Zagreb, and the memoirs of Vladimir Teliakovsky, the director of the Mariinsky Theatre between 1901 and 1917.

An important reference work has been the comprehensive "International Encyclopedia of Dance", edited by Selma Jeanne Cohen, with its authoritative entries on individual dance artists and choreographers, and on countries, including Yugoslavia. It has been especially useful for information on individuals, such as Christian Johansson, for whom there is a paucity of other material available in English. The "Hrvatski biografski leksikon" has provided profiles on dancers in Croatia.

While care must be exercised in consulting Wikipedia, often those articles provided the starting point in the search for other sources. Online material has burgeoned in the past twenty years and has been particularly valuable for websites such as that hosted by the Petipa Society, and for serious historical research which may not be accessible in original sources (for example, the articles on dance in Yugoslavia by Kosik, Milin and Mosusova). Historical descriptions based on archival material are available online for theatres such as the Mariinsky in St Petersburg and the National Theatres in Zagreb and Belgrade. It was possible to study with ease performances posted online of the Legat brothers' ballet "The Fairy Doll", by the Vaganova Academy in St Petersburg, and of the opera "Ero the Joker" by the Croatian National Theatre in Belgrade. A subscription to Ancestry.com has been particularly helpful for chronological details, while the searchable records of the *London Gazette* have provided information on military ranks and honours.

My research on the activities of Zybina's friends who worked with the Special Operations Executive during the Second World War has also focused on first-hand accounts and memoirs. Sources include Roderick Bailey's "Forgotten Voices of the Secret War, an Inside History of Special Operations During the Second World War" (2008), Flavia Kingscote's "Balkan Exit" (1942), Bickham Sweet-Escott's "Baker Street Irregular" (1965) and Edward Wharton-Tigar's "Burning Bright" (1987). The BBC documentary "The Sword and the Shield" (1984), on SOE activities in Yugoslavia, includes interviews with Zybina's close friend Duane Tyrrel Hudson OBE and a number of his colleagues who also wrote about their experiences in Yugoslavia, as well as contemporary film footage. Although Hudson did not leave a memoir, the archives of the Imperial War Museum, London, are an important source of background material on him (IWM document reference 12691). More general works include M.R.D. Foot's "SOE An Outline History of the Special Operations Executive 1940–46" (1984), which has a section on SOE endeavours in Yugoslavia, and Malcolm Atkin's "Section D for Destruction: Forerunner of SOE" (2018), which has short profiles of a number of SOE agents, including Hudson and Katherine Mason's father, William Morgan.

CHAPTER 2
HALF-FORGOTTEN MEMORIES

... the art of [the dancer] cannot be recorded on canvas or on paper; it lives in our bodies and in our hearts...

Nicolai Legat, "The Story of the Russian School".

The telling of this story began as a light-hearted exploration of my ballet heritage, my ballet "roots". It was sparked by an unexpected virtual reunion with Christine Stripp (*née* Tout), a former classmate at Maria Zybina's ballet school, and the realisation that, through Zybina's own principal teacher, Nicolas, or Nicolai Legat, a pupil of Pavel Gerdt and Christian Johansson in St Petersburg, Russia, I was separated from the great Imperial Russian classical ballet tradition of the late nineteenth century by only two generations. The renewed contact with Christine came about as she was searching one of the early social networking websites for someone else at my secondary school and came across my brief profile.

> "Do you remember me?" she emailed – we had not seen or heard of each other for something like thirty-five years. "Of course, I remember you," I responded. "I think of you often because I use wide elastic for my ballet shoes, just as you did."

That started an exchange of "Do you remember...?" But we quickly appreciated that we really did not know a great deal about our much-loved teacher beyond that she was Russian, was a student of Legat, had been ballet mistress to the ballet company in Split, Yugoslavia, and, at some point, had moved to England and started her own school in the London suburb of

Beckenham in Kent. Apart from remembering Legat's photograph on the wall of Zybina's studio, we heard a few stories about him – that he had had his front teeth knocked out by his partner as she turned a *pirouette*; that his feet were so well turned out that he could balance a glass of water on his instep in *attitude en avant*, which also meant that, when he died, his feet had to be tied together to stop them falling into first position and hitting the sides of his coffin; and that he would knock his wedding ring on the piano if he wanted to stop the class in the middle of an exercise – but little else.

At first, I thought I might write up some of my research in an article or two but, as in the way of these things, once I started writing in earnest, I saw that it would have to be a book about Zybina in the form of a series of stories about her and the people she knew, and the people who influenced her as a dancer and teacher. In their own ways, the stories of these people are as important as those whose names are better known in the ballet world. They helped shape Zybina's character – particularly her clear-headed determination that was hardly apparent in the graceful and gentle teacher my friends and I knew and held dear. So, while it may seem a digression to delve into the experiences of Zybina's first husband, Hugh Pearse, in the trenches of Flanders in the First World War, these illuminate the personality of the man who supported her ballet training and the training of her friend, the Yugoslav ballerina and teacher Ana Roje. Since so many of Zybina's close friends worked in intelligence during the Second World War, I have included descriptions of their activities and an account of how many Britons left Yugoslavia after the German invasion in April 1941; while Zybina did not undertake that journey, a number of her friends did – and it is a story in itself that deserves to be more widely known.

Such digressions simply emphasise that history is rarely linear or neat, and that this book is more akin to a tapestry, with its many interlinking threads, than a single skein of wool. These threads link revolution and war, displacement and loss, and the making and remaking of new lives in unfamiliar surroundings. As a tapestry, it spans three centuries, from its beginnings in the nineteenth and its conclusion in the twenty-first with the installation of a heritage plaque on the building where Legat had his London studio.

The First World War and the Russian Revolution shaped Zybina's early life, as they did for so many Russian *émigrés* who settled in Western Europe, and who then had to find new homes when the Second World War caught up with them. Like Zybina, they had resilience and determination, and the dancers among them strove to pass on their artistry to a generation of students far from the Imperial Theatres of St Petersburg and Moscow. I was intrigued by the close and enduring relationships between ballet students and their teachers, and how so many of those students went on to become teachers themselves. They passed on their experience by example, honouring the generations who came before them – each a link in the chain of teachers' teachers. The story of Nicolai Legat and those of the people around him, some of whom were also part of Zybina's life, are inseparable from her own. His story is a thread that runs from the Russia of Zybina's birth and through her career in the decades after his death. It relates closely to the stories of her other teachers, Evgenia Eduardova in Berlin, Elena Poliakova in Belgrade and Olga Preobrazhenskaya in Paris, and of her colleagues, both dancers and teachers, in Yugoslavia and England. Their stories are equally inseparable because what shaped them influenced Zybina in turn. She would have known much of the background of these stories, although perhaps not all the details. I hope that she would have enjoyed reading them. As an individual, Legat became somewhat overshadowed by Enrico Cecchetti, at least in England, where he spent much of his later life, and this is an opportunity to acknowledge Legat's contribution to a generation of young dancers in the 1920s and 1930s. In a wider context, the diaspora of which he, Eduardova, Poliakova and Preobrazhenskaya were part, to say nothing of Anna Pavlova and Serge Diaghilev's Ballets Russes, inspired countless others in Europe and the Americas.

⁓

Realisation that I had a link to Marius Petipa through Zybina and Legat came from a passage in Diane Solway's biography of Rudolf Nureyev ("Nureyev: His Life"), where she refers to Legat as Petipa's student and successor. But a more subconscious train of thought had been developing as I got older and as my twice-weekly ballet classes were increasingly important to my well-being – as a physical and mental challenge, certainly, but also as a means to balance the demands of work and family. I appreciated that, then in my fifties, I was relatively free of injury and reasonably able to hold my own, at least at the *barre*. Not only that but, to my great surprise, the mental and physical challenge of class was, if anything, more enjoyable than in earlier years. I knew that it stemmed from my training with Zybina and, by extension, from her training with Legat. Having taken classes some years earlier with a Russian teacher trained in the Vaganova method in Leningrad, I suspected that Zybina's classes probably were very similar in structure and approach to the older style of Legat's. While pursuit of that thought has guided much of my research, the evidence remains convincing but circumstantial. Importantly, too, I came to appreciate that what Zybina taught me extended even to my working life – memory, the importance of teamwork, the importance of presentation, the importance of completing a task as correctly and accurately as possible – all things I drew upon without thinking that they came from her. Indeed, in remembering her classes and the work she put into our performances, those of her students with whom I am in touch have expressed much the same appreciation of her guidance and inspiration.

As Christine and I browsed the internet endlessly to find out what we could about Legat we stumbled across nuggets of information which intrigued us further and then brought us into contact with people outside our immediate circle but who were connected not only to Legat but to Zybina as well. What began as an amusing exchange of reminiscences took on a life of its own as we pieced together Zybina's story and found out more about her career and her life as a dancer and teacher. The next summer Christine and I met in London and went on a frustrating mission to find Legat's studio at 46 Colet Gardens in Barons Court. We did not know then that Talgarth Road had been built along the southern arm of Colet Gardens. We should have been looking at the imposing row of buildings on the south side of Talgarth Road rather than the Victorian terraced houses on the west side of Colet Gardens, and looking at 151 Talgarth Road, which is what 46 Colet Gardens became as a result. (Nor did we know then that Legat lodged for a time in one of those terraced houses in Colet Gardens.) We were joined for lunch by Katherine Mason, who we knew as Katherine Morgan, another classmate from Zybina's studio – and for me, through both primary and secondary school – and with whom I had also re-established contact through a social networking site. Christine and I shared with her the fruits of our research so far and we were able to get in touch with Zybina's daughter Tamara Jakasha in Milan through Brenda Olivieri (*née* Sanger), and through Tamara with another contemporary at Zybina's school, Cheryl Schildknecht (*née* Mudele), in Switzerland. I was able to reach out to Jill Lhotka, who had studied with Ana Roje and Oskar Harmoš and, as a result of a fortunate internet discovery, I was able to contact Claire Faraci (*née* Courtney), a near-contemporary of Tamara who studied with Zybina as well as with Ana Roje and Oskar Harmoš.

Of course, none of this would ever have happened in the first place without the internet and would have continued unimaginably slowly without access to increasing volumes of material made available online. As it is, researching and writing has taken something approaching twenty years, although most intensely over the past ten. It would have been nice to be able to travel more because it really is important to see the places being written about, and not to rely on written descriptions and the internet. As it was, I was able to go inside 151 Talgarth Road on two occasions, and by lucky chance, on a work-related trip, to see the outside of the house where Zybina lived with her family at number 7 Pokrovsky Boulevard in Moscow. I also drew on memories of family holidays in Yugoslavia when we visited Zagreb and Split, and travelled as far south as Cetinje in the mountains of Montenegro. More recently, a few days in Trieste gave the opportunity, also, to see the rugged landscape of the limestone plateau which surrounds it. However, constrained by the demands of work, extensive travel for research was a luxury I had to do without.

As the details started to fall into place, opening up other avenues of research at the same time, it became an all-absorbing challenge. Not at all gripped by history at school, with limited formal knowledge of ballet history and trained as a geologist, suddenly I found myself becoming a self-taught amateur historian, though trying hard to maintain rigour and accuracy in my research. Half-forgotten memories surfaced: sitting at the feet of Tamara Karsavina at the age of nine, at the annual certificate-giving of the Federation of Russian Classical Ballet, and then realising that, through her, my degrees of separation with Diaghilev's Ballets Russes, Vaslav Nijinsky and Serge Diaghilev, himself, were very few; that because Jill Lhotka had danced for Nijinsky in one of many attempts to bring him out of his state of withdrawal, and getting to know Jill much better than I could ever have known Karsavina, the gap closed a little more. I was overcome to hear Zybina's voice, and her Russian accent, on the tape-recorded interview made by Patricia Deane-Gray MBE and was eager to put those memories of Legat, her first marriage and life in Belgrade, into context. I remembered that Zybina's first husband was an Englishman and was happy that, when she gave his full name, I could research his early life. I was shocked and delighted when I first came across a picture of Zybina's close friend and Special Operations Executive agent Colonel Duane Tyrrel Hudson OBE and could then recognise him in other photographs. I learned about the other friends in her circle who worked in intelligence during the Second War, including Katherine's parents. And, given my working career as a geoscientist, the way in which mining engineers and mining companies come into this story has also been interesting and yielded some unexpected leads to relevant information sources far removed from classical ballet.

As my researches progressed, I was especially drawn to first-hand accounts and descriptions – Zybina's own in the interview, Legat's in his memoir, "The Story of the Russian School", the memoirs of his friends and colleagues, and importantly, the articles written by Legat and Karsavina about their contemporaries and teachers. I came to understand for myself what trained historians know well – personal reminiscences are just that and may not refer to events that others saw, or see, as important, and that details may conflict with other accounts. For example, while Legat describes in some detail how he taught the ballerina Mathilde Kschessinskaya to successfully turn thirty-two *fouettés* (rapid turns on one leg), she does not refer to his help at all in her own memoir, "Dancing in Petersburg", saying simply that the critics said she was the first, after the Italian ballerina Pierina Legnani, to execute them perfectly. Legat describes the suicide of his beloved younger brother Sergei in 1905 but does not dwell on the events which led to his death. It is Karsavina who writes in "Theatre Street" of the divisions between the dancers of the Mariinsky company at this time of political upheaval, but Michel Fokine, who was very much involved with one of the dancers' factions, makes no mention at all of this period in his own memoir.

In researching and writing this, I have come to learn, too, that memory is both powerful and fallible at the same time. Mine is as blurred in places as it is clear in others. I have supplemented and confirmed my own memories, and those of my classmates, with as much documentary material as possible, a process akin to researching family history which can pose its own challenges. But in exploring those memories we have each discovered that Zybina's influence was of great benefit to us, whether or not we went on to professional careers as dancers.

My last meeting with Maria Zybina was quite by chance. We ran into each other in Piccadilly in London sometime late in 1977. She looked very elegant in a Russian fur hat set at a stylish angle. She told me that her second husband, Germano, had died at the end of the previous year and that she had been in London to sell an emerald ring, a family heirloom. I was lucky to have been looking up references at the library of the Geological Society in

Burlington House and out of my usual office routine. A cup of tea across the road at Fortnum and Mason seemed a good idea and we caught up a little on the years since we had last seen each other – Zybina remembering that she still had a wedding present waiting for me at home. It did not cross my mind that I would not see her again. Now, of course, it is a great and lasting regret that I did not make the effort to do so. My story about Maria Zybina is dedicated to her with love and with thanks for her teaching which go much, much deeper than a simple "Thank you" could ever convey.

CHAPTER 3
EARLY DAYS IN MOSCOW AND BERLIN

...I came out of the theatre as if in a dream.

**Entry in the diary of Maria Zybina on seeing
Anna Pavlova dance in Berlin on 1 December 1926.**

Madame Maria Zybina, Madame to her pupils, Mary to her family and friends, established her ballet school in Beckenham, Kent, in 1950 – but, since she was Mary in her wider circle, Mary she must be from now on.

Broad stone steps led to the front door of a large detached Victorian house at 7 Copers Cope Road and into the rather dark hall from which the changing room opened on the left and the studio on the right. The studio was probably typical of many in England at the time – not very large but large enough, equipped with *barres* of varying heights and, leaning against the wall, two of those big old-fashioned mirrors which had previously hung over a mantelpiece. The other walls were lined with photographs of Mary's friends and contemporaries from ballet companies in England and abroad, and of Nicolai Legat, with whom she had trained in London in the 1930s when she was already a professional dancer. Although Mary was born and spent her early childhood in Moscow, her ballet training started in Berlin and continued in Belgrade, with Russians who taught in the style and method of the Imperial schools. They, like Legat, were among the dancers who had performed with Anna Pavlova, with Serge Diaghilev in the Ballets Russes and with other groups throughout Europe and the Americas, and who, like her own family, left Russia after the revolution of 1917. Mary always referred to Legat as Mr Legat, or Nicolas Legat, pronounced as in 'begat', not 'Degas'. But, since only the last fifteen years of his life were spent outside Russia, I have chosen to use Nicolai rather than Nicolas or Nikolai.

Mary was born on 2 May 1910 (New Style), in Moscow. The weather would still have been wintery and overcast but the first buds would have started to appear on the trees outside the Zybin family home in Pokrovsky Boulevard near the centre of the city. Her family and their friends may have remarked on the recent appearance of Halley's comet. The fact of it becoming much brighter as it neared the earth was the source of anticipation mixed with some fear and trepidation given the association of comets with momentous events. The comet would have had particular significance for the Zybins since a shooting star is part of their family crest. However, *The Times* of London published no news from Moscow in the last week of April or early May so that, to the outside world at least, the city was going about its business as usual. The Ballets Russes were preparing for the opening night of "Le Carnaval" in Berlin and looking forward to the *premières* of "Schéhérazade" and "The Firebird" in Paris in June. Mary was not associated directly with Diaghilev's company, or any of the successor companies to the Ballets Russes, but it is worth placing her birth within the timeframe of Diaghilev's work outside Russia since her training and professional career were very much part of the Imperial tradition, which he introduced to new audiences. Later, in Yugoslavia, she would have performed at least some of the works of his company.

Mary's parents were Nicolas and Maria, who was called Mussia or Mussi within the family. (Mary's father's name is given as Nicolas on his German death certificate, which also provides details of his marriage and his parents' names.) He was born in Moscow on 22 June 1874, and his own parents were Nicolai and Katharina, *née* Lilienthal. Nicolas and Maria, whose maiden name was Ragnoff, were married in Moscow on 28 April 1899. Mary was their second daughter. Her elder sister Tatiana was born on 25 December 1902 (New Style), her brother, Vyacheslav or "Slavchik" in late 1903, and her younger sister, Katerina, or Kitty or Katusha, in December 1914. All the children were born in the imposing house with its neoclassical facade at 7 Pokrovsky Boulevard. They did not attend school but were educated by governesses or tutors. The family was well-to-do and owned a glass or crystal factory. Nicolai was well connected and had business in Spain for which he was the honorary consul, and he probably spoke fluent Spanish and English. Summer holidays were spent at a *dacha* outside Moscow, the location of which is unknown. The family had been granted lands and estates dating from 1617, possibly including the *dacha*, and a coat of arms with the Latin motto *Fuimus*, literally translated as "We have been" or "We were". A document in the family archive notes that the Zybins served the Russian throne and were included in the Voronezh Nobility Council, essentially the record of noble families in the Voronezh region of central Russia. Almost certainly, the motto refers to a specific event related to the elements of the coat of arms, which include a shooting star over a river, a sword and a serpent being cut in two.

Pokrovsky Boulevard is part of the Boulevard Ring that surrounds the centre of Moscow and the Zybins' house is about two kilometres east of St Basil's Cathedral and Red Square. The streets of the Boulevard Ring were completed in the 1820s, replacing the medieval walls of the city after the disastrous fires of Napoleon's siege in 1812. Rows of stately buildings on either side of this part of Pokrovsky Boulevard still overlook the wide strip of mature trees and grass that separates the two lanes of traffic. A map of Moscow from the mid-1800s shows that the trees had already been planted along the southern section of the street, while an early postcard shows a double-deck, horse-drawn tram. Number 7 is located just north of Durasovsky Pereulok on the eastern side of the boulevard and is by no means the least imposing of the buildings on that stretch of the street. When Mary went on a ballet teachers' tour to Russia at the end of 1964, the family learned that, after the revolution, number 7 became the Persian, and then the Iranian embassy, as it is today. Katherine Mason came across the account of Farhad Sepahbody, son of Persia's last ambassador to the USSR, who, on a visit to Moscow almost at the same time in 1965, went to the house where his father had been ambassador in 1936, and which he remembered as a child. Sepahbody describes the building as drab and grey, both in his memory and on his visit. The present exterior paintwork in cream is closer to what it would have been before the revolution, before decades of grime had accumulated (see Sepahbody, "Will Anyone Miss Us?").

The centre of Moscow was dominated, as it is now, by the massive walls of the Kremlin, St Basil's Cathedral and Red Square from which the main streets radiate. It was relegated to the position of Russia's second city when Peter the Great founded St Petersburg as the capital in 1712; Catherine the Great, in particular, regarded Moscow as backward and provincial. But the destruction in 1812 resulted in rebuilding on a grand scale, though many small, irregular streets remained. As Napoleon's army entered the city, fires were set that destroyed two-thirds of it, leaving the residents without shelter or food, but ultimately victorious, since Napoleon retreated a few weeks later. Emancipation of the serfs in 1861 also shaped Moscow as freed serfs flocked there to work in the factories. Gradually, they prospered and moved into trade, banking and publishing. By 1900, Moscow had a population of over one million, though still smaller than St Petersburg's, and Nicolas's consular responsibilities would have brought him in contact with people from diverse business and national backgrounds.

In 1917, the Provisional Government was established by the Duma, or legislative body, in what had become Petrograd in 1914 (renamed to remove the German connotation of "Petersburg") as Tsar Nicholas II was increasingly unable to exert his rule. In general, events unfolded more slowly in Moscow than in Petrograd, partly because the city itself had an established business and professional class and a more diverse workforce, so that the gulf between the court, and its bureaucracy, and the populace was less pronounced. A State Conference of representatives was held in Moscow in August 1917 in which participants represented a cross-section of interests from commercial and military interests, the church and the intelligentsia. But change was inevitable. A strike of nearly half a million workers called by the Bolsheviks brought the city to a standstill. Bread was rationed, as in Petrograd, and food and fuel were scarce. As the Bolsheviks continued to gain support in Moscow, Mary's father would have closely analysed the news in both cities, as he would have done during the events of the 1905 Revolution. The Pokrovsky Barracks are close by, and the family would not have been able to ignore the movement of soldiers and the fighting of the October Revolution of 1917 as unrest spread to Moscow from Petrograd. Nicolas may have gone to the Bolshoi Theatre to hear Alexander Kerensky exhort the population to patriotism; however, it is less likely that Mussia went with him and followed the lead of ladies in the audience who threw their jewellery on the stage in support (see Lockhart, "Memoirs of a British Agent").

Nicolas foresaw the implications of political turmoil and the First World War on the future of his family. Under no illusions as to their fate if the Soviets prevailed, the Zybins were among the hundreds of thousands who left Russia to settle all over Europe, or to travel further to North and South America. Although she was only sixteen, a suitable match was found for Tatiana in Robert Smith, an English merchant originally from Gateshead in Durham. He had business in Moscow and was over ten years older, but he must have been able to speak good Russian. He and Tatiana were married in Moscow in 1918 and went to England together shortly afterwards. Nicolas arranged for Mussia, Mary and Kitty to travel via Petrograd to Finland under Spanish diplomatic protection in December 1918. Despite Mary's own recollection given in the interview recorded by Patricia Deane-Gray, family history has it that Nicolas did not accompany his wife and younger daughters but travelled separately and slightly later with Slavchik. Slavchik's passport, dated 14 November 1918, states that he is the son of the Spanish consul, and that his destination is England for the purposes of study. It records his exit from Bergen in Norway on 7 January 1919, with permission to enter the United Kingdom. In the chaos of 1918, the railway journey between Moscow and St Petersburg may well have taken much longer than the twenty-four hours scheduled when the line first opened in 1851. To add to their worries, the Spanish influenza epidemic was still claiming large numbers of victims.

Mary's own account suggests that they walked most, if not all, of the way from Petrograd to the border with Finland. At the time, the Sestra River formed the border and the town of Beloostrov on the railway line from the Finlyandsky terminal in Petrograd was the nearest settlement to the border, and was around thirty kilometres from the city. As Mary says:

We came out on my father's papers who in the last year, it was '17, it was 1917. He was asked, as a very well-known citizen, to continue with the Spanish consulate to help the Spanish people to get out. And we left because we basically knew we were going to be, well... eliminated. In the last two hours we left Russia in a hurry. My father, my mother, myself and my younger sister. And we went out towards Finland where we found some guides who, for a lot of money, it was, of course, all pre-arranged, we went on foot to cross the frontier. And we came in Helsinki. And we walked for hours... and we walked for hours to come to a place near Helsinki, and there we had, for the first time since we left our house, something warm to drink. My sister was three and a half years and she did not talk for about forty-eight hours. Not just did not talk – she was completely frozen up. They put a bit of brandy in and she then started to come to.

Family documents show that they left in 1918 rather than 1917. They had to leave behind most of their possessions but took small valuables, including jewels and heirlooms. Mary's description suggests that they walked from Petrograd to the border. A distance of about thirty kilometres would have been possible, if demanding, on foot in the winter with two small girls. However, Helsinki (then Helsingfors) is three hundred kilometres overland from St Petersburg and it seems unlikely that they walked for the whole distance. Their guides may have used sleds and been able to take a slightly shorter route across the northern shore of the frozen Baltic Sea. Mary's daughter Tamara believes that they slid down a snowy bank at the border, which suggests that they travelled by train from Petrograd to Beloostrov but then left the railway and crossed the frozen river on foot. On Nicolas's own journey with Slavchik, when nearing the border with Finland, Nicolas realised that they would certainly be searched, and any valuables confiscated. Among their valuables was a box containing the family jewels. These were significant pieces since, following Russian custom, Nicolas would buy a jewel in a Fabergé egg for Mussia every Easter. He had no choice but to throw the box out of the train into a snowbank just within Finland. The first time he went back to the border to enquire if a box had been found, the snow was still thick on the ground, but a little later he learned that it had been discovered. When asked how he could prove ownership, he countered by suggesting that, if the key he was carrying opened the box, that should be proof enough. It was handed over. The jewels, still safely inside, helped to underpin the future of the Zybin family outside Russia.

After moving around Europe "looking for a new home", in 1921 or 1922 the family settled in Berlin, where there was an established Russian *émigré* community centred around Kurfürstendamm and Charlottenburg. Through the remainder of the 1920s, they lived at Motzstrasse 61 in the nearby Schöneberg district. (Views online show it as part of a five-storey apartment block, which, because of the ornamental stonework around the windows, is probably similar to how it looked then – except that the stonework would have since been cleaned.) By 1932, the family was living at Hallesches Ufer 27 but moved to number 58 a few years later. Nicolas continued to represent Spain as consul and had his own telegraph address, "Zybin Hallesches Ufer 58". Motzstrasse lies south-east of the centre of Charlottenburg, which was founded in the early 1700s and remained a separate town until 1920 when it became a borough of Greater Berlin. Hallesches Ufer runs along the north bank of the Landwehrkanal between Potsdammerstrasse and Mehringdamm. Nicolas bought a number of properties and set up holding companies for them in his wife's name, including the building at Hallesches Ufer 58. Not surprisingly, he had banking arrangements with Dresdner Bank, Baring Brothers in London and Skandinaviska Kreditaktiebolaget of Stockholm.

With its theatres and restaurants, and the Deutsches Opernhaus which was built in 1912, Charlottenburg was a centre of recreation and nightlife. The baroque Schloss Charlottenburg or palace stood in Spandauer Damm and the Tiergarten just to the east. (Badly damaged by bombing in the Second War, the present building has been carefully reconstructed.) In the 1920s, that part of Berlin was culturally rich, with Russian-language newspapers and journals, bookshops and publishing houses, schools and an Orthodox church in Nachodstrasse in the Wilmersdorf district. Nicolas may have frequented the cafés, Café Leon, the Café Landgraf or the Prager Diele, and the family may have known some of the Russian writers, musicians and artists who also made their homes in the city. At the same time, of course, Berlin was also a centre for experimental theatre and cabaret, and had a gritty underworld which would have been inescapable – Schöneberg was well known for its gay bars. The bustle of Motzstrasse would have felt very different from the elegant mansions and breadth of Prokrovsky Boulevard but the family's comfortable life was supported by Nicolas's business activities, although perhaps it became somewhat less comfortable by the end of the 1920s, when economic conditions deteriorated sharply.

How did Mary know that she wanted to dance? Although this was not possible when she was a young child in Moscow, and was discouraged by her father, she may have been taken to performances at the Imperial Bolshoi Theatre, which, after major reconstruction in 1856 following a fire, would have appeared much as it does today after the restoration work completed in 2011. Many years later, she told her family that she was impressed by seeing the Tiller Girls in Berlin. The English troupe of high-precision, high-kicking dancers regularly appeared in the Haller Revue at the Theater im Admiralspalast from 1923. But the Zybins would have made a point of going to performances of Russian dancers and musicians whenever they came to the city – Anna Pavlova, Tamara Karsavina and the Ballets Russes among them. Mary kept a diary, which she wrote in German, although what remains of it covers only the period between August 1926 and May 1927. It does not mention the Tiller Girls but Mary does record that she saw Pavlova perform in Berlin on 1 December 1926, saying that she left the theatre "as if in a dream". Afterwards, her father arranged a meeting with Pavlova; they spoke in Russian but, without giving any reasons, Mary says that she was so disappointed that she could not mention it any further.

It was in Berlin that, at last, Mary was able to study ballet. She says:

> I always wanted to dance and I couldn't. Because when we left Russia my parents, who left during the Revolution, went through Europe looking for a new home. And we went through many places where we could not settle down, but we settled down in Germany and there I stayed. And there for the first time, I went to a ballet school myself with Evgenia Eduardova who was a very famous teacher from the Kirov [Mariinsky] ballet.

While Eduardova was the first of Mary's teachers, they all, Nicolai Legat in London, Eduardova in Berlin, Elena Poliakova in Belgrade and Olga Preobrazhenskaya in Paris, came from the Imperial Theatre and its school in St Petersburg. Their training was rooted in the traditions of the late 1800s and the era of the Mariinsky Theatre under Marius Petipa and Christian Johansson. Despite the differences in their ages – Eduardova and Poliakova were more than ten years younger than Legat and Preobrazhenskaya – they were colleagues in St Petersburg. Legat frequently partnered Preobrazhenskaya, both at the Mariinsky and on tour, and Eduardova, Poliakova and Legat toured together with the Imperial Russian Ballet of St Petersburg in 1909. Vladimir Teliakovsky, director of the Mariinsky Theatre between 1901 and 1917, saw the young dancers as promising soloists, in company with Olga Spessivtseva, Lydia Kyasht and Lydia Lopokova (or Lopukhova). Legat started teaching at the Imperial Theatre School in 1896 and both Eduardova and Poliakova would have taken his *classe de perfectionnement*, or class of perfection, for dancers in the company when he took it over from Johansson, even if they had not been in his classes at the school. As their contemporary, Poliakova would have had the same teachers as Karsavina and her great friend, Lydia Kyasht. In her memoir, "Theatre Street", Karsavina lists them as Pavel Gerdt, Johansson and Enrico Cecchetti, as well as Evgenia Sokolova and Legat. Before leaving Russia and establishing her famous studio in Paris, Preobrazhenskaya taught at her own school in St Petersburg. A bond between Mary and her teachers was that all of them had fled the Russian Revolution or its aftermath; she was much younger, of course, and their shared experiences may have been accepted implicitly rather than discussed explicitly, but it would have been a bond nevertheless.

Evgenia Platonovna Eduardova was born in St Petersburg in 1882 and graduated from the Theatre School in 1901. A contemporary of Pavlova and a few years older than Poliakova, Karsavina and Kyasht, she was taught by Gerdt and Johansson at the Theatre School, and then by Legat in the *classe de perfectionnement*. As a student in the school, Vaslav Nijinsky's younger sister, Bronislava Nijinska, recalls being allowed to watch Eduardova rehearsing her graduation performance, which was staged by Gerdt, although she gives no other details. Eduardova became a noted character dancer and was a character soloist in the tours of the Imperial Russian Ballet of St Petersburg in 1908 and 1909 organised by the Finnish impresario Edvard Fazer and which visited the northern and central European capital cities. In 1908 the group included Pavlova as the principal dancer with Adolf Bolm, Mikhail Obukhov, Elena Poliakova, Elsa Vil (Elizaveta Will) and Alexander Shiryaev, who was particularly known as a character artist, and his wife, Natalia Matveeva. The tour started with performances in Scandinavia, in Helsinki, Stockholm and Copenhagen, before going on to Prague and Berlin. The following year, Bolm went to Paris to join Diaghilev's Ballets Russes and Nicolai Legat took his place as ballet master and Pavlova's partner for performances in Berlin, Leipzig, Prague and Vienna. Some accounts of these tours suggest that this was Pavlova's own company but, as the Finnish dance historian Johanna Laakkonen makes clear in her study of these tours in her book, "Canon and Beyond. Edvard Fazer and the Imperial Russian Ballet 1908–1910", they were organised by Fazer. Laakkonen's work is especially valuable since she describes in detail the tours of a company, rather than just a few dancers, and uses reviews and reports in Scandinavian languages and German that were not followed by the writers who documented the early seasons of the Ballets Russes. She notes that the *répertoire* included the popular ballets of the nineteenth century, such as "Halte de Cavalrie", "Coppélia" and "Paquita" together with shorter *divertissements* and character pieces. Theatregoers were particularly taken with Eduardova's character dances. In Stockholm, one newspaper article called her the "Russian darling" of the audience and she was also very popular in Copenhagen, where her style was seen as somewhat reminiscent of the Danish school. Indeed, it seems that there was some rivalry between Eduardova and Pavlova as audiences loudly demanded encores of the character numbers that Eduardova danced with great spirit and verve. Various accounts, including Legat's own (see his tribute to Pavlova published in his memoir "Ballet Russe", and in the *Dancing Times*, March 1931), note that Pavlova was also a very able and dramatic character dancer.

The writer Franz Kafka was particularly taken with Eduardova when she appeared at the Neue Deutsche Theater in Prague in 1909. In a letter to his lover, Felice Bauer, written in January 1913, he looks forward to seeing the Russian ballet "tomorrow" and remembers the performance in Prague. He recalls dreaming about the company, and especially Eduardova, who he describes as a very wild dancer. His diaries of 1910 also recall the dream, noting that he asked Eduardova to dance a *czárdás*, "just one more time", but they do not shed light on the performance itself since it took place before the time of his extant diaries. In "A Franz Kafka Encyclopedia", the authors indicate that Kafka saw Eduardova perform on 25 May 1909. However, it seems there is no record of the programme since Laakkonen notes specifically that no information on the *répertoire* was given in a review in Vienna's *Neue Freie Presse*. But the works performed in the last week of May in Vienna, immediately following the engagement in Prague, were "Giselle", the second act of "Swan Lake" and "Paquita", each followed by *divertissements*. In writing about his dream, Kafka suggests that in the street, rather than on the stage, Eduardova appeared pale and dowdy because of the way she dressed, even though at the time she would have been only twenty-seven, barely a year older than Kafka himself. In an interesting connection to this story, the frontispiece to Max Brod's edition of the diaries, 1910–1913, for Schocken Books is a reproduction of Kafka's manuscript referring to his dream of Eduardova.

Eduardova also appeared in the first London season of Pavlova's company in April 1910, when she and Alexander Monahoff (Monkhov) led performances of character dances from Russia, Poland and Hungary. The *Daily Mail* commented on the performance on 18 April when the leaders of the troupe, Eduardova and Monahoff, danced to the "Second Hungarian Rhapsody" of Franz Liszt, which was a popular number in Fazer's tours. (This might have been the *czárdás* dreamed of by Kafka.) *The Times* noted that the welcome accorded to Pavlova and Mikhail Mordkin was rightly extended to Eduardova and Monahoff (see Macdonald, "Diaghilev Observed by Critics in England and the United States 1911–1929"). Eduardova danced briefly with the Ballets Russes but, unlike some of the other dancers of this period, she elected to return to St Petersburg and the Mariinsky Theatre.

Eduardova became the second wife of Alexei Davidov, a prominent banker and industrialist who was also a musician and founder of the St Petersburg Music Society. She retired from the theatre in 1917 and they left Russia, settling in 1920 in Berlin, where she had enjoyed such success in 1908 and 1909. Eduardova's life after she left Russia is described by Marion

Kant in "Joseph Lewitan and the Nazification of Dance in Germany" in "The Art of Being Jewish in Modern Times", and in Kant's work with Lilian Karina, a student of Eduardova, "Hitler's Dancers: German Modern Dance and the Third Reich". They write of how Eduardova's lover Josef Davidovich Lewitan came to Berlin at the same time, noting that Eduardova lived with him, and not her husband. Lewitan was over ten years her junior and, during the First World War, he had worked in the government department which supplied the army and, afterwards, in education. Once in Berlin, he became involved in the dance world and started an entirely new career as a dance critic and commentator at a time when classical ballet was being challenged by the German expressionist dance movement led by Rudolf Laban and Mary Wigman. Lewitan founded the magazine *Der Tanz: Monatsschrift für Tanzkultur*, which first appeared in October 1927. His aim was to produce a serious journal covering all aspects of dance, rather as Philip J.S. Richardson was doing with the *Dancing Times* in England and as Akim Volynsky had done in Russia as editor of *Severnyi Vestnik* (*Northern Herald*). Through *Der Tanz*, Lewitan tried to provide a balanced discussion of both classical ballet and German modern dance, though his own preference was for ballet.

Importantly, Lewitan helped Eduardova to establish her school, which was one of the first of its kind in the city and which went on to become one of the largest in Berlin. She and her school were sufficiently well regarded outside Germany to be listed in Arnold Haskell and P.J.S. Richardson's "Who's Who in Dancing 1932". She had two studios, both located within the Russian community, at Kalckreuthstrasse 11 and Eisenacherstrasse 36–37. (Views online show an ornate art nouveau-style wooden door and the number 11 for the Kalckreuthstrasse address, although the building itself appears to have been extensively modernised.) Eduardova also danced with the Berlin Grosse Volksoper, and Haskell and Richardson note that she staged and arranged ballets for the theatrical producer Max Reinhardt, the Grosse Volksoper and the Scala and Wintergarten variety theatres. They note, too, that in 1931 Eduardova founded the Anna Pavlova Association in Berlin, which may not have continued to operate when she and Lewitan left the city. Lewitan refers to the activities of the association in some of his reports to the *Dancing Times* in the 1930s. Ludmilla Chiriaeff, founder of Les Grands Ballets Canadiens and Vera Zorina (Eva Brigitta Hartwig), Balanchine's second wife, were among Eduardova's students. (Both were younger than Mary; she may have known Zorina at Eduardova's school, and they may have met up again at Legat's studio in London.) As events in Germany unfolded and Hitler gained power, however, Eduardova would have been dismayed to follow the career of another student, Leni Riefenstahl, who became a noted director of Nazi propaganda films.

Lewitan also worked for a Russian publishing house in Berlin and, among other works, translated Volynsky's "Book of Exultation: A Primer in the Classical Dance" ("Kniga likovanij") into German as "Buch des Jubels". Through the mid-1930s, he regularly wrote on dance in Germany for the *Dancing Times* but his position as a critic and essayist became increasingly precarious. In January 1933 he was officially declared a Jew and, though he still owned *Der Tanz*, it was seized and his responsibilities taken from him. The proponents and supporters of modern dance in Germany became more vocal and took on philosophical and racial positions. Lewitan finally sold the magazine three years later. There followed a period in which he managed tours for dance companies, including the Ballets Jooss and Eduardova's own troupe. In 1937, he was invited to work at Les Archives Internationales de la Danse in Paris and managed to leave Germany on French identification papers. In common with other Russian *émigrés*, including the Zybin family, Eduardova held a Nansen passport, which, although it protected the holder from deportation and allowed crossing of borders in order to find work, did not allow free travel in and out of Germany. (The Norwegian Arctic explorer, Fridtjof Nansen, was appointed as the High Commissioner for Refugees of the League of Nations in 1920. One of his initiatives was the creation of a document for stateless persons that became known as the Nansen passport.) Mary suggests in the interview with Patricia Deane-Gray that Eduardova was able to travel – possibly because she could demonstrate to the authorities that it was for work. Meanwhile, throughout this period, Eduardova had secured all the necessary permits and certificates to continue to run her school, she became a member of the Reich Theatre Chamber, and a member of the professional association, Fachschaft Tanz. She was not Jewish herself, was not married to Lewitan, and had no need to leave Germany. But she decided that she could not live without him and joined him in Paris in October 1938, leaving her school in the hands of Sabine Ress, a student and one of her daughters-in-law.

In Paris, Eduardova struggled to establish a ballet studio but she and Lewitan lived there for only a few years. Once again fearing for his safety, they managed to leave France ahead of the advancing German army and reached Casablanca in May 1942. At the end of that year, British and American forces landed in Morocco and Lewitan secured work as a purchasing agent for the Naval Construction Battalion of the United States Navy. Davidov's death in Berlin in 1940 allowed Eduardova to convert to Judaism so that she and Lewitan could marry in a Jewish ceremony in September 1943. His work allowed them finally to reach the United States in May 1947. They anglicised their names and made a home in the Upper West Side of New York City. He was a translator for the United Nations for the next twenty years and wrote occasionally for American dance magazines. Eduardova tried to re-establish herself as a ballet teacher but with limited success. By then she was becoming elderly and, if Lewitan had a regular income, perhaps teaching was not a financial necessity. In her essay on Lewitan in "The Art of Being Jewish in Modern Times", Marion Kant observes that he never really settled in America, although he became more in touch with the Russian community in New York and less committed as a Zionist. Eduardova may have been similarly unsettled, particularly if she could not repeat the success of her school in Berlin. She died in New York on 10 December 1960 after a fall in her bathroom at the age of seventy-eight. Lewitan died on a visit to Paris in April 1976. A collection of their papers and photographs is held at the Jerome Robbins Dance Division of the New York Public Library.

While studying with Eduardova and like all young dancers, Mary looked forward to the opportunity to perform and was able to join her teacher's touring company. She recalls:

> And when I was sixteen, several of the pupils of Eduardova were chosen to make a company which travelled around and was also in the stationary theatres. And I could not go with them because I had a Nansen passport which did not allow these people to go to another country, because we were not belonging to any country.

It seems that Mary was able to perform with Eduardova's company within Germany, in Hamburg as well as in Berlin. There are few details available, although a note in the *Dancing Times* of February 1928 reports on the collaboration of dance groups, including Eduardova's, in the German Lace Fair, and in which Mary may well have participated. (This would have been one of the performances in venues other than "stationary theatres"; the writer expresses disapproval at serious and reputable dancers and companies being involved in a commercial enterprise to promote textiles.)

Mary's great interest in and knowledge of character dancing originated with Eduardova. Her belief in the value of character dance to the development of a ballet dancer also stemmed from her early training with Eduardova, from whom she learned the special character exercises at the *barre* that she says were used by Pavel Gerdt at the Imperial Theatre School (see *Dancing Times*, June 1963). Since much of Eduardova's performing *répertoire* was made up of the character dances that were so popular in Fazer's tours, Mary would certainly have learned these and absorbed some of Eduardova's verve and interpretation. Among them was what we knew as the Russian court dance and which was the Russian dance variation from the second act of "Swan Lake". Character variations were an integral part of the Mariinsky ballets, notwithstanding Petipa's tendency to make them more balletic, and highly regarded ballerinas like Kschessinskaya and Pavlova were also accomplished character dancers. Interpretation of roles in ballets which had important non-classical elements was an appreciated skill. Legat writes of Pavlova as a "passionate dancing-girl" in the first act of "La Bayadère" and a "burning Spaniard" in "Don Quixote". (That the quintessential ballerina was well able to work in the stylised choreography of these roles is shown in full-length portraits painted by Max Slevogt of "La Bayadère" and by John Lavery in an untitled dance.) Eduardova was a relatively junior member of the Mariinsky company when Nicolai and Sergei Legat published their

folio of caricatures between 1903 and 1905 but the brothers capture the vivacious aspect of her character which audiences enjoyed and which inspired Mary as a student and as a performer, although it is impossible to identify the ballet in which she appears from her simple costume.

Since Eduardova talked about exercises for character dance, she would also have talked to her students about Alexander Shiryaev and Pavlova, with whom she toured in 1908 and 1909, as well as about Legat, Poliakova and Karsavina. It is unlikely that Mary ever met Shiryaev but when she came to

Mary in costume for the Russian court dance, collection of Tamara Jakasha.

know Poliakova and Legat, and then Karsavina a few years later, she would have heard more about him and his work.

Even in those early days, Mary may also have seen from Eduardova's example that teaching often follows a professional career, and to appreciate the importance of performing experience to the development of a good teacher. Later, she always maintained that performing was not only important but essential experience for a teacher.

☙

Despite the restrictions of their Nansen passports, Nicolas arranged for both Mary and Kitty to attend a girls' boarding school at Crowborough in Sussex, perhaps for as long as a year, for them to learn English. But the opportunity not only to travel but to live and, ultimately, to perform outside Germany came with Mary's marriage to her first husband, Hugh Armine Wodehouse Pearse, an English diplomat who was invited to visit the Zybin family at New Year 1928. In the interview Mary describes how she decided to accept his proposal, saying:

> I wanted to get married to an Englishman... And he [Hugh Pearse] came from Belgrade to Germany to spend the New Year with his friends who were my sister [Tatiana] and her British husband. He came to Germany to practise his German, which he knew very well indeed, and have a good time with my family because, of course, my sister and her husband always came every Christmas.
>
> When he, after ten days, he asked if I would marry him, I said, "I don't know, you have to ask my mother", and I ran out of the room. And he bowed and he said, "Please may I ask for the hand of your daughter?" My mother was just as surprised as I am because we knew him only ten days. Anyway, we decided that we will not arrange for a marriage, not for three months at least, or six, but that he would write to me and, after six months if I decided that I would like to marry him, we... he will be very happy. And his was a very, very, very old British family. And after six months, before then, he wrote to me and said, "Well, have you thought, you will marry me or not?" And I said quickly, "Yes", because I wanted in all, all the things in the world is to be belonging somewhere. Yes, to a country. And I knew I would get a British passport, although it did not mean to me as much as it means now. But I said, "Yes, yes, yes, I will marry you".

While Mary's account shows her surprise, and suggests that Hugh may have acted impulsively, family history suggests that his visit and his proposal had been carefully planned by her parents. Tatiana and her husband may well have been enlisted to help find an eligible bachelor since Robert's passport was renewed in Belgrade in 1930 and he could easily have met Hugh there a few years earlier. Mary's mother's apparent surprise would have been part of the plan, as well as the three- to six-month interval for Mary to think over Hugh's proposal. Hugh's widowed mother would also have been consulted and must have approved of the marriage. By then, Mary spoke German and some English, as well as Russian, and Hugh may already have been able to speak and write some Russian for his work in Belgrade. Mary tore the pages following May 1927 out of her diary. Her daughter, Tamara, suspects that they may have mentioned the plans for her marriage to Hugh and were too private to risk being seen by anyone. Apart from the entry for 1 December 1926, when Mary saw Pavlova perform, and the disappointing meeting afterwards, her thoughts are mostly very personal, as might be expected of a sixteen-year-old.

Hugh and Mary were married less than six months from when they met, on 20 April 1928, at the Russian church at 10 Nachodstrasse. While the wording is formal, the wedding invitation gives Mary's name as Mussia. In

Hugh and Mary on their wedding day, 20 April 1928, collection of Tamara Jakasha.

a photograph, Hugh is quite serious at the age of thirty-six and Mary, not quite eighteen, looks almost playful in her wedding dress and stylish veil.

Both the Russian and Greek Orthodox churches were located within an imposing but not obviously ecclesiastical building that would have been a short walk from the Zybin's home in Motzstrasse. Because their wedding was a Russian Orthodox ceremony, Hugh and Mary would also have been married in a civil ceremony at the British consulate to conform with British legal requirements. But all church records were lost when the building was destroyed during the Second War and that part of Nachodstrasse is now lined with modern office buildings.

∽

Shortly afterwards came the Wall Street Crash of 1929, with its repercussions on the German economy that had relied heavily on American loans for the previous five years. Perhaps the family continued to be reunited at Christmas during the 1930s (although latterly without Slavchik, who died in 1936) in spite of difficult economic conditions, the gathering clouds of Hitler's regime and his frequent speeches in Berlin. Mary's father died unexpectedly in Dresden in 1938 while visiting the city on a business trip. Such a sudden death suggests that he suffered a heart attack. Mussia continued to live in the flat in Hallesches Ufer. By then, and with both Mary and Kitty living in Belgrade, she may have been particularly interested in the visit of Prince Paul of Yugoslavia to Berlin early in June 1939 and watched the military parade between the Brandenburg Gate and Charlottenburg, and the accompanying squadrons of war planes which flew low overhead. (Sir Paul Dukes, who comes into this story much later, describes the event in his "An Epic of the Gestapo".) Having survived most of the Second War without her husband and far from her daughters, Mussia died in Berlin on 7 January 1945. It is thought that she also died of a heart attack following bombing nearby since she was found alone, sitting at her table, with the samovar still boiling, although all the windows had been blown out in the explosion.

In 2004, Tamara Jakasha arranged to have headstones with Russian crosses installed for her grandparents in the Russian Orthodox cemetery in Berlin. Nicolas's original grave was a concrete slab, while Mussia's was only a mound of earth.

CHAPTER 4
AN ENGLISH DIPLOMAT,
HUGH ARMINE WODEHOUSE PEARSE

And his was a very, very, very old British family.

Maria Zybina, interview with Patricia Deane-Gray.

When Hugh visited Mary's family that Christmas in Berlin, he was living and working in Belgrade as a member of the British legation. (In those days, a legation, led by a minister, was somewhat less important than an embassy at which the British government was represented by an ambassador.) Thanks to his unusual full name, which Mary gives in the interview, it has been possible to piece together something of his family background and his life before his proposal of marriage. By then, the First World War had been over for ten years and the interview was not an occasion for her to mention that Hugh fought throughout the war on the Western Front in Flanders and north-eastern France. Who knows if he had been disappointed in love before, or if the effects of his wartime experiences had prevented him from marrying earlier? Indeed, he may not have spoken much to Mary about the war since many who survived did not. They were together for less than ten years, but, without him, Mary's career as a dancer would have been very different – if she had been able to dance professionally at all – and she would not have had the lasting benefits of holding a British passport. And, without Hugh's support for the training of Mary's friend Ana Roje with Nicolai Legat in London, the development of ballet in Yugoslavia would have been quite different too.

As Mary says, Hugh's was a very old family that can be traced back to King Edward III and had a crest and the motto *In Deo Confido* (I trust in God).

In spite of its aristocratic connections, Hugh's own family was comfortably well-off, but not particularly wealthy. His father, Hugh Wodehouse Pearse, was a career soldier who served in the East Surrey Regiment. He fought in the Afghan and South African wars and received a number of military honours, including the Distinguished Service Order for his services in South Africa. He also wrote several books on military history. (The famous Jeeves books would have been more widely read; the great-grandfather of the author, P.G. Wodehouse, was the Reverend Philip Wodehouse, brother of Hugh's great-great-grandfather.) Hugh's older sister, Dulcibella, was born in 1890 and named after her great-grandmother and her aunt. Hugh was born on 27 January 1892 and, like Dulcibella, he was baptised at All Saints Church, Kingston upon Thames. The family lived in a house called Penleigh in Crescent Road, Kingston Hill.

Hugh went to St Bernard's School, a small preparatory school at Star Hill in Woking, about twenty kilometres away. Then, between 1904 and 1910, he attended Wellington College at Crowthorne in Berkshire. He was in Beresford House and was a dormitory prefect in 1909, an early indication of his leadership and sense of responsibility. The college was named after the Duke of Wellington and had strong military links but it also provided a well-rounded education (several pupils went on to become writers and historians) and Hugh himself taught history there after the First World War.

Mary's family history relates that Hugh was educated with Edward, Prince of Wales, who became King Edward VIII in 1936. They were not schoolboys together but were contemporaries at Magdalen College, Oxford. Hugh went up to Magdalen in 1911 and the Prince of Wales a year later. The family story of them being "in the same class" suggests that they may have been in the same small tutorial group, and they were undoubtedly friends. In her book "Oxford", Jan Morris notes that the prince enjoyed driving around the city in his open Daimler. Very few undergraduates had cars in those days and Hugh may well have joined him on these drives and been invited to the suite of rooms in college that was reserved for royalty. The Magdalen College archive holds a collection of photographs taken by the prince, who was a keen amateur photographer. It includes one dating from June or July 1914 of Hugh with two others at a regimental summer camp. Hugh and another man are in uniform, so the picture may have been taken very shortly after he and his friends joined up, just before war was declared on 4 August 1914. By then, Hugh would have completed most of his undergraduate studies but had not received his degree.

The *London Gazette* records that, as of 15 August 1914, Hugh was to be a second lieutenant in the Bedfordshire Regiment, for which war diaries, field notes and other records are collected on www.bedfordregiment.org.uk. Hugh served with the First and Second Battalions and the diaries provide glimpses into his experiences. The entries are succinct but, in a way that school history lessons had failed to do, they provided a moving reminder that my own grandfathers and great-uncles also fought in the Great War. The low-lying region of north-eastern France, now green farmland, is underlain by heavy clay and rainfall averages over two hundred days a year, but the years of the war were particularly wet and cold. The ground did not provide firm footing for men or artillery and the defensive trenches in which the soldiers had to spend most of their time had no natural drainage. Terse entries in the war diaries hardly convey the appalling conditions in which Hugh and his companions were living, fighting and dying at a rate of one in ten. The rate at which soldiers were seriously wounded or suffered from exposure to poisonous gas was much higher and many of the survivors never fully recovered. Hugh was one of the lucky ones; a total of seven hundred and seven former pupils of Wellington College lost their lives in the war, as did two hundred and seven members of Magdalen College.

The First Battalion fought in the first battle of Ypres in October and November 1914, in which the objective was to hold the ports of the English Channel and British supply lines against the Germans in the "race to the sea". Losses were heavy on both sides. A poignant entry in the war diaries for 22–23 November reported that the battalion was billeted at Locre and attempts were made to "get all ranks washed" despite heavy frost and lack of accommodation. On Christmas Day, cards from King George V and Queen Mary were distributed to all the soldiers. A hard frost lasted all day. Semaphore signals were received from the Germans that they would not fire and there is a note that a private diary recorded fraternisation between men of B Company and the Germans in No Man's Land. However, the war diaries do not suggest that Hugh's battalion witnessed the singing of carols that brought "Silent Night", "Stille Nacht, Heiliger Nacht", to represent the brief moments of truce.

The first note on Hugh himself appears when, having come through the worst of the fighting in April and May, he was wounded on 25 June 1915 on Hill 60 at Ypres in what was known as the second battle of Ypres, although there is no indication of how seriously he was injured. The second reference is to when he joined the Second Battalion from England in May 1916, by which time he held the rank of captain.

In July 1916, Hugh was in the Battle of the Somme when he had command of B Company which was establishing positions in the rear of the attacking battalions in trenches that had been taken from the Germans. On 10 July, however, he had to retire to the transport lines because of a sprained ankle. Given the thick, slippery mud and uneven ground, simple sprains would have been common and only serious injuries warranted a note in the diaries. On 11 August, at Lestrem, Hugh was appointed adjutant of the 30th Division Infantry School but returned to command A Company on 30 October and the battalion moved to the trenches at Berles (or Berles-au-Bois) to relieve battalions of the Lincolnshire Regiment. Hugh was given two weeks leave on 9 January 1917, rejoining the battalion at Beaurepaire.

On 1 March 1917, Hugh was sent to the 89th Infantry Brigade Headquarters for instruction in "Q", or quartermaster, duties. At the end of the month, he was reported sick and admitted to hospital but no details are recorded. He is next mentioned on 10 June when he rejoined the First Battalion at Camblain-Châtelain – the diary notes that a swimming parade took place before breakfast and church parade at 11.15am. At Camblain-Châtelain, the battalion was not in the trenches, but in camp and doing training exercises, although it had come under aerial and shell attack just before Hugh's return. The short interval of relative calm did not last and, in early July, the battalion moved to the trenches east of Willerval. A month later, on 24 July, at Beaurepaire, Hugh was honoured with the Military Cross, as noted in Divisional Routine orders. The citation reads:

> For conspicuous gallantry and devotion to duty at a critical moment during our attack. Seeing that the front line was held up, he quickly realised and restored the situation by throwing in his reserves at the right moment, which resulted in sixty-three of the enemy surrendering. He showed splendid dash and determination in the attack, and skilfully organised the work of consolidation afterwards. He has shown great coolness and gallantry on all occasions and can be trusted in any emergency. (Recorded in the Supplement 30287 to the *London Gazette*, 14 September, 1917)

October saw the battalion in the third battle of Ypres (the battle of Poelcapelle) when it was subject to heavy shelling. On 10 October 1917, the record notes: "Total casualties – 4 officers Killed, 6 wounded, 35 [Other Ranks] Killed, 97 wounded, 4 missing." Hugh was among the officers listed as wounded but, again, no details are given. He is not mentioned in the available war diaries after October 1917.

The First Battalion was at Louvignies-Quesnoy when the armistice was declared on 11 November 1918. It was signed in a Wagon-Lits railway carriage in the forêt de Compiègne, about one hundred and fifty kilometres to the south-west. By the end of 1918, the battalion had moved to Gembloux in Belgium, although it was not until the middle of April 1919 that it finally left for Antwerp and then, on 30 April, embarked on the crossing to England. The war diaries suggest that much of the time was spent in training and sports, and demobilisation activities, although there was a divisional dinner for officers in Brussels on 12 March, which Hugh may have attended.

Like her brother, Dulcibella lost no time in coming forward to contribute to the war effort. She joined the Voluntary Aid Detachment of the British Red Cross Society only two days after war was declared and then worked as an orderly on ward duty until March 1919. At first, VAD members were generally not allowed to serve overseas or in military hospitals, but Dulcibella spent six months to April 1917 at the Scottish Women's Hospital at Abbaye de Royaumont in France, near Asnières-sur-Oise in Val-d'Oise, about thirty kilometres north of Paris. It is impossible to know if it was coincidence that she was posted to Royaumont or whether she requested it in order to be near to Hugh. But, surely, they were able to meet when he had leave in January 1917, and, surely, she was able to see him when he was ill later that year before her tour of duty ended.

In addition to the Military Cross, Hugh received the Star Medal, the Victory Medal and the British War Medal, which were awarded to all ranks who served in the war. Dulcibella was also awarded the Victory and the British War Medals for her work.

ᑯ₯

It seems that Hugh may not have remained with the battalion until April 1919 since the Magdalen College records indicate that he was back at Oxford in 1918, matriculating as a Bachelor of Arts the following year. Once Hugh's medal record had been found online, with his address given as Somerleigh Court in Dorchester, it was possible to identify the building in a photograph sent by Tamara Jakasha and to find its location in the centre of the town.

The house was built in 1860 for a local banker named Edward Pearce, later Pearce-Edgcumbe, of the landed gentry Edgcumbes of Tavistock in Somerset. Extended in 1889, Somerleigh Court was originally made up of three main buildings, including Edgecumbe Manor, built for Robert Edgcumbe Pearce. There is no way of knowing why Hugh's family moved there from London and, while it is tempting to think there was a link between a family which spelled its name Pearce in the eighteenth and nineteenth centuries, and the Wodehouse Pearse family, it has not been possible to confirm a connection. Perhaps the name is a coincidence and, on his retirement from the army, Hugh's father simply wished to be closer to his mother and his sister, who had moved from Norfolk to Parkstone in Dorset sometime before 1901.

Hugh's father lived in Dorchester for just a few years and was only sixty-four when he died in October 1919. As a soldier, he would have had no illusions as to the dangers of active service but he must have been shocked at the horrors endured in Flanders and thankful to have seen his son return home with honours, and to have completed his degree at Oxford. Hugh's mother, Ada, and Dulcibella remained at Somerleigh Court until 1945 when the property was purchased to become the maternity unit of the Dorset County Hospital. Although the Dorset History Centre does not have a record, the building almost certainly was bought from Ada. She and Dulcibella moved to Heddington, 6 Clarence Road, now renamed Clarence House, an imposing double-fronted late Victorian house not far from Somerleigh Court.

Hugh returned to Wellington College for a short time to teach history and became assistant master (assistant headmaster). Not surprisingly, given his war record and his family background, he was also involved in running the school's Combined Cadet Force (then the Junior Division of the Officer Training Corps). This suggests, too, that his wartime experiences had not dulled his sense of duty and patriotism. The college yearbook for 1923 records:

At the end of the Summer Term Mr. H. A. Pearse resigned. He had only been on the Staff for four years, but his personality quickly won him a distinct place. He was an able historian, who combined teaching History to the Army Sixth with the instruction of the Middle Fourth in most things. He was a keen soldier, who gave much time to the Corps. To Wellingtonians past and present, especially to members of the Beresford, his old dormitory, to whom he was under-tutor, his hospitality was unlimited. He has given up schoolmastering and intends to read for the Bar. (Wellington College Archive)

Apart from Mary's brief comments in the interview, this paragraph and the citation for his Military Cross are the only first-hand insights into Hugh's personality and character. While he may have read for the Bar, he does not seem to have become a solicitor or barrister and, between his time at Wellington College and his marriage to Mary in 1928, there are just a couple of glimpses into his life. With Ada and Dulcibella, he travelled from Hong Kong to London on the SS *Patroclus*, landing in April 1925; his occupation is given as "merchant" and the home of all three of them as Somerleigh Court. Not long after that trip, Hugh bought an elegant 1924 two-seater A.C. sports car but, at the beginning of 1931, he placed an advertisement for its sale at a price of thirty-five pounds and with the phrase "stored four years". He may have taken it out of storage to drive Mary around Dorchester when they were first married – and he may have regretted that it had had so little use.

CHAPTER 5
DANCING IN BELGRADE

I also decided that I will have a go at the theatre and see
if they have me... And we had the engagement and we
slowly went into the *répertoire*."
Maria Zybina, interview with Patricia Deane-Gray.

After their wedding in Berlin, Hugh took Mary to England to spend some time with his family at Somerleigh Court before they travelled on to Belgrade. If they started their journey in London and connected with a luxury sleeper on the Simplon–Orient Express, they may have left Paris just before midnight and arrived in Belgrade in the morning, about thirty hours later. Breakfast would have been served as the train went along the north shore of Lake Geneva, and they would have caught a glimpse of the Château de Chillon before travelling through the Simplon Tunnel and across northern Italy to reach Venice and Trieste in the evening. They may have broken the journey for a few days in Venice before going on through Zagreb to Belgrade. Alternatively, they may have taken the Orient Express route from Ostende via Cologne and Vienna. Almost certainly, Hugh would have taken the Simplon-Orient Express on his first journey to Belgrade to join the legation staff sometime in the mid-1920s. (Writing of the journey in 1921, Tamara Karsavina's husband H.J. Bruce says, however, that the luxury of good food and spotless tablecloths lasted only until Venice.)

In Belgrade, a new British legation and residence had been recently completed at 46 Resavska ulica (street) in the centre of the city. (Consular and commercial services are now housed in the building after a new residence was constructed in the 1950s.) By then the city was no longer a border town on the edge of the Ottoman Empire but was modernising rapidly and emerging as the cultural and political centre of what was to become Yugoslavia. Industry and trade were boosted by completion of the railway to Niš in 1884, while electricity and tram service and the founding of scientific and cultural institutions followed. Its principal street, Knez Mihailo ulica, was named after Prince Mihailo Obrenović and many of the city's more important buildings were and are found there. Republic Square, formerly known as Theatre Square to commemorate the establishment of the National Theatre, is dominated by the statue of Prince Mihailo and is one of the focal points of the city with a number of streets running to or through it. Traditional single-storey houses remained in the side roads, away from the broad streets and imposing buildings of the centre. The population of about two hundred thousand was a diverse mixture of the well-to-do wearing the latest European styles, and men and women dressed as they would be in the villages – loose shirts and baggy trousers (*čakšire*) for the men and colourful embroidered skirts and head scarves for the women. The city is still dominated by the Turkish fortress of Kalemegdan, which was built above the confluence of the Danube and Sava rivers. By then it was surrounded by public gardens with views that stretched over the plain north-west to Hungary. Far though it was from Western European cultural centres like Paris and Berlin, after 1917 Belgrade became home to thousands of Russians, who, like the Zybins, left at the time of the revolution. In Serbia, however, rather than simply being accepted or tolerated, Russian emigrants were made welcome in light of the historical links between the two countries and they quickly contributed to the development of science and the arts, including music and ballet. Mary would have seen for the first time the influences of the Ottoman Empire but she was also surrounded by more familiar Russian influences in the architecture and language, a small Russian church, a recently-built but still unfinished Orthodox cathedral, and in the theatre. (See David A. Norris, "Belgrade, A Cultural History".)

At the time of their marriage, Hugh was living in Višegradska ulica rather than in the legation itself. But in the interview, Mary says that she and Hugh then lived in a villa in Topčider or Topčidersko brdo (Topčider Hill). The area was named from the casting of cannon (*top*) during the siege of 1521. Topčider, with Košutnjak and Senjak, make up the area of Dedinje which, in the early 1900s, was known for its orchards and vineyards. The Topčider valley had been used by the rulers of Belgrade for centuries for hunting and country pursuits and, emulating the country estates of Western

Europe, Prince Mihailo built a residence there in the early 1830s. Dedinje became even more desirable when King Alexander Karađorđević built a new family home overlooking the leafy valley in 1929. The elite of Belgrade society built their own villas and summer houses, and foreign representatives and embassies followed, establishing their residences in the 1930s. Hajd ("Hyde") Park was set in the nearby parkland for walking and riding. Mary also mentions the racecourse, or Belgrade Hippodrome, which was located near Senjak at the beginning of the twentieth century.

She describes how she tried, not very successfully, to assume the role expected of a wife of a member of the legation staff:

"After the marriage, and of course there was a honeymoon and everything very big, and then I went to live with him in Belgrade. He wanted me to go to… after I had called on all the people, because he was a member of the embassy… And, of course, after I had called on all the people whom he knew, he wanted me to go to a hospital, which was run by a Scottish doctor and try and help her as a voluntary person… And I could not, could not do it. Although I am very, very gentle myself, I am not very good with ill people. I have a lot of patience, but not with ill people who are, who are always wanting, asking for something and then being brought to them the medicine and saying, "No, I will not have it".

Hugh's suggestion may have originated with Dulcibella, who Mary knew as Jenny, and her work at the Scottish Women's Hospital in France, since other hospitals had been set up in Serbia during the First World War and several Scottish women doctors remained in the country afterwards. It is possible that Mary volunteered at the hospital for women and children that had been set up in 1919 by Dr Katherine MacPhail with the support of the Scottish Women's Hospitals. (The industrialist and philanthropist Georg Weifert, who makes a brief appearance later in this story, was instrumental in setting up hospitals in Belgrade.) After the war, Dr MacPhail remained in Serbia, running her own small hospital, the Anglo-Serbian Children's Hospital in Belgrade, with some funding from the Scottish Women's Hospitals.

If being a volunteer at the hospital did not suit her, living in Belgrade did provide the opportunity for Mary to continue her ballet training. Perhaps Hugh had attended ballet performances at the National Theatre, or he may have seen the Ballets Russes or Pavlova's companies in London.

Nonetheless, he supported Mary's ballet training at the studio run by Elena Poliakova who had settled in Belgrade after the Russian Revolution. Despite the upheavals of the revolution and leaving Russia, through news exchanged among *émigré* communities and mutual friends, Eduardova in Berlin almost certainly would have been able to tell Mary that her former colleague from the Mariinsky and the Ballets Russes was in Belgrade, and it would not have been long before Mary sought her out. Hugh also created a practice studio in their house – he may have been indulging his young wife, but he must also have taken her aspirations seriously.

⁂

By the late 1920s, ballet in Yugoslavia and especially in Belgrade and Zagreb, had benefitted for nearly a decade from the energy and creativity of Poliakova and another Russian dancer, Margarita Froman (Frohman). Not only could Mary take classes with Poliakova and build on what she had learned with Eduardova, but there was growing interest in and support for ballet performances and the National Theatre was expanding its *répertoire*. It was not long before she became friends with two other young dancers, Ana Roje and Oskar Harmoš, and over the next fifteen or so years, until after the Second World War, they trained and then worked together, and they remained close friends for the rest of their lives. As dancers, and then as teachers, they were shaped by the dancers, teachers and choreographers who came before them, including Michel Fokine from St Petersburg and the American dancer Isadora Duncan – but their experience was rooted in the Russian classical tradition as a result of the arrival in Yugoslavia of the Russians who formed the nucleus of permanent companies and established ballet schools and studios. These Russian dancers came into an environment which was ready to accept and support them. And while Belgrade and Zagreb may have remained outside the mainstream of ballet performance and pedagogy between the late 1800s and the end of the First World War, a number of internationally recognised dancers emerged in later years, including Milorad Mišković, Mia Corak Slavenska, Igor Youskevich and Jelko Yuresha (Željko Jureša), as well as Ana and Oskar themselves. As the careers of Mary, Ana and Oskar progressed, they were shaped also by the development of dance in Yugoslavia through the 1930s: Mary's interest in character dance, which had been fostered by Eduardova, developed into a life-long study of European and Yugoslav regional folk dances; Ana focused on ballet in the Russian classical tradition and went on to become one of the country's foremost performers and teachers; while Oskar embraced the new modern style which originated in Germany, and brought that experience to his choreography.

Both opera and drama were regularly performed in the larger cities, with the National Theatres opening in Zagreb in 1860, in Belgrade in 1869 and Ljubljana in 1892. In the nineteenth century, ballet was produced for opera and some touring groups visited. Regular performances of ballet took place earlier in Zagreb than in Belgrade, but then languished between the end of the century and the early 1920s. Classical ballet was not performed regularly in Belgrade until after the First World War. Poliakova and Froman, who settled in Belgrade and Zagreb, respectively, may not have known each other in Russia since Poliakova's training was in St Petersburg and she danced with the Mariinsky company, while Froman trained in Moscow and danced with the Bolshoi. But they were colleagues in Diaghilev's Ballets Russes and brought that common experience to Yugoslavia, staging ballets by Fokine, Léonide Massine, David Lichine and Boris Romanov. They are both important in Mary's story – Poliakova because of her studio in Belgrade and Froman because of her choreography of new works based on Yugoslav themes, including the ballet "Svatovac" (a wedding dance) and the dance sequences for the comic opera "Ero s onoga svijeta" ("Ero the Joker"). "Svatovac" and the final *kolo* (a traditional circle dance) from "Ero the Joker" were performed many times by Mary's students in England from the 1950s to the late 1970s.

In Belgrade, a ballet company attached to the opera of the National Theatre was formed around 1920 and a ballet school was established under the direction of Claudia Issachenko (Klavdia Isačenko), a principal dancer. Shortly afterwards, having first worked at the National Theatre in Ljubljana as a dancer and choreographer, and then as a teacher at the Conservatory, Poliakova arrived in Belgrade in February 1922. Born Elena Dmitrievna in May 1884, in St Petersburg, she graduated from the Theatre School in 1902 in the same class as Tamara Karsavina and Lydia Kyasht under Pavel Gerdt and Enrico Cecchetti and, after graduation, in the *classe de perfectionnement* taught by Christian Johansson and Nicolai Legat. After much thought, and reluctant to hurt Legat's feelings, Karsavina decided she needed a female teacher and moved to Evgenia Sokolova's class. Poliakova may well have followed suit. At the Theatre School she must have taken her academic studies seriously since Karsavina says that she prepared for their final exams with "Elena", calling her the "clever girl" of the story of Batioushka, a Russian holy man. In a photograph of the graduating class, Poliakova sits between Karsavina and Kyasht, with Alexandra Cherniatina, Ekaterina Prudnikova and Alexandra Fedorova standing behind them, and Evgenia Lopukhova (elder sister of Lydia and Fedor) seated to the left. Karsavina, Kyasht and Poliakova, are shown in a studio portrait from around the same time. Their graduation performance, held at the Mikhailovsky Theatre, was the "In the Kingdom of Ice" scene from "The Sparks of Love", revived by Gerdt. Karsavina had appeared in the graduation performances of Fokine and Pavlova in 1898 and 1899, and it is probable that Poliakova did as well.

Poliakova, Karsavina and Kyasht often danced together. At the beginning of 1903, they and Evgenia Lopukhova were Lace Dolls in the "The Fairy Doll" choreographed by Nicolai and Sergei Legat, and Poliakova danced with Karsavina and Mikhail Obukhov in the *pas de trois* in the revival of "The Haarlem Tulip" in the same year. Nicolai Legat, Vera Trefilova and Lydia's brother Georgi (Georgy Kyaksht) were in the leading roles. Poliakova took part in Edvard Fazer's tour of northern Europe in May and June of 1908, together with Eduardova and Legat. She returned to the Mariinsky for the 1908–1909 season when she was joined in "La Source" by Karsavina, who had just come back from Prague. (Lydia Kyasht had taken up a contract in London and did not return to St Petersburg except for short visits before the First World War.) Poliakova also danced in "La Esmeralda" and "The Sleeping Beauty" before joining the Ballets Russes, where she was among the principal dancers in the company's first season, in the *première* of "Schéhérazade" on 4 June 1910 at the Opéra de Paris (Paris Opera). Serge Grigoriev, *régisseur* (responsible for productions) with the Ballets Russes, describes an early rehearsal for "Schéhérazade" in St Petersburg; Sophie Fedorova was brought in from Moscow to join Vera Fokina (Michel Fokine's wife) and Poliakova in the *pas de trois* for the Odalisques in the opening scene, in which Fokine required them to sit on the stage and use only their arms, heads and upper bodies – an idea that was strange to all three (Grigoriev, "The Diaghilev Ballet 1909–1929"). Poliakova danced as Myrtha in "Giselle" in Paris on 17 and 18 June, when Karsavina and Nijinsky took the roles of Giselle and Albrecht. That she danced the third principal role in "Giselle" with Karsavina and Nijinsky shows that she was not merely a capable dancer but a ballerina in the St Petersburg tradition, as well as being able to embrace the sensuousness of Fokine's choreography for "Schéhérazade". Having danced with the Ballets

Russes for its first season, on her return to Russia, she gained the rank of soloist with the Mariinsky.

Poliakova left Russia with her family in 1920 and settled in Belgrade, where she was offered an engagement with the National Theatre beginning in September 1922. She choregraphed for the opera, and then staged "The Nutcracker", "Schéhérazade" and "Les Sylphides" to the appreciation of Belgrade audiences. Historian Viktor Kosik and musicologists Melita Milin and Nadežda Mosusova provide insight into Poliakova's work over the next few years, which included performance as well as choreography and staging for opera. She danced the role of Swanhilda in "Coppélia" in June 1924, in "Swan Lake" in the following year and in her Ballets Russes role of Myrtha in "Giselle". Her contract was not renewed in 1927, although she continued to appear as a guest artist. Her last performance was in May 1929, when she danced in "The Little Humpbacked Horse" before King Alexander of Yugoslavia, the same ballet as the gala performance for the Tsar in 1902. Poliakova taught at Issachenko's school shortly after her arrival in Belgrade but established her own studio in 1927, not long before Mary joined her class. Her students were both Russian and Yugoslav and, like Eduardova's school in Berlin and the studios of Olga Preobrazhenskaya and Mathilde Kschessinskaya in Paris, it became well respected. Later, she taught ballet at the Belgrade Academy of Music between 1937 and 1940.

Another Russian, Alexander Fortunato, came originally from Lviv (now in western Ukraine). As the first director of the Belgrade ballet, he staged the Russian works in which Poliakova performed, including "Coppélia" (the first full-length ballet mounted in the city), "The Polovtsian Dances" and "Swan Lake", and "Giselle". Nina Kirsanova also shaped the company over the many years from when she joined it in 1923. Somewhat younger than Poliakova and Froman (she was born in 1898), Kirsanova trained in Moscow with Lydia Nelidova. She was accepted into the Bolshoi company but left Russia shortly after with her husband Boris Popov an opera singer. They went first to Poland and then moved on to Belgrade where she danced until 1926. She and Fortunato then left to dance elsewhere in Europe. Kirsanova went on to tour with Pavlova, dancing with Pierre Vladimiroff, Leon Woizikowski and Cleo Nordi, among others. It may have been just before she joined Pavlova's company that she took classes with Nicolai Legat in Paris in 1927 since, in "The Legat Saga", John Gregory quotes a letter in which Legat wrote that Kirsanova was "going over" to Pavlova, at the loss of another three hundred francs in income. She was Pavlova's principal dancer and another particularly brilliant character dancer. Kirsanova returned to direct the Belgrade ballet in 1931, by which time Mary and Ana and Oskar were all in the company. She led the company's first international tour to Athens, in 1933; Froman's "Licitarsko srce" ("The Gingerbread Heart") was among the ballets performed and this may well have been when Mary visited Greece, as mentioned in E.C. Mason's profile in *Dance and Dancers* (October 1957). Kirsanova left three years later to go the opera company in Monte Carlo and the National Theatre in Kaunas, Lithuania. But by the late 1930s the rumblings of war in Europe drew her back to Belgrade, which she regarded as her second home.

Although Mary was not directly associated with the theatre in Zagreb, development of ballet in the city and the people involved bear on her story since it was Oskar's home, he and Ana worked there later, and it was where "Svatovac" and "Ero the Joker" were first performed. Dancing was an important aspect of social life in Zagreb, perhaps more than in Belgrade, which was less influenced by the customs of Austria-Hungary. In her book "Zagreb: A Cultural History", Celia Hawkesworth describes how traditional dance forms became a symbol of Croatian national unity in the nineteenth century when the region was still part of the Austro-Hungarian Empire, and notes that dance was an integral part of the Illyrian Movement which promoted Croatian linguistic and cultural unity among the South Slavs. A permanent opera ensemble was established in 1870, although the first ballet master and choreographer Pietro Coronelli had arrived earlier, in 1859, maintaining a dancing school there until his death in 1902. A ballet ensemble for the opera company was formed in 1876 for which Coronelli became the ballet master. Ivana Freisinger was engaged for the 1876–1877 season, when she was recognised as Croatia's first ballerina, although she came originally from Budapest. Coronelli revived the "Hrvatsko Salonsko Kolo", a version of the *quadrille* which incorporated elements of Croatian folk *kolos*, but which had been suppressed for political reasons in the mid-1800s. This led him to embark on a study of Croatian dances, foreshadowing others' work in the period between the First and Second World Wars. A ballet ensemble and a ballet school were established by Stjepan Miletić when he was appointed manager of the National Theatre in 1894. He engaged Emma Grondona, who had trained at La Scala in Milan as principal dancer, and she danced in the first performances of "Coppélia" and "Giselle" and a number of other ballets. The first Croatian ballet, "na Plitvičkim jezerima" ("At the Plitviče Lakes"), with choreography by Bela Adamovic and music by Srećko Albini, was staged in 1898.

With the departure of Miletić and the death of Coronelli, however, ballet lost its momentum in Zagreb until Margarita Froman led a resurgence of interest and activity and fostered a national approach which was influenced both by folk tales and melodies, as well as by the German contemporary dance movement. Margarita Froman was born in Moscow on 27 October 1890. The daughter of a Swedish father and Russian mother, she was accepted into the Imperial Theatre School at the age of eight, where she studied under Vasily Tikhomirov, graduating into the Bolshoi company in 1909 and quickly becoming a soloist. Both she and her brother Maximilian, or Max, who also danced in the Bolshoi company, were engaged as principals with the Ballets Russes and appeared in a number of the *première* performances between 1911 and 1914. Margarita was a princess in "Sadko – In the Underwater Kingdom" on 6 June 1911 at the Théâtre du Châtelet in Paris and both Margarita and Max appeared in the season at the Royal Opera House, Covent Garden, in June and July 1911, where the programmes included "The Polovtsian Dances", "Le Pavillon d'Armide", "Schéhérazade", "Les Sylphides" and "Le Spectre de la rose". Like Elena Poliakova, Margarita and Max experienced the excitement and challenges of performing with the Ballets Russes in its earliest days when it was taking Paris and London by storm, leaving audiences astonished by the music and costumes, as much as by the dancing. They would have enjoyed the freedom of costumes that were light and unstructured for "Daphnis et Chloé" and cursed the difficulty of moving in the heavy and cumbersome costumes of "Sadko" and "Le Rossignol". They would have struggled, with the rest of the company, to learn Nijinsky's choreography to Igor Stravinsky's score for "The Rite of Spring".

In October 1916, Margarita and Olga Spessivtseva were engaged by the Metropolitan Music Bureau for a gruelling cross-country tour of the United States for which their first performance was in "Les Sylphides" in New York. However, the tour ran into financial difficulties and both dancers were dropped from the troupe in San Francisco at the end of the year as the company and Metropolitan tried to cut costs. Margarita toured in Europe and the United States with the Ballets Russes in 1917 but then returned to the Bolshoi for a short time, when she danced the title role in Mikhail Mordkin's "Legend of Aziade" and in performances of "Coppélia" and "The Sleeping Beauty". The Fromans' brother, Valentin, also a student at the Theatre School, was not associated with the ballet in Yugoslavia for an extended period but later went on to dance with a successor to the Ballets Russes after Diaghilev's death, Colonel de Basil's Ballets Russes.

Margarita, Max and Valentin arrived in Yugoslavia in 1921 with another brother, Pavel. Melita Milin, Nadežda Mosusova and Viktor Kosik, writing about how Russians contributed to music and ballet in the country, note that Margarita came to Zagreb with a company formed with Max and Valentin. She was appointed head of the Zagreb ballet, Max was engaged as *danseur*, Pavel as designer (he worked on over forty productions) and Valentin as choreographer. At the time, the National Theatre was directed by Julije Benešić and ballet received strong support. Over the next ten years, the Fromans staged works by Arthur Saint-Léon, Marius Petipa and Michel Fokine from the Russian and Diaghilev *répertoire*, including "Swan Lake", "Coppélia", "Schéhérazade", "Le Papillon", "The Polovtsian Dances", "Petrushka" and "Le Carnaval". Margarita choreographed "Cvijeće male Ide", based on Hans Christian Andersen's "Little Ida's Flowers", in 1925. "Le Boiteau" and versions of "Raymonda" (1927), "The Little Humpbacked Horse" (1928) and "Les Noces" (1932) are also credited to her.

Margarita Froman was the first to choreograph major theatrical works based on Yugoslav themes to music by Yugoslav composers. She built on the interest in national dance that had been fostered by the popular character *divertissements* performed by the Russian touring groups before the First World War and her own experience with the Ballets Russes, as well as the resurgence of interest in Croatian dance and music. As Mosusova notes in "Are Folkloric Ballets an Anachronism Today?", the use of orchestral music for these works was particularly important. Ivan Zajc wrote the music for "Svatovac", which was orchestrated by Krešimir Baranović and first performed in 1922, while Baranović composed the music for "The Gingerbread Heart" in 1924, for which he also wrote the libretto. "Svatovac", a "dance of the wedding guests" is based on a village marriage broker's attempt to marry a rich bachelor to a young girl, with a supporting cast of friends and relations, while "The Gingerbread Heart" brings together the Russian classical ballet tradition, a score based on folk melodies and a village love story. Having retired from the stage in the mid-1930s, Froman remained as choreographer and ballet mistress, and directed opera at the Zagreb theatre until after the Second War. Among the operas was "Ero the Joker", for which she choreographed the dances, including the final *kolo*. Its composer, Jacov Gotovac, conducted the first performance on 2 November 1935 at the Croatian National Theatre in Zagreb. He had come from the coastal town of Split to Zagreb in 1923 and remained the conductor of the opera of the theatre there until 1958. "Ero the Joker" opened in Belgrade in

April 1937, when Mary may well have danced in it for the first time. Froman also choreographed the ballet "Imbrek z nosom" ("Imbrek with a Nose" or "Long-nosed Imbrek"), to music by Baranović, in 1935.

As well as dancers trained in the Russian tradition, the husband-and-wife team of Pino and Pia Mlakar was another important influence on the development of dance and ballet in Yugoslavia. Pino Mlakar was born in Novo Mesto in Slovenia in 1907. Although at first he studied science, he went to Germany in 1926 to train with the modern dance theorist Rudolf Laban at the Rudolf Laban Choreographic Institute in Würtzburg where he met his wife *née* Maria Luiza Pia Beatrice Scholz, who was born in Hamburg in 1908. They were also students of Poliakova in the 1920s but divided their time between Yugoslavia and Germany. By 1929, they had been appointed directors of the ballet company in Darmstadt and from there went on to hold similar positions in Dessau, Zurich and Munich. Their first chorographic success came with the second prize awarded at the choreographic competition in 1932, sponsored by the Archives Internationales de la Danse, with "Un Amour du moyen âge" ("A Ballad of Medieval Love") to music by Vivaldi and Bach. The first prize in that competition was awarded to the expressionist choreographer Kurt Jooss for his best-known work, "The Green Table". They were invited to Belgrade to stage "Die Josephslegende" ("The Legend of Joseph") and "Till Eulenspiegel" to Richard Strauss's music in 1934. This was followed by "Đavu u selu" ("The Devil in the Village") with music by Fran Lhotka. The *première* was in Zurich in February 1935, and the ballet was performed in Zagreb in 1937 and Belgrade in 1938. "A Ballad of Medieval Love" was mounted in 1937 and "The Arc" in 1939. "The Devil in the Village" remains in the *répertoire* of the Croatian National Theatre and was later staged by the composer's son Nenad Lhotka for the Royal Winnipeg Ballet in Canada, and by Oskar Harmoš for the inaugural performance of the Bermuda Civic Ballet.

New dance styles of the early twentieth century had been brought to Yugoslavia before the arrival of the Mlakars, however, and in the period between the wars ballet in Croatia was influenced by dancers who trained in the expressionist style with both Mary Wigman in Germany and Gertrud Bodenwieser in Austria. Maga Magazinović studied with Isadora Duncan and set up a school in Belgrade in 1910 that later became the Škola ritmiku i plastiku Maga Magazinović (School of Rhythmics and Plastics of Maga Magazinović, *plastique* being a term used to describe flowing dance movements) and, in 1912, she travelled to Germany to study with Émile

Jaques-Dalcroze. Magazinović was a pioneer in more than modern dance. She was the first woman to graduate from the Faculty of Philosophy in Belgrade, the first woman to write for the *Politika* daily newspaper and the first woman librarian at the National Library of Serbia. She was born in Užice in 1882 and died in 1968. Issachenko had introduced a modified form of the Duncan style to Belgrade. Her student, Ana Maletić, studied with Laban in Berlin and returned to Zagreb, where she established her own school in 1932.

It was Margarita Froman and the Mlakars who led the development of Yugoslavia's own ballet tradition based on regional folk tales and the music of contemporary composers including Baranović, Gotovac, Stevan Hristić, Lhotka, Alfred Pordes and Svetomir Nastasijević. Mosusova describes how, as dancers, Alexander Fortunato and Anatoli Zhukovski (a student of Poliakova) were also particularly interested in traditional folk dance. In the early 1920s, Fortunato spent time in southern Serbia around Lake Ochrid on the border with Albania conducting research for Hristić's "Ohridska legenda" ("The Legend of Ochrid"), although this was not produced as a one-act ballet until 1933, when he had already left Belgrade. By then, Zhukovski was the leading soloist in Belgrade and worked closely with Kirsanova on its production. He also travelled to study the dances of southern Yugoslavia and the area around Lake Ochrid and trained some of the dancers in the company in Belgrade in these folk dances. Later, he went further afield to Greece, Bulgaria and Romania. Although Zhukovski is mentioned only briefly by Mary in the interview with Patricia Deane-Gray, she clearly knew his work as a choreographer and is likely to have danced in "The Legend of Ochrid", and may even have been among the dancers to whom he taught the pieces which he had learned in his field studies. It was not until after the war, in 1947, that Margarita Froman brought the full-length version of "The Legend of Ochrid" to the stage. Popular for many years, it continues to be restaged by other choreographers.

Mary describes the first time she met Ana Roje in 1929 or early 1930, not long after she started to train with Poliakova at her studio in Kosovska ulica, not far from the National Theatre, saying:

"She was there when I came, and we, well we looked at each other for perhaps a month, maybe six weeks, something, and I always admired her line, in dancing, but she was always very sad. So, on that day, when we really met, and why we came together, is because she fainted in the school... She was fading away completely. And I could not speak any Yugoslav. I spoke Russian of course, but not Yugoslav. And I asked a friend of mine whether she would ask her why she fainted. And she said, "I have nowhere to go and live, because I was here at my Aunt's and we had this disagreement and I don't know where to go". So, I said, "Tell her not to be sorry, tell her not to worry; I just would like her to dress, and I take you to my home". I told Madame Poliakova that I am taking her with me home, and my chauffeur was waiting outside in my car, and I took her home to my villa in Belgrade, outside Belgrade, opposite the racing place, where the [horse] races were held... Topčider. And she stayed with me... My husband said, "Whom have you brought?" And I said, "This girl will stay with us." "Oh!" he said, "All right. How long is she going to stay?" And I said, "Well, we see what we are going to do." And, anyway she stayed with us for about a year I should think. And we went together to the school, and Ana was waiting to get an engagement to the theatre...

Yes, it must have been that year, that I also decided I will go and have a go at the theatre and see if they have me. And, we then, you see, went together to the theatre, we had the lessons there and we had the engagement, and we slowly went into the *répertoire*... In the opera, in the ballet, in Belgrade... We danced not the first roles but, you know, solo parts... And from there out, we decided to have concerts of our own. And we travelled round together with Oskar... Either we went as three of us, or we went with some of the soloists of the Belgrade ballet.

Eduardova's teaching in Berlin had given Mary a firm and thorough foundation and Poliakova's classes were what she needed at an advanced level on a day-to-day basis. Although Hugh was prepared to provide for Mary's advanced training, it may have been Ana and Oskar who gave her the support she needed to seriously pursue a career as a dancer. The three of them rapidly became friends and, as they started to perform together, both with the ballet company of the National Theatre and in their own engagements, they became professional colleagues as well.

It seems that, as a member of Hugh's household, Ana was invited to legation functions, although Oskar was not. Mary goes on:

> All my life in the theatre and all my life with my first husband was very, very busy… and my life was socially going, as much as ballet, which was very difficult because I had social, social obligations, yes, and I had also those of the dance… So, it was very difficult. Yes, [we had] a very social time, of which Oskar was very jealous!

In agreeing to give Ana a home, Hugh again showed his willingness to support an aspiring dancer – it has to be supposed that their house could comfortably accommodate a long-term guest without Hugh feeling that his home life had been too disrupted. His official duties at the British legation would have been reasonably demanding in the 1930s, giving Mary time for classes and rehearsals during the day. But she would have been expected to accompany Hugh to evening functions and perhaps to host some of them.

Ana's home was in Split, where she was born on 17 October 1909 at 23 Vrhmanuška ulica (now 27 Tolstojeva ulica), not far from the walls of the palace of the Roman Emperor Diocletian. As described in the biography, "Ana Roje", by Davor Schopf and Mladen Mordej Vučković, she was brought up with her elder sister, Jelka, and three brothers, Jakov, Tonči and Bogumil. She apprenticed as a milliner but, through a colleague, heard about an audition to be held by the conductor Ivo Tijardović for female dancers at the theatre. Then completely untrained, she was accepted and allowed to enter the theatre under the watchful eyes of her brothers. She danced in opera and operetta and one of her first roles was the "Kraljica lopte", or "Queen of the Ball", in Tijardović's operetta about football of the same name and which had its *première* in August 1926 to mark the fifteenth anniversary of the Hajduk football club. With a scholarship from the city of Split and support from some private sponsors, Ana was able to go to Zagreb in 1927 to study with Margarita Froman and it was at the theatre there that she met Oskar Harmoš. Almost immediately, they started to practise together and then danced together as partners in Dalmatia. Oskar recalls in his unpublished memoir (referenced by Schopf and Vučković) that when he first saw Ana she was wearing a black dress, a wide-brimmed black hat, black shoes (bought two sizes too big so that they would last) and carried an umbrella with which to protect herself. In Zagreb, she became known as the "Black Natasha" ("Crna Nataša") on account of a recent popular novel which featured a girl in a black dress. The protective umbrella would later appear in Nicolai Legat's caricature of Ana drawn in London. Zagreb had a lively café scene; the Theatre Café (Kazališna kavana), opposite the National Theatre, opened in 1906, and became something of a cultural institution among students and theatre people, Ana and Oskar included, for long conversations and debate.

Ana Roje, caricature by Nicolai Legat, courtesy of the Legat Foundation.

There is little readily accessible biographical material in English on Oskar Harmoš, although a biography is in preparation by Mladen Mordej Vučković and Davor Schopf. In addition to the limited information in Ana's biography, confirmation of dates and some other details of his work are given in the entry in the "Hrvatski biografski leksikon" ("Croatian Biographical Lexicon"). Just a little younger than Ana and Mary, he was born in Zagreb on 25 February 1911. He acted as a child and was a pupil at the ballet school of the National Theatre in Zagreb from the early age of six, where he was taught by Josefine Weiss. He joined the ballet company in Zagreb around 1922, when Froman was ballet mistress. Then, from 1928 to 1930, he and Ana toured in India, Japan and China performing their own pieces. A note in the *Dancing Times* (July 1960) says he danced with the short-lived Ballet Russe de Paris. Froman's obituary in the *Willamantic Daily Chronicle* (25 March, 1970) notes that she formed a touring troupe with her most talented pupils and this may well have included Ana and Oskar.

Oskar was tall and striking-looking, though not conventionally handsome. He had high cheekbones, large eyes and a pronounced aquiline nose, and he used these features to advantage in the roles of the Devil in "The Devil in the Village" by Pino and Pina Mlakar and Death in Kurt Jooss' "The Green Table". Jill Lhotka, who knew and worked with him some years later, describes him as a "big bear of a man" not having the typical build of a dancer, a man whose philosophy was to enjoy life to the full and who was an immensely gifted character artist. He was a prolific choreographer, starting in his late teens with the pieces he developed for performances with Ana,

Self-caricature by Oskar Harmoš, collection of Katherine Mason.

progressing through ballet for opera and operetta, short dances and variations from "Swan Lake" and "The Sleeping Beauty", and restaging works by Froman. Although Oskar trained in classical ballet, physically he was better suited to modern dance, which he studied with Laban in Germany and possibly with Maletić in Zagreb. Later, he appeared in two films, "Barok u Hrvatskoj" ("Baroque in Croatia") with Ana in 1942 and a full-length comedy "Bakonje fra Brne" ("Ivo, the Monk") in 1951, in which the husband of Mary's sister Kitty Viktor Starčić had the more prominent part of Kusmelj.

Ana's ambitions soon extended beyond Zagreb, however, and Margarita Froman's return at the end of the 1920s from a couple of years working in Belgrade was not enough to keep her there. She was ready to audition for the National Theatre in Belgrade, as was Oskar. They presented his choreography for a *pas de deux* to Frédéric Chopin's waltz in C flat minor, a piece that they had already performed in Dalmatia. Not only were they successful in their audition but, as Mary mentions in the interview, all three of them went on to become soloists with the company in Belgrade. Ana and Oskar trained with Kirsanova, as well as with Poliakova, and they also took private lessons with Nataša Bošković. Almost certainly, Mary worked with Kirsanova and Bošković as well. But Ana was looking even further afield and particularly wanted to study with Nicolai Legat, whose reputation as a teacher would have come to Yugoslavia with Poliakova and Froman, and other dancers from Russia.

CHAPTER 6
IN ENGLAND WITH NICOLAI LEGAT

Steak and artichokes and *sauce hollandaise*

Ana Roje writes in her article on "The Art and Science of Teaching Ballet" (reproduced in the biography by Schopf and Vučković) that, while it had seemed impossible that she might study with Legat, "as in a fairy tale, destiny one day brought me to the great Legat in his London studio". "Destiny" was manifest in Mary and Hugh, who, having given Ana a home in Belgrade, were instrumental in realising her ambition to work with Legat. Hugh undertook to support Ana's professional training for a year. Even if his resources were such that the cost was not a major consideration, this commitment cannot have been taken without careful thought. He must have seen for himself that Ana was unusually talented and worthy of his assistance. Without Hugh's support at a critical time in her career, Ana's life would have been very different and her contribution to the development of ballet in Yugoslavia and to a generation of students, both there and in the United States, would have been much less. Mary describes how it came about, probably in the summer of 1933:

> She [Ana] was always talking about, "I do not want to stay in the Belgrade theatre. I want to go higher. I want to go to Nicolas Legat. He is a wonderful teacher". And when we [Mary and Hugh] went before – we went several times a year to London and to his family in Dorchester, because they had a very enormous house [Somerleigh Court] in Dorchester – in Dorset, Dorchester. I made... I tried to find out through the theatres and everything where Legat was. At

first it was thought he was in France. Then we knew he had opened a school in London. So, when we knew that the school was in London, I said, "Now comes the moment, Ana, when we can go to London and you can meet Legat and we shall arrange a meeting and see if he will have you". But, for myself, no, there was no question that I could stay, you know, stay in London because he [Hugh Pearse] had to go back. Because, in the meantime, he had changed... He said, "It is not fair that the embassy will send you somewhere else. I want you to have your own life with me and not being always responsible to all the social things that go on. And we will go back, of course, to Yugoslavia." ...So we brought Ana then, it was arranged that we go in the summer to see my mother-in-law, my sister-in-law... that we take Ana.

She goes on:

[We] made an appointment to see Mr Legat... in his school [in] Colet Gardens. Now it is completely different. It doesn't really exist anymore. Well, it does exist, but it is not a school, a ballet school. And there he talked to her – I think he took her into the class. I don't think that I watched it, I was too busy. And we arranged with an English friend of mine that she would stay with her. I mean, she would have a room there... And we would pay the fees... for a year. And from then on I left her.

Mary must have been able to find out about Legat's studio in London, only a year or so after he had, in fact, moved from Paris in 1930. It was located in Colet House, 46 Colet Gardens in Barons Court. Not only does the red brick and sandstone building still stand at the western end of the terrace known as St Paul's Studios, both the exterior and interior are largely unchanged from Legat's time, although the address became 151 Talgarth Road when the busy artery out towards London Airport was built along the southern arm of Colet Gardens in the 1960s. While Ana came to Legat looking for a final polish to her technique, his first reaction was to tell her that she had to relearn everything that she already knew, that she did not even know how to stand correctly. But he clearly recognised that Ana was particularly gifted. The first few months were spent working only at the *barre*, studying the most basic positions of the feet and the purpose of each exercise. The issues which Legat identified must have originated with her earliest training. But, unlike Froman, Kirsanova and Poliakova, Legat was unencumbered by the responsibilities of running a company and he had the time and patience to work intensively with her. Through those years, Ana became a beloved pupil, working hard to improve her technique, learning to speak Russian with him and being introduced to Russian literature.

Mary's recollection in the interview of her own classes with Legat captures his liveliness and sense of humour:

Oh yes, that was an absolutely special person. He was small, very small. Not, not bigger than about five foot... five... I don't know whether it was before or what, but when I met him, he had not one single hair on his head. Completely bald and... his arms and his eyes, and his face was never still. When he talked, it was living, his whole body moved, and his face moved, and his hands moved and his fingers moved to explain something, whether it was about dancing or about something funny, or how he would do all the caricatures. Yes. Because there was a trunk [torso] and from a trunk was a face, usually a friend, who was mixed in with it... And of course, it was always wonderful for anyone to come along and meet him. And in the school, when he played the piano, he was even more alive. Because he gave the piano, he gave the rhythm, and he gave the steps. And the steps were never... we had never to wait for steps, he just gave us the *enchaînement*, and when it was ready, he said, "Now then, this one comes and that one comes." He did not talk much because he did not speak English very well. Well, we had so many things because we had a man in there who could never move his foot. And he called him "The Iron" [for pressing clothes]. Yes, I don't know whether he is still dancing... [Another] was so thin, he called him "a Thread". But he used to say it in Russian, "The Thread, of course, does not do that *pirouette* as I told him..." Yes, nicknames for most people he could make a caricature from. But he could not from me. But of course, there is that lovely one from Ana... many... from Ana. He could caricature her and many other people. He sits in the restaurant and he makes the picture – something special. Because he caricatured Ninette de Valois... [and many others in the ballet world].

Ana's particular nickname was kinder than "The Iron" or "The Thread". Legat called her "Zaika", or "Dear Little Rabbit" because she would listen and take home all of what he said during the day and then work through it for herself and prepare her questions. He called Mary "Mussia", the same endearment as her mother's. Unfortunately, there are no caricatures of Mary and, as she says, he could not capture her likeness successfully. Anton Dolin, by then dancing with the Vic-Wells company, was given the nickname "Piccadilly" after the statue of Eros in Piccadilly Circus, although it was a couple of years before he understood what his nickname actually meant. Legat's caricatures reference his acrobatic abilities, which Bronislava Nijinska drew on for "Le Train bleu" ("The Blue Train"); one of them shows him wearing only shorts and ballet shoes (and white socks wrinkled at the ankles) in a handstand with his legs arched over his back.

∽

After the year of financial support from Hugh ended, Ana made some money by dancing at private parties and receptions because she could not perform publicly under the terms of her immigration status in Britain. Oskar joined her in London around 1935 after he had completed his national service. A photograph of him with Legat at one of the two wrought-iron gates on either side of Colet House is given in both Ana's biography and in "The Legat Saga". While he and Mary were not in England with Ana continuously through this period, they also enjoyed a close relationship with Legat that extended beyond that of teacher and student. Despite her limited opportunities to perform in public, Ana was already noted for her lightness and line and was a source of amazement at the studio for the time that she could balance in arabesque *en pointe* – long enough to enjoy a cigarette. She had become Legat's trusted assistant and the biography also quotes, or paraphrases, Legat as saying, "When I die, she will be the only one who has the knowledge and will be able to continue and prolong the momentous school and system that was left as inheritance to me by the great masters." In "My Life in Ballet – A Russian Heritage", Anna Lendrum, also a student of Legat, remembers Ana as a brilliant technician, but who was always ready to assist anyone who needed help with a particular movement.

For Mary, however, by the mid-1930s, the struggle of reconciling her life as a dancer and in the theatre with that of a diplomat's wife resulted in her separation from Hugh – as she says in the interview, "It was too much for

Mary Pearse!" In the early days, the social life of a diplomatic service wife in a city with a diverse and lively cultural scene must have been an exciting contrast to family life in Berlin. Belgrade was the centre of commercial and diplomatic activities and, at first, Mary's social obligations would have been amusing and interesting, notwithstanding her failed attempt as a hospital volunteer. But as time passed, and as she became more established in the theatre and in performing, she would have been increasingly aware of the near-impossibility of reconciling the two parts of her double life, or even of reconciling her own ambitions and personal growth with what Hugh was able to offer. By the middle of the decade, too, the circle of Mary's friends included Yugoslav and Russian dancers from the ballet company in Belgrade. Through Hugh and her brother-in-law Robert Smith she had friends in the British community and she also had Russian friends who were not dancers. By then, she would have met Viktor Starčić, an actor and the future husband of her younger sister Kitty. The difference in the ages of Mary and Hugh may well have been a factor in their separation; he was established in his career and approaching middle age while she was at the beginning of her own career as a professional dancer and needed to train and perform as much as she could.

Hugh's photographs suggest a very kind, but serious person; his war record shows a clear-headed man of courage; the note in the Wellington College Yearbook describes a man with a sense of responsibility and genuine interest in his pupils and the school community, and his financial support of Ana's training in London shows a real interest in ballet and, it must be assumed, in Mary's own aspirations as well. But as Mary's husband, and as an individual, he remains in the shadows. The rather enigmatic suggestion from Mary that he might leave the diplomatic service or move from Belgrade – "I want you to have your own life with me and not being always responsible to all the social things that go on" – could imply that he was considering leaving the service so that she would have a more stable life. But by 1936, however, the wording of a letter from Hugh written in Russian from Somerleigh Court to Katherine Mason's mother in Belgrade suggests that he was no longer working there and, from this point on, he fades from the scene.

⁓

As she separated from Hugh, Mary decided that she would also study with Legat. She recalls:

I was going everywhere... travelled an awful lot, but I came to England to settle because I wanted to continue the dancing. And we met with Ana, who by that time was, I mean, more than a year passed... she was already his [Legat's] assistant... He was very, very, very interested in her and thought her very, very talented. And we lived all together in a Russian pension in Colet Gardens, at the beginning of Colet Gardens. I think that was two or three Colet Gardens but I don't remember the number of the school. It was also in Colet Gardens... It was a little, like a little boarding house... but I think Oskar was living there.

The "little boarding house" was number 1 Colet Gardens, the home of Mrs Viatkin and almost certainly the same house where Ana had stayed. Mrs Viatkin is listed in the Kelly's Directory from 1931–1932 to 1937–1938 living at number 1, which is the third house south from Hammersmith Road. Kelly's Directory for the early 1930s also lists numbers 1a and 1b, and the houses remain numbered this way, with 1a and 1b coming before number 1.

A somewhat more formal perspective of how she came to train with Legat is given in Mary's recollection in "Heritage of A Ballet Master: Nicolas Legat" by André Eglevsky and John Gregory:

From the moment I joined Mr. Legat's Class of Perfection in London a new life seemed to open before my eyes. I had been trained by several eminent Russian teachers on the continent and enjoyed their classes at which we all worked until we were exhausted. However, this was something different; here with Legat we felt refreshed after finishing a lesson. After several months I still felt the same remarkable effect, so I decided to stay in England and train regularly with Legat. As it happened, I was one of the lucky people who lived for a time in the same boarding house as the master.

I found him a most warm-hearted person, but he did not mix easily. Once you knew him and he regarded you as a friend, his personality was exuberant. Then he would open up and expound his inexhaustible knowledge and experience. We often sat up late into the night talking about every kind of dancing, theory, history and temperaments and habits of different countries and their dancing cultures. Mr. Legat was not only a teacher of classical ballet he also had a wide knowledge of national character and mime. Although he did not give a character class with *barre* and centre work, as we do today, I am sure that his talks with us had a great influence on my character work. When he choreographed a national dance, his persuasiveness and explanations were all-embracing.

Mary's conversations with Legat in London, and his classes, would have deepened her interest in character dance which she learned first with Eduardova and was reinforced with the *répertoire* of the company in Belgrade.

In the interview, Mary describes how she, Ana and Oskar enjoyed Legat's company, and he theirs:

[Legat] loved his food but he wasn't very happy with the food that we got in that boarding house, so in the evenings, most evenings, he used to send Oskar and buy some more steaks, and we used to do it in our rooms and he would like something special like artichokes and *sauce hollandaise...* And he would say, "When are you coming, I would rather not eat, I love your company, but come on or I stay here. I can smell the lovely things that are coming." So, it was a wonderful, wonderful time – a wonderful time. Then I was living in the same house as Mr Legat because he, long into the nights, he used to sit and talk to us about... even about character dancing and about the life in Russia, and we just simply took it all in.

Oskar, being the cook that he was, would not only have bought the ingredients for a meal but would have prepared it too. Those long conversations would have been in Russian, or a mixture of Russian and Croatian, and certainly were important to Mary's development as a dancer and as a teacher. That she spoke Russian would have helped to cement her friendship with Legat, which is illustrated not only by sharing steaks and artichokes and *hollandaise* sauce in their boarding house but also by the photograph of the two of them in a playful embrace. It must have been taken in one of the little gardens at the back of Colet House that are separated only by a high brick wall from the rail lines in Barons Court Underground station. In my search for first-hand accounts of Legat's classes in London, I have been unable to find references to suggest that

Mary and Legat share a kiss. The Royal Ballet School Special Collections: Mimi Legat Collection. Photographer unknown.

any of his students, other than Mary and Ana, enjoyed such a degree of close friendship with him.

As well as Eduardova in Berlin and Poliakova in Belgrade, Mary also studied with Olga Preobrazhenskaya, Legat's former partner at the Mariinsky. This would have been in Paris in the 1930s rather than in Berlin, where Preobrazhenskaya taught briefly in the early 1920s. Like the Zybins, she made her way with her dog, Kleva, from Russia to Finland on foot in the bitter cold and snow early in 1921. At the border, however, she found that an exit permit was needed for Kleva. She returned to Petrograd but, by the time Kleva's papers were prepared, her own were out of date. Rather than risk never having both sets of papers in order at the same time, she crossed the border illicitly with the help of friends. In her biography, "Olga Preobrazhenskaya", Elvira Roné suggests that she walked all the way from Petrograd and that it was a "long journey" but gives few details. From Finland, where she had to sell a diamond necklace in order to live and to continue her journey, Preobrazhenskaya travelled to Latvia and then to Berlin. (The selling of a diamond necklace echoes the importance of jewellery as a means of survival to Mary's family, and to many other Russians fleeing Russia with only such valuables as they could easily carry and conceal on a long and unpredictable journey.) Preobrazhenskaya first opened a studio in Charlottenburg, and then in an annex to the Theater des Westens in the centre of the city. She also danced in cabaret but struggled to make ends meet. At the end of the year, she went to La Scala in Milan to work as a choreographer for a short period and danced in a festival in her honour at the Teatro del Popolo. She returned briefly to Berlin but moved permanently to Paris in 1923. One of her last performances was given in 1925 at the Théâtre des Champs-Elysées when she demonstrated old-fashioned dances for a lecture given by the critic André Levinson. In Paris she established a successful school in a large studio above the Olympia Theatre and then moved to the studios of the Salle Wacker near the Paris Opera. (Wacker was a maker of pianos and the lower floors of 69 rue de Douai were taken up with a piano showroom and storage.) Preobrazhenskaya's studio on the fourth floor was reached by a steep iron staircase and had windows on two walls and a mirror on the third. For her classes, she always wore a simple brown tunic over a white top and, being quite short, photographs show her standing on a chair so that she could see her dancers almost as if in a theatre. She is well known for the fact that among her pupils in Paris were two of the three famous "baby ballerinas" of the Ballets Russes de Monte Carlo, Tamara Toumanova and Irina Baronova (the third, Tatiana Riabouchinskaya, studied with Mathilde Kschessinskaya), but her students also included Igor Youskevich and Mia Slavenska from Yugoslavia both of whom became principal dancers with the Ballets Russes de Monte Carlo. (See also Franc L. Scheuer's "Two Celebrated Nurseries of Russian Ballet", *Dancing Times,* December 1933.) Surely Preobrazhenskaya and Mary shared the experiences of their winter journeys across the border into Finland and, surely, she appreciated a student who had trained with her former friends and colleagues.

Having learned all she could from Christian Johansson at the Theatre School, Preobrazhenskaya regarded Enrico Cecchetti as her most important teacher, while in contrast Legat, having learned much from Cecchetti, remained a devoted student of Johansson. Writing in his introduction to Roné's biography of Preobrazhenskaya, the critic Fernau Hall suggests that Cecchetti's approach gave Preobrazhenskaya the strength that she needed to overcome a deformity of the spine and one knee that was particularly hyperextended. Legat, on the other hand, was immensely strong physically, but needed the grace and elegance that only Johansson could give him. They shared the embodiment of what Legat calls *russkaya dusha* or Russian soul, as well as a similar approach to their own teaching. Kathleen Crofton, who appears later in this story, studied intensively with Preobrazhenskaya and writes that she had a gift for understanding the particular requirements of every dancer who came to her, whether an established star or a student (*Dancing Times*, January 1951). Her classes had a natural flow which avoided strain or overworking so that, having finished, her pupils felt strengthened rather than exhausted by their hard work. Similar observations have been applied to the classes of Johansson, Gerdt and Legat. Like Legat, but unlike Cecchetti, Preobrazhenskaya never repeated the centre work for a class so that the *enchaînements* were always "fresh and varied". As at Legat's studio in London, her classes were attended by numerous established dancers who valued her gifts as a teacher; for many of them she was simply Madame Preo.

Preobrazhenskaya was a very private person and rarely invited anyone to visit her in her flat, but those who were allowed in were amazed to find that it was filled with birds in cages. Roné's picture of Madame Preo in her later years is of a sad, rather lonely figure who rebuffed even her friends. It would have been much earlier, in the 1920s, that this happened to Legat, who she had invited to visit but then did not answer the door when he knocked. To comfort him as Legat lay dying in 1937, she sent him her own diamond lyre brooch, the emblem of the Mariinsky presented to principal dancers on the twenty-fifth anniversary of their joining the company, to replace the one he had lost in the revolution; it must also have been a gesture of reconciliation and regret that they had become estranged. Preobrazhenskaya's aversion to visitors was not universal, however. Her former student Irina Baronova relates that, when she and her husband visited in the 1950s, they were given tea and were eyed by her pet parrot Popka. Preobrazhenskaya also clearly enjoyed the opportunity to give class to the Moiseyev Ensemble when they visited Paris in 1955 – Pierre Tugal, founder of the Archives Internationales de la Danse and Paris correspondent for the *Dancing Times*, writes in a note for the *Dancing Times* (December 1955) that she picked up her skirts to demonstrate character steps and the young Russian dancers "listened to her with the utmost respect".

Preobrazhenskaya never married, though she lived for many years with Alexandre Labinski, who played for her classes. According to Roné, she regretted, to the point of bitterness, that she was no longer able to dance on stage and could not experience the magic and beauty of performing with an orchestra for an audience. Only when teaching did she show her humour and wit, and she taught until the age of eighty-eight, when she became too weak to continue. John Gregory and his wife, Barbara, visited her in 1959 with their small daughter Paula but found her "frail and weary", struggling up the stairs to her studio and teaching a handful of pupils when she deserved to rest in comfort. Like Legat, she was surrounded by Russians, but was cut off from Russia and cut off from the theatre, teaching out of necessity to make a meagre living, rather than being able to select her pupils. Roné was almost the only person she accepted in her old age, particularly after a stroke in 1955. Preobrazhenskaya lived to the age of ninety-one; she died on 27 December 1962 and is buried at the Russian Cemetery, Cimetière de Sainte-Geneviève-des-Bois, in the Île-de-France. She was made an Officier du Mérite Civique de France in 1955. Beloved by many English students, she only appeared in London for one early season in 1910, in a variety programme at the Hippodrome Theatre which included an abridged version of "Swan Lake" and which was the first time any part of the ballet had been seen in England.

✑

After her separation from Hugh, Mary divided her time between London and Belgrade, where she had progressed to the rank of soloist and then principal dancer in the National Theatre. She says:

> Yes, during these three years [approximately between 1935 and 1938], I was still living in London quarters [but] still living in Belgrade and travelling…

Ana spent most of the period between 1933 and 1937 in England, studying with Legat and performing at private functions when she could. Oskar also trained with Legat in London, but he remained connected with the theatre in Zagreb, where Margarita Froman continued to choreograph ballets and to direct opera. Legat was probably less influential on Oskar's performing career than on Ana's, and he was already interested in German contemporary expressionist dance. However, he would have learned much about double-work and how to perform daring and spectacular lifts, as the photographs in Ana's biography show – but without these appearing contrived or showy, in accordance with Legat's emphasis on artistry. Dolin particularly acknowledges Legat's teaching of *pas de deux*, "for which I am so grateful". Oskar would have shared the sentiment and would also have absorbed Legat's approach to teaching since, after Legat's death, he assisted his widow Nadine Nicolaeva-Legat (or Nicolaeva Legat) by teaching *pas de deux* at the studio. Later he and Ana used their experience to advantage at their schools in Yugoslavia. Mary may have been looking ahead as well, to a time when she would be running her own school rather than performing, and made a conscious effort to learn what she could from Legat and about what made him so successful as a teacher.

Mary, Ana and Oskar lost a dear friend when Legat died of pneumonia at eleven o'clock on a mild but grey Sunday, 24 January 1937. They were still young, only in their twenties. Mary remembers:

> I was in England just by good luck, or bad luck, until he died... Yes, it was 1937 when he died ... It is always cold in England! I can't remember. It was the beginning... it was not the summer... I am not quite sure... Yes. I know that everyone went to see the ashes in the wall [at Hendon Crematorium] and they were there.

Legat's nephew, "G.S." (George, or "Grisha", Shidlovsky), describes how Legat had become ill with double pneumonia and pleurisy in the previous May. He went to the spa at Baden-Baden in Germany for a cure and returned to London much improved but, at the end of the year, he again became ill with pneumonia and pleurisy. (See the Introduction to Nicolaeva-Legat's "Ballet Education".) Legat's last illness is poignantly described by Alan Carter, then a young student, in "Heritage of a Ballet Master". He forced himself to get up or, failing that, sat up in bed to give a class to Ana. Nicolaeva was called back from engagements in Europe. To some it seemed callous and inappropriate that she threw a party to celebrate the Russian New Year in the large studio above Legat's bedroom while he was so gravely ill. But New Year celebrations had always been very important to her and it may have been her way of wishing her husband back to health, and of celebrating the New Year looking forward with hope. Mary and Ana may have been at Nicolaeva's New Year party, and possibly Oskar as well. Barely ten days later, they would have said silent prayers as Legat lay in his open coffin in the studio surrounded by wreaths and bouquets of flowers. It was placed below Valentin Serov's full-length portrait of Pavlova as "La Sylphide", which was hung to lean out from the wall, and which Carter likens to a guardian angel watching over him.

The funeral was held at St Philip's Russian Orthodox church, which was then at 188 Buckingham Palace Road. Legat would have attended Pavlova's funeral service there just six years before in January 1931, and another ballerina and teacher from the Mariinsky, Seraphina Astafieva's in September 1934. Mary would have known the prayers, the psalms and the hymns, and Ana would have understood the Russian. Their tears and their loss would have been heartfelt. Carter describes the service, with the choir and the "great bass voice" of the priest ringing through the shadowy interior of the church. Though he was only about sixteen at the time, he observes that many of the mourners who lined up to kiss Legat's body must have been weeping "crocodile tears" in light of the less-than-kind treatment they had given him when he was alive. Another student, Dorothy Lysaght, remembers the church being so crowded that it was fortunate that the congregation remains standing throughout an Orthodox service because there was no room for pews or seats at all. The coffin was covered by over two hundred wreaths. Legat was cremated at Hendon Crematorium and his ashes placed alongside those of his father-in-law Admiral Briger. They were later moved and now are located with the remains of Nicolaeva-Legat and her family at the Kent and Sussex Cemetery and Crematorium at Tunbridge Wells.

CHAPTER 7
NICOLAI LEGAT AND THE RUSSIAN CLASSICAL SCHOOL

My family's association with the Imperial Ballet dates back
over a hundred years. My grandfather, who was a Swede,
was invited into the Imperial ballet company by the Emperor
Nicolas I."

Nicolai Legat, "The Story of the Russian School".

L egat's death in January 1937 marked a turning point for Mary, Ana and
Oskar. They would not have considered spending a long time in England,
or living there permanently, but they may well have wished that they could
have had more time to work with him. Then, as 1938 followed 1937, they
could not ignore the events that were unfolding in Germany and central
Europe, and which ultimately took them back across Europe to Yugoslavia.
Notwithstanding the relatively short period in which Legat appears directly
in Mary's life, his story is integral to it because of his importance to her own
development as a teacher. Because of his influence, the environment in which
he grew up as a dancer, as well as the people and events which influenced
him subsequently, are an important part of Mary's background. She may not
have known the all the details of his life, but through her conversations with
him, and with Eduardova and Poliakova, she appreciated and acknowledged
that heritage.

From the time he entered the Theatre School in 1880, Legat was
surrounded by the great dancers, teachers and choreographers of the second
half of the nineteenth century. Four outstanding personalities – Christian
Johansson, Marius Petipa, Pavel Gerdt and Enrico Cecchetti – shaped the

theatre and the ballet company in those years, as they would shape Legat's own career. Legat embodied the Russian Imperial classical ballet tradition and even those, notably Fokine, who rebelled against what they felt to be rigid and old-fashioned in his ideas, had his and Johansson's training as the foundation for their own technique which allowed them to move in new directions. From the Imperial Theatre School in St Petersburg, Legat rose through the ranks of the Mariinsky ballet company in the period when Petipa held sway as *premier maître de ballet* and Cecchetti was one of the leading dancers. The great ballerinas of the time, from Mathilde Kschessinskaya to Anna Pavlova, appreciated Legat's skill as a partner, while audiences applauded his technical brilliance and his mime. He became one of the preeminent teachers of his generation and, as he says in his memoir, he saw himself relating back directly to August Bournonville and to Auguste Vestris, through his father and Johansson. He was the link between the era of Johansson and Petipa and that of his own pupils who, themselves, went on to become well-known pedagogues. Within Russia, these were Mikhail Obukhov, Vladimir Ponomarev and Agrippina Vaganova (who, of course, went on to develop her own teaching method) and the somewhat younger Alexander Pushkin.

Sir Paul Dukes had known Legat in St Petersburg and encouraged him to write his memoir, "The Story of the Russian School", translated it and arranged for its publication in 1932. Dukes also arranged the publication of a posthumous edition, "Ballet Russe", in 1939. Legat's language is informal and conversational and gives an idea of his irrepressible sense of fun. John Gregory published "Heritage of a Ballet Master: Nicolas Legat" with André Eglevsky in 1978 to preserve a series of four classes which Legat wrote out for Eglevsky in London in 1933. Eglevsky had asked for a single lesson that he could use while on tour and was delighted to receive four classes, although Legat really did not believe in committing his lessons to paper. The book also includes classes remembered by Alan Carter, Barbara Gregory (*née* Vernon) and Cleo Nordi, along with music for a class, written down and arranged from Legat's own improvisations by his friend, the composer and conductor Vladimir Launitz. Gregory's "The Legat Saga", published in 1992, draws on Russian sources for Legat's early life, as well as on the personal knowledge of his widow Nadine Nicolaeva-Legat. In the book, Gregory also references and quotes from Legat's unpublished memoirs written in 1930 which must have formed the basis for "The Story of the Russian School". These passages particularly relate to Legat's childhood and family life. The chapter on

Legat and his contribution as a teacher in the Imperial School in Gennady Albert's book on Alexander Pushkin, "Alexander Pushkin: Master Teacher of Dance", is particularly valuable since it gives a contemporary Russian perspective, available in English, on a pre-revolutionary figure. (Pushkin was the foremost teacher of his generation; Rudolf Nureyev and Mikhail Baryshnikov were among his students at the Leningrad Choreographic Institute.) Memoirs written by or about Legat's colleagues, teachers and students shed more light on the environment in which he worked and the influences on his development as a dancer, choreographer and teacher. Otherwise, biographical material is limited to encyclopedia and dictionary entries, which tend to be brief and somewhat repetitive.

Thirty years before his memoir appeared, Legat and his younger brother, Sergei, published a series of caricatures as "Русскій балетъ въ каррикатурахъ", or "The Russian Ballet in Caricatures", from 1902 to 1905. Not always kind, but witty and keenly observed, they are beautifully drawn and coloured, and record the principal personalities in or associated with the Mariinsky ballet at the time. Published as a folio of chromolithographs, the set of originals is held in the A.A. Bakhrushin State Central Theatre Museum in Moscow. In London, a copy of the folio is accessible online through the Victoria and Albert Museum. In the United States, the Library of Congress and the New York Public Library hold copies. (According to the New York Public Library notes, the plates for Alexander Chekrygin, Evgenia Eduardova, Lubov Egorova, Ekaterina Geltzer, Christian Johansson, Tamara Karsavina, Anna Pavlova, Vera Masolova and Vera Trefilova are missing from that copy.) Among other institutions, the Special Collection of the Toronto Public Library also has a copy. In 2021, the Noverre Press republished the caricatures in book format. Legat was always drawing and, as well as caricatures of dancers, the selection reproduced in "The Legat Saga" shows sketches of animals dressed up and behaving as if they were human, and round faces which were drawn on boxes for cheese. He would also sketch on restaurant serviettes or even, according to Nicolaeva, on the cuff of his shirt.

Gregory set up the Legat Foundation in 1994 with the objective of advancing the education of the public about the life and teachings of Legat and the Johansson-Legat system of classical ballet. He was one of the founding trustees with Moya Vahey Beynon, Beverley Galante, Carol de Fusco and Paula Gunawardena. As chair of the foundation, Moya Vahey Beynon was invited to a conference at the Vaganova Academy in St Petersburg in 2014 to celebrate the one hundred and forty-fifth anniversary of Legat's birth and the hundredth anniversary of his last performance on the Mariinsky stage. To mark the occasion, she assisted the rector of the academy, Nikolai Tsiskaridze, in arranging the publication of translations into Russian of "The Story of The Russian School", "The Legat Saga" and "Heritage of a Ballet Master". A collection of Legat's papers, photographs and caricatures from his life outside Russia is held in the National Arts Education Archive at the Yorkshire Sculpture Park at West Bretton near Wakefield. In 2012, an archive of papers and photographs, and a bronze bust and portrait in oils by Auguste Albo, were given to the Royal Ballet School Collections by Mimi Legat, granddaughter of Nicolaeva and Legat. She also donated a copy of Albo's bust to the Vaganova Academy. Among materials relating to Legat at the Jerome Robbins Dance Division of the New York Public Library is a sixteen-millimetre film, with sound, of Eglevsky teaching one of the classes which Legat wrote down for him to two of his students. It appears as Class III in "Heritage of a Ballet Master". The class is preceded by a brief biographical sketch of Legat with a few still photographs. In 2018, Patricia Deane-Gray drew on her own experience as a teacher to publish "The Legacy of Legat" as a tribute to Legat and her own teachers, Nadine Nicolaeva-Legat and Ana Roje, bringing together many aspects of Legat's pedagogical approach.

Nicolai Gustavovich Legat was born on 15 December 1869 into a family of theatrical entertainers, dancers and teachers. Sources differ as to whether he was born in Moscow or St Petersburg, although Moscow is believed to be correct. His parents were both dancers and the theatre was in his blood. His paternal grandfather was Johann-Anders Lundquist-Legat, who married Constance Katharine Afrosyne Lede (or Lédé, or Ledet), a ballerina at the Paris Opera in 1836. His great-uncle Samuel Lundquist-Legat married Sophie Teresa Isadora Lede (Ledet), the two brothers marrying two sisters. The hyphenated family name arose because, although Dorothea, mother of Johann-Anders and Samuel, was married to Joseph Legat, the father of her two sons was Johann Lundquist. Following the death of Johann in 1820, the brothers decided that Legat was the better stage name and they dropped Lundquist. To confuse matters further, Johann-Anders took the name Ivan. As Ivan Legat, he became a ballet master and scenery designer, while Samuel became a theatrical engineer. Together, they staged shows and performances at carnivals and feasts in Scandinavia and Russia. Legat himself says that Johann-Anders (Ivan) was invited to join the St Petersburg ballet company as ballet master by Tsar Nicolas I, perhaps in the 1830s. Although not authenticated, Gregory notes that Samuel Legat invented a hot air balloon and it was on one such flight over St Petersburg that both Ivan and Samuel met their deaths.

Legat's father Gustav, a son of Constance and Ivan, was a pupil of Marius Petipa at the Theatre School in St Petersburg and graduated into the ballet company in 1857. He performed some of the roles danced by Petipa and Johansson but because he retained his Swedish citizenship he was not promoted and taught classes privately in order to supplement his income. (The family did not become members of the Orthodox Church. Their plot in the Smolenskoe Lutheran Cemetery has the graves of both Gustav and his wife Maria, and Nicolai's brother Sergei, as well as Samuel and Ivan, and his aunts Sophia Legat and Adelaida Legat-Obukhova and uncle Konstantin Legat. The headstone for Adelaida Legat-Obukhova shows that the family was related by marriage to the Obukhov family of dancers; Legat's nephew Mikhail Obukhov was a student in his classes and later taught at the Theatre School, while Mikhail's nephew Anatole makes a brief appearance later in Legat's story.) Gustav married Maria Semenovna, a character dancer whose stage name was Grankina or Granken, in 1865. For about seven years, they lived in Moscow, dancing with the Bolshoi company of the Imperial Theatre and Gustav taught at the school of the Bolshoi Theatre. Those days in Moscow were reasonably comfortable. Constance lived with them and Gustav kept his own horse and a carriage used for family outings. However, he was unable to renew his contract in 1875 and returned to St Petersburg with his family, which by then included seven children. Gustav held the position of first dancer and teacher with the Mariinsky Theatre, while Maria was employed as a mime. In 1886, Gustav retired with a pension but he continued to teach privately, including in Helsinki. Nicolai's descriptions of his childhood show a close and happy family, despite being less well-off in St Petersburg than they had been in Moscow.

Gustav and Maria had fourteen children in all. She continued to perform during her pregnancies, as did many other dancers. Seven of the surviving children, Vera, Maria, Nicolai, Evgenia, Ivan, Sergei and Nadezhda, went to the Theatre School in St Petersburg and danced with the Mariinsky. Vera was the first of the siblings to graduate, in 1884, and she became a character dancer before her marriage to Count André Shuvalov. Kschessinskaya, who was the lover of the young tsarevitch before his marriage, recalls in her memoir that supper parties with the tsarevitch sometimes included Vera and Count André. (Gregory tells of a meeting much later in Paris at the time when Nicolai Legat was ballet master for the Ballets Russes in 1925 when Vera and her husband appeared in the lobby of their hotel. Despite Count André's aristocratic background, like many other Russian *émigrés* in Paris, the Shuvalovs were very short of money and may have been hoping for Legat's help.) Nicolai was the third surviving child. He graduated into the company in 1888. Evgenia was barely a year younger; she was born in 1870 and was in the company in the early years of the twentieth century since her caricature is included in the brothers' folio, although she was dismissed for lack of talent in 1908. She married Ivan de Lazari, a composer and musician in the orchestra of the Mariinsky Theatre whose caricature also appears in the folio. Ivan Legat was born in 1872 and, while he joined the company in 1890, he suffered from periods of mental instability and retired to become a monk. The third son, Sergei, was born on 15 September 1875. He enjoyed an illustrious career with the Mariinsky from 1894, as a dancer as well as a teacher at the school. Ivan's instability and the tragedy of Sergei's suicide in 1905 were not the only manifestations of mental illness within the family, however. Petipa recalls in his memoir that at the second performance of his ballet "The Daughter of the Snows" the wings and set at the back of the stage collapsed. The machinist at the time, named Legat and a relative of the Legat dancers, was affected so severely that he lost his mind on the spot. (Gregory notes that a cousin of Gustav, L.I. Legat, was an engineer responsible for scenic effects at the Imperial Theatres.) Nadezhda became a character dancer like Vera but seems not to have had a long or notable performing career. Some sources refer to the Legat brothers in performance as Legat I, II or III: Nicolai was Legat I; during the time that he was performing, Ivan was Legat II; Sergei was Legat III, or Legat II after Ivan's retirement. Similarly, when the sisters were both in the company together, Vera was Miss Legat I and Evgenia, Miss Legat II.

Before they entered the Theatre School in St Petersburg, Gustav taught Nicolai and Sergei, and presumably his other children as well, though Maria may have helped to train their daughters. For Nicolai and Sergei, their father was a hard task master – "merciless in his severity" – and the brothers' caricature of themselves in his lesson shows them sweating profusely. Gustav accompanied himself on the violin, as did all dance teachers at the time, and

The Legat brothers taking class with their father, caricature by Nicolai Legat, courtesy of the Legat Foundation.

the caricature shows the watering can used to moisten the wooden floor at the ready to avoid any slipperiness, as well as the family dog and a younger sibling calling from the doorway. (In those days, rosin was not used and the sprinkling of water from a watering can to prepare the floor for class was something of a ritual for many teachers.) Both Nicolai and Sergei wear Bournonville-style ballet shoes, which, with the white V-shaped inset on the toe, give an elegant line to the leg. Gregory describes how Gustav tied Nicolai's feet to the bed frame in order to increase his turnout of his hips while he slept and that, as a result, Nicolai did, indeed, have remarkable turnout. As Mary told her students, he could balance a glass of water on his foot in *attitude en avant* and when he died, his feet had to be tied together when his body was laid out to stop the toes falling apart.

෴

At the Theatre School, Johansson and Gerdt were the senior teachers, and Petipa had held the position of *premier maître de ballet* for ten years. Gerdt was Russian-born, though his father was German. Johansson and Petipa, originally from Sweden and France, respectively, spent the greater part of their long careers in St Petersburg. Among the Italians who frequently performed in Russia, Cecchetti was asked to join the company as a principal dancer in 1887, just before Legat's graduation. His time with the Mariinsky spanned only fifteen years but he had a lasting influence on how the Russians developed their technique. All were highly-regarded performers, although Petipa's stage career was shorter than the others'. Legat was too young to have seen Johansson and Petipa on stage in their prime but he was much impressed by Cecchetti – "literally staggered", as he says in his memoir – at the age of about sixteen when he first saw him dance. Legat also performed with Gerdt on numerous occasions. In his earlier years at the school, he was taught by Nikolai Volkov and Gerdt, but he had a particularly close relationship with Johansson, who was the most important of his teachers and colleagues, especially with regard to his own development as a teacher. Legat points out that neither Johansson nor his own father produced a single ballet, while Petipa was a mediocre teacher. They each excelled in their chosen *métier* and in the fifty or so years that they worked together they brought the St Petersburg theatre to new heights, laying the foundation for ballet in the twentieth century both within and outside Russia. He notes that, during the course of their long careers, Petipa and Johansson essentially become Russians and died in their adopted country. In contrast, Cecchetti and his compatriots came to Russia as Italians, but they left as Italians too.

Per Christian Johansson first came to St Petersburg from Stockholm when he was twenty-two. He was born in 1817 in the southern part of the city and entered the school of the Royal Swedish Ballet (Kungliga Baletten) in 1829. He studied with Sophie Daguin, who had come to Stockholm with a French company when she was seventeen, and Per Erik Wallquist, a Swedish dancer. Daguin had trained with Charles-Louis Didelot in the short period in which he worked in Paris and went on to enjoy a long career as a dancer and ballet mistress with the Royal Swedish Ballet. Didelot himself studied with Jean-Georges Noverre and was a dancer and ballet master with the Imperial Theatre in St Petersburg between 1801 and 1837 except for a period during the Napoleonic Wars when he had to leave Russia. Crown Prince Oskar of Sweden took a personal interest in Johansson's studies. He supported Johansson's further training in Copenhagen with the renowned Danish teacher and choreographer August Bournonville, who had obtained the bursary from the prince and took him into his own home. As a result, Johansson enjoyed a particularly close relationship with Bournonville. (See Gregory, *Dancing Times*, February 1986; Karsavina, *Dancing Times*, July 1964; Kulakov in "International Encyclopedia of Dance"; and Zozulina in

Sovietsky Ballet. Gregory also wrote a series of articles for the *Dancing Times* on the letters of Johansson to Bournonville, March through July 1986.)

Johansson's debut was with the Royal Swedish Ballet in 1836 in a *pas de trois* in "The Marriage of Figaro" and even then his elegance and precision were noted. As early as 1838, he staged Bournonville's "Soldier and Peasant" in Stockholm, as "Hemkomstem". In 1841, he accompanied Marie Taglioni to St Petersburg as her partner but, while she continued to tour in Europe, he remained there for the rest of his life. Johansson first performed on the Bolshoi Kamenny stage in 1841 with Elena Andreyanova in Filippo Taglioni's "La Gitana" and it was this performance which secured his place in the Imperial Theatre. The fact that his relationship with Anders Selinder, the ballet master in Stockholm, was stormy and unproductive, and that he regarded Selinder as incompetent, would have made St Petersburg a more congenial place in which to build his career. Johansson's lightness and technical abilities were immediately recognised and, as well as Marie Taglioni, he partnered the other three great Romantic ballerinas, Fanny Elssler, Fanny Cerrito and Carlotta Grisi, as well as the Russians Adèle Grantzov, Tatiana Smirnova, Marfa Muravieva and Nadezhda Bogdanova.

Despite his strong technique, Johansson's style was considered exaggerated in St Petersburg and he evidently had less mastery in acting and mime than was expected by Russian audiences. He worked hard to understand the Russian approach to performing and, as a result, he quickly became one of the stars of the St Petersburg theatre, enjoying a stage career that lasted over forty years. His last performance was in 1883 although the role has not been identified. The *répertoire* in the mid-1800s was dominated by the Romantic ballets of the French choreographers and his roles included Ahmet in "La Péri" and Gringoire in "La Esmeralda", as well as Rajah Dugmanta in Petipa's "La Bayadère". Johansson was among the male dancers, with Jules Perrot, Arthur Saint-Léon and Lucien Petipa (brother of Marius), whose artistry went beyond their skills as partners.

Johansson taught at the Imperial Theatre School in St Petersburg from 1860 until shortly before he died in 1903. He retained his Bournonville background, blending it with the Russian style and developing an aesthetic and academic approach that would last until the early years of the twentieth century. In this, Johansson was joined by Petipa, who was intensely interested in both Johansson's teaching methods and the inventive *enchaînements* which inspired his own choreography. In his memoir, Legat recounts how Petipa would watch Johansson's classes, taking notes, after which Johansson would say, "The old man's pinched some more". Accompanying himself on his pocket violin, Johansson never repeated a class and he approached each student as an individual, trying to bring out their best, while overcoming their deficiencies. As well as Nicolai and his brother Sergei, just a few of his students who went on have long and illustrious careers include Pavel Gerdt, Mathilde Kschessinskaya, Petipa's elder daughter Maria, Olga Preobrazhenskaya, Michel Fokine, Anna Pavlova, Tamara Karsavina, Ekaterina Geltzer and his own daughter Anna Christianovna. The Italian ballerina Pierina Legnani, who danced with the Mariinsky in the 1890s, also worked with him.

Nicolai Legat notes that his father was Johansson's most trusted pupil before he attained that position himself, and that, if Johansson was unable to accept a private engagement, he would always send Gustav Legat in his place. He remembers too that, though both his father and Johansson were Swedes, they conversed together in French, which in earlier years had been widely used among well-educated Russians. He describes Johansson as being of medium height with a powerful chest, grey-haired and with light blue eyes and, occasionally, demonstrating a series of "flashing" *pirouettes* in class to finish in a perfect *arabesque* – all of this when he was over sixty. His strength and vitality were legendary; Legat recalls that he did not remember Johansson having a day of illness and that into old age he still ran up the steps to the school two at a time. "Don Quixote" was performed for his farewell benefit performance on 20 January 1902.

∽

Less than a year younger than Johansson, Petipa was born in Marseille in 1818. He was taught ballet by his father, Jean-Antoine, who had his own troupe, which toured in Western Europe and in America. Marius first appeared on stage as a child and then as a young man he travelled extensively, both with his father's company and for his own engagements. He was energetic and ambitious and, when only sixteen, secured a contract with the theatre in Nantes, where he choreographed three ballets, "Le Droit du seigneur", "La Petite Bohémienne" and "La Noces á Nantes". He also produced ballets with the Grand Théâtre in Bordeaux and the Teatro del Circo in Madrid. When he was twenty-two, Petipa studied for a short period with Vestris and he drew on that experience throughout his career. He was invited to St Petersburg in 1847, where he staged "Paquita" (which had been mounted two years earlier in Paris by Joseph Mazilier) and appeared in it as Lucien, partnering Andreyanova in September of that year. His father joined him shortly afterwards and was appointed as ballet master for senior classes in the school. Marius took over that position on his father's death in 1855 and he continued to teach until 1863 when Johansson officially took over his classes. In 1854, he married Maria Surovshchikova, who had succeeded Andreyanova following her retirement. His daughter from this first marriage, Maria Mariusovna, became a noted ballerina and character dancer and was the common-law wife of Sergei Legat.

Saint-Léon succeeded Perrot as ballet master and choreographer at the Mariinsky in 1859 but Petipa was then able to choreograph and stage a number of his own full-length works, as well as shorter pieces. His first important ballet, "La Fille du Pharaon" ("The Pharaoh's Daughter"), based on a story by Théophile Gautier and with music by Cesare Pugni, opened in January 1862. Petipa danced the principal male roles of Ta-Hor and Lord Wilson himself. Shortly afterwards he was appointed second ballet master. In February of the following year, he staged his own version of Perrot's "Le Corsaire" in which his wife and Johansson took the leading roles and Adolphe Adam's score was modified and supplemented by Pugni. Petipa retired from the stage as a *premier danseur* in 1869. Although he was compared with Johansson, his strengths as a performer were in character and in mime. His interpretation of Conrad in "Le Corsaire" was particularly well received by audiences and critics, as well as by his colleagues.

On Pugni's death in 1870, the Austrian composer Ludwig Minkus was appointed to the position of ballet composer of the Imperial Theatres, while Petipa was promoted to the position of first ballet master in the following February. As well as staging "Don Quixote" in 1871, Petipa collaborated with Minkus on a series of ballets, including "La Bayadère" in 1877, of which the third act, "The Kingdom of the Shades", may be considered Petipa's first masterpiece, although he does not describe it in his memoir. Minkus's contract was not renewed in 1886 when the then director of the Mariinsky, Ivan Vsevolozhsky, abolished the position of ballet composer and appointed the Italian Riccardo Drigo as director of music. Drigo's first full-length ballet score was for Lev Ivanov's "La Forêt enchantée", created for the graduation performance of the Theatre School in April 1887. This was followed by the score for Petipa's "Le Talisman", which had its first performance in February 1889. Petipa and Drigo collaborated on "Le Réveil de Flore" for the wedding celebrations of the Grand Duchess Xenia Alexandrovna to the

Grand Duke Alexander Mikhailovich at the Peterhof Palace in August 1894, and the ballet was then taken into the *répertoire*. Dancers from both the Moscow and St Petersburg companies, including Nicolai and Sergei Legat, took part in the performance of "La Perle" ("The Miraculous Pearl") for the coronation of Tsar Nicholas II and Empress Alexandra in Moscow in May 1896. Next came "Les millions d'Arlequin" which had its first performance on 10 February, 1900 at the Imperial Theatre of the Hermitage.

While Petipa's working relationships with Pugni, Minkus and Drigo were productive and successful, his most famous ballets are to Pyotr (Peter) Tchaikovsky's scores – "The Sleeping Beauty" was staged in 1890, "The Nutcracker" in 1892 and "Swan Lake" in 1895. They were produced in the later part of Vsevolozhsky's time as director and he wrote the libretto for "The Sleeping Beauty" as well as designing the costumes. The first version of "Swan Lake" was choreographed by Julius Reisinger in Moscow in 1877 and was regarded as a failure, but Petipa persuaded Vsevolozhsky that Tchaikovsky's music deserved restaging in St Petersburg. This took place not long after Tchaikovsky's death. Strangely, Petipa does not mention it in his memoir but it must have been a blow when that important and productive working relationship was cut short. As for his other ballets, Petipa was meticulous in his instructions to Tchaikovsky. The editorial notes for his memoir show how he set out the number of bars, for example, in the mime scene between the King and the Master of Ceremonies, and his suggestions of music for mewing and clawing in the "Puss in Boots and White Cat" variation in "The Sleeping Beauty".

Petipa's talent for staging works that were attractive crowd-pleasers ensured his long career. In addition to his original ballets, he was responsible for the revival of many others, including "Giselle" and "Le Corsaire", the choreography of dances for opera, as well as *divertissements* for various occasions. Particularly in his first decades in Russia, he worked frequently in both Moscow and St Petersburg. As first ballet master at the Mariinsky, Petipa was assisted by a succession of second ballet masters: Lev Ivanov, Achille Coppini, Alexander Shiryaev, Nicolai Legat and Nicolai Sergeyev (Sergeeff). For reasons that are debated among dance historians and commentators, Ivanov's contribution to some of the great works of the Mariinsky is less acknowledged than he may deserve. As second ballet master, Ivanov was subordinate to and overshadowed by Petipa; he was also eighteen years younger, remaining very much the junior until Petipa's ill health brought him forward. Writing in "The Life and Ballets of Lev Ivanov", musicologist and historian Roland John Wiley notes that Ivanov's memoirs focus on his early years, hardly discuss his own work and do not even mention "Swan Lake" and "The Nutcracker", for which his contributions were particularly notable when Petipa fell ill. Petipa hardly refers to him, and Tchaikovsky not at all. But Ivanov had a long performing career in St Petersburg between 1852 and the 1890s (his last appearance was in a benefit performance dancing a Spanish *pas de deux* with Maria Petipa in 1893). For a short period, he was *régisseur* but was happy to be demoted to second ballet master in 1885 and relieved of administrative responsibilities to which he was not suited. Ivanov seems to have been an unambitious man who accepted that he was not ambitious, did not want or aspire to be in a position of authority and appears not to have been embittered by others' success.

Both Wiley and Vera Krasovskaya (in her entry in "The International Encyclopedia of Dance") set this modest and unassuming man against the backdrop of the Imperial Theatres. They describe how Ivanov's work progressed to its culmination in his choreography for the second and fourth acts of "Swan Lake" and parts of "The Nutcracker" that are seen as equal to any of Petipa's and contributed to the lasting popularity of these ballets. "The Waltz of the Snowflakes" in "The Nutcracker", for eight female soloists and a fifty-strong *corps de ballet*, was Ivanov's great masterpiece. White pompoms on the *tutus* and more pompoms on the wands, or icicles, which they carried, were particularly effective. The scene is described in detail by Volynsky in "Ballet's Magic Kingdom" and is recalled by Karsavina in a note in the *Dancing Times* of July 1958, while a caricature of O. Levinson appears in costume in "The Russian Ballet in Caricatures". Ivanov also choreographed "The Polovtsian Dances" for the *première* of the opera "Prince Igor", which Natalia Roslavleva believes Fokine subsequently strengthened and embellished (see Roslavleva, "Era of the Russian Ballet").

Accounts of Petipa's character are mixed and difficult to reconcile. Kschessinskaya refers to him as "all-powerful", able to retouch the ballets of Ivanov and then claim them as his own. In an article in the *Dancing Times* (March 1928), Prince Serge Volkonsky, director of the Imperial Theatres between 1899 and 1901, recalls a visit to the school and describes Petipa as having sparkling but "wicked little eyes" and indulging in "self-worship", not taking kindly to any suggestion that his staging might be improved. While appreciating that Petipa furthered her career by choreographing some effective pieces for her, the ballerina Ekaterina Vazem does not mince words in describing him as ready always to look after his own family, in particular maintaining the position of his daughter Maria as first character soloist when more able dancers were available, and refers to his many amorous conquests, whether these were ladies in society or humble workers in the theatre (see Wiley's "A Century of Russian Ballet. Documents and Eyewitness Accounts, 1810–1910"). On the other hand, in an interview with Pierre Tugal, Olga Preobrazhenskaya remembered Petipa as a "perfect gentleman" and believed that he and Ivanov were good friends as well as colleagues (*Dancing Times*, April 1952). In "Writings on Ballet and Music", Fedor (Fyodor) Lopukhov, brother of Evgenia, Lydia and Andrei, notes that Petipa respected Ivanov adding that if Petipa did not have confidence in Ivanov's work, he would not have permitted him to collaborate on ballets such as "Swan Lake" and "The Nutcracker". He writes, too, that he spoke with Gerdt, Legat, Shiryaev and others who had worked with both Petipa and Ivanov, all of whom assured him that this was the case. According to Legat, Petipa was popular with the dancers, was "the life and soul of every gathering" and was known, familiarly, by his first name. He says he "never allowed the least favouritism" but Petipa was also a family friend of the Legats and godfather to one of Legat's sisters.

Ivanov and Petipa did approach their choreography differently. Wiley emphasises that Ivanov was a gifted musician who became a dancer and, since he was intensely musical, he may have been inspired by Tchaikovsky's music as he had never been inspired before. Petipa's choreography was inspired by movement and the groupings of his dancers, rather than by the score. As noted above, the music was often composed to his specifications after the steps and groupings had been worked out. In his memoir (included in "Alexander Shiryaev: Master of Movement"), Shiryaev describes Petipa's careful and painstaking approach in which he used small paper dolls to represent the dancers when working out his *enchaînements* for the *corps de ballet* and would call a pianist and violinist to his home to provide the music. He had his own notation for movements, marking women with a zero and a dagger for the men. Shiryaev also notes that if Petipa did not like or was not inspired by a particular piece of music he would assign the choreography to Ivanov or himself. Shiryaev choreographed a number of the character dances in Petipa's ballets, although Petipa was fundamentally interested in character or national dances, he approached them from a classical point of view and was supportive of Shiryaev's efforts to have more authentic character variations.

Petipa, Johansson and their colleagues established a company of highly trained soloists and *corps de ballet*. Petipa's choreography shows that technical standards at the Mariinsky were exacting or he could never have contemplated such sequences as the entrance of the Shades in "La Bayadère", or the travelling *arabesques* of the *corps de ballet* in the second act of "Giselle". But the rules of the theatre itself imposed high standards; as members of the Imperial Theatres, the dancers were essentially employed directly by the tsar and a slip on the stage could result in a fine for poor execution.

Cecchetti was some thirty years younger than Johansson and Petipa, and was already married to his partner, Giuseppina de Maria, when he was engaged at the St Petersburg theatre in 1887. Other Italians had come before him, but in the fifteen years that he lived in St Petersburg Cecchetti brought the *bravura* style of the Italian school into the Mariinsky and the Theatre School. Like Petipa, he came from a family of dancers and was born in the Teatro Tordinona (later the Teatro di Apollo) in Rome in June 1850. His mother, Serafina Casagli, was a dancer and his father, Cesare, was a dancer and choreographer. Cecchetti's own stage career started early with a performance in Genoa at the age of five as a child in "Il Giocatore". He was then sent to be formally educated at schools in Fermo and Florence but his heart was set on being a dancer. Eventually, his father allowed him to study with Giovanni Lepri, a pupil of Carlo Blasis, at the École de Danse in Florence. As Cecchetti relates in his memoir, Blasis was in his seventies when Cecchetti first met him and the young man was exhorted to work hard and not to heed or have his head turned by the applause of the audience. He describes Blasis as elegant and cultured, a collector of books and pictures, and a friend of artists, musicians and writers. At the age of twenty, Cecchetti appeared at La Scala in Milan in the leading role in Pasquale Borri's "La Dea del Valhalla". Already noted for his strong technique, he then toured through Denmark, Norway, the Netherlands, Germany and Austria, before going to St Petersburg for the first time in the summer of 1874.

In the summer of 1887, Cecchetti and one of his brothers took a company of Italian dancers to the Acadia Theatre in St Petersburg. (According to Karsavina, however (*Dancing Times*, December 1964), Cecchetti and Giuseppina de Maria had already danced for four consecutive summer variety seasons at "Demidov's Garden", the Demidov Botanical Garden in Moscow.) Giovannina Limido was *première danseuse* and Giuseppina was principal mime. The season at the Acadia was followed with great interest by the dancers of the Mariinsky, Petipa and the director, Vsevolozhsky, when the technique and virtuosity of the Italians created a sensation. Legat was taken by his father to meet Cecchetti even before he graduated from the Theatre School and later the two became good friends. Legat considers Limido to be the greatest of the Italian ballerinas because of her pure technique. In the interview with Tugal, Preobrazhenskaya agrees, but remembers Virginia Zucchi as her favourite because of her elegant style and the expressiveness of her mime. The Italians' technique was not entirely to the taste of the Russians, however. Karsavina notes that one critic particularly objected to Cecchetti's Italian style of *entrechats* in which the beats (quick changes of the legs while in the air) were done with the heels and the knees drawn up. While she says that he did not teach his students to do *batterie* with drawn-up knees, in her article for the *Dancing Times*, November 1964, on Madame Caterina Beretta, with whom she studied in Italy, however, she describes *petit allegro* with the knees not fully stretched, allowing for greater speed. Mary described this way of jumping as the Cecchetti or Italian style, although it must have been largely abandoned by the early twentieth century.

Cecchetti was immediately engaged at the Mariinsky, where his debut performance was in November 1887 in Ivanov's "The Tulip of Haarlem". He was appointed principal dancer and then, in the following year, to the position of second ballet master. Notably, in 1890, he danced in the first complete performance of Petipa's "The Sleeping Beauty" when he appeared both in the character role of Carabosse and in the virtuoso role of the Bluebird in the *pas de deux* of the third act. He staged numerous revivals, including Perrot's "Catarina, ou La Fille du Bandit" in 1889, and "Coppélia" in 1894. He also collaborated with Ivanov on dances for the opera-ballet "Mlada" by Rimsky-Korsakov in 1892 and, with Petipa and Ivanov, on an elaborate version of "Zolushka" ("Cinderella") in 1893, in which Pierina Legnani danced the leading role and first performed thirty-two *fouettés* for a Russian audience. Between 1892 and 1902, he taught at the Theatre School while continuing to tour outside Russia during the summer months, appearing at the Empire Theatre in London in 1888, 1891 and 1892. Cecchetti's last performance at the Mariinsky was as the Marquis in Ivanov's "La Flûte magique" in May 1902.

⌒

Pavel Andreyevitch Gerdt worked alongside Johansson, Petipa and Cecchetti and enjoyed a long and celebrated career in the Mariinsky Theatre. Born near St Petersburg in November 1844, he was a student in some of the earliest classes taught by Johansson and also trained with Alexander Pimenov (himself a student of Didelot) and Jean-Antoine Petipa. Gerdt graduated in 1860 and his elegant style became a model for future dancers. He created the leading male roles in many of Petipa's ballets, including Prince Désiré in "The Sleeping Beauty" at the age of forty-six and Prince Siegfried in "Swan Lake" at fifty. While still performing regularly, he taught at the Theatre School for nearly twenty-five years, from 1880 to 1904, where, as well as Nicolai and Sergei Legat, his pupils included Fokine, Karsavina, Pavlova, Vaganova and Georgii Balanchivadze (George Balanchine), as well as Eduardova and Poliakova. Having given up teaching in favour of performing, his last appearance in 1916, at the age of seventy-two, was as Don Gamache in "Don Quixote". Karsavina writes that, while she could not have seen Gerdt performing in his prime, his *pirouettes en dedans* were legendary, particularly in Albrecht's solo in the second act of "Giselle" when the *pirouette* ended with the working leg à la *seconde* and was followed by two *fouettés renversés en dedans* each ending in *developé à la seconde* (see *Dancing Times*, June 1964).

CHAPTER 8
CLASS AT THE IMPERIAL THEATRE SCHOOL

We have had the story of the stage, but we have never had
the story of the class-room.

Sir Paul Dukes, foreword to "The Story of the Russian School".

The Imperial Theatre School and the Mariinsky Theatre were dependent
on a Ministry of the Imperial Court, as were their counterparts in
Moscow. The Mariinsky Theatre had been built to replace the wooden Circus
Theatre, which had been destroyed by fire. Designed for opera and ballet
by Alberto Cavos, it opened in 1860, taking its name from its patroness,
the Empress Maria Alexandrovna. The ballet company was then transferred
from the Bolshoi Kamenny, or Big Stone, Theatre in 1886. The Mariinsky
has the classical horseshoe shape, with the box in the centre of the dress
circle first reserved for the Imperial family, and later for political dignitaries,
although the Romanovs preferred to use their family box to the left of the
stage for non-official occasions since it brought them much closer to the
performers. Ballet and opera were also performed in the Maly, or Little
Theatre, the Bolshoi Kamenny and the Alexandrinsky Theatres, as well as
at the private court theatres, the Hermitage, Tsarskoe Selo Chinese Theatre,
Gatchina and Krasnoselsky.

In St Petersburg, the school was located near to the theatre in Architect
Rossi Street, also known as "Theatre Street", and had been built in 1832
by the Italian architect Carlo Rossi. The school, with its traditions of
teaching that were embodied in Johansson, Petipa and Gerdt, provided the
foundation for the Mariinsky ballet company through the second half of
the nineteenth century and into the early years of the twentieth century,

when Legat came of age as a dancer, teacher and choreographer. Over thirty-five years from 1880, the principal teachers of advanced students were Christian Johansson, Marius Petipa, Pavel Gerdt, Nikolai Volkov, Lev Ivanov, Platon Karsavin (Karsavina's father), Alexander Shiryaev, Alexei Bogdanov, Samuil Andrianov, Enrico Cecchetti, Michel Fokine, Leonid Leontiev and Viktor Semenov, as well as Nicolai and Sergei Legat. Although Nicolai Legat entered the Theatre School nearly twenty years earlier than Tamara Karsavina and Bronislava Nijinska, their books "Theatre Street" and "Early Memoirs", respectively, describe student life that would have been little changed from his own time. In this respect, they both write essentially as historians, in contrast to others, such as Kschessinskaya in "Dancing in Petersburg" and Kyasht in "Romantic Recollections", whose focus is more on their own interests and achievements. Students spent the first two years (or sometimes three) of their eight-year training on trial, living at home. Once accepted as boarders, they were fully supported but were allowed very little contact with their families. Until the age of fifteen, they were allowed home for Saturday and Sunday, but after that they were given only three days' holiday at Christmas and Easter. Parents were permitted to visit twice a week and, while brothers were also allowed to enter the school, no male cousin could go in.

Students' days started at eight in the morning and were highly regimented. Breakfast at eight-thirty consisted only of tea and a roll. Dancing classes started at nine, followed by music and practice. School work followed lunch and lasted until five, although that did include lessons in ballroom dancing, singing, acting and fencing. There was a break of half-an-hour for a walk, either in the streets of St Petersburg or in the garden of the school. There was no time for play, but Karsavina suggests that the boys' lives might have been slightly more relaxed than the girls' since occasionally "horrid boyish pets" like white mice or guinea pigs were smuggled into ballroom dancing lessons. (See also Karsavina's article "Imperial Schooldays", *Dancing Times*, December 1927.) Students quickly became familiar with the theatre since *divertissements* for children were frequently included in the last acts of the ballets. They could be selected to take part in performances of opera and drama as well, and were paid for this work at the end of each month.

Both Karsarvina and Nijinska describe the students' clothes. For ballet class, the junior girls wore light grey/brown dresses, graduating to dresses of white lawn with pink spots for the senior students and then to starched white organdy dresses for those in the graduating year or, exceptionally, before their graduation year. Nijinska notes that their "semi-hard" shoes were made of coarse unbleached linen with hard soles. The girls' school uniform consisted of a long dark blue dress with a full gathered skirt and a white starched *fichu* around the neck which crossed in front of the bodice. (Karsavina remembers the dresses as "sky blue" cashmere.) A black alpaca apron covered the dress. Hair was parted in the centre and tightly braided. In their graduation photograph, Karsavina and her classmates wear long white starched aprons over long-sleeved pale silk dresses. Nijinska describes the boys' uniform of dark grey wool trousers, a shirt held with a wide belt of black patent leather which had a square copper buckle, a blue cap and high boots. The boys were also provided with a summer vacation uniform, even down to handkerchiefs, although the girls were not similarly fitted out. The boys' graduating class wore suits with the fastenings concealed in a placket down the right side of the chest and a stand-up velvet collar on which the silver lyre, the insignia of the Theatre School, was pinned on both sides. On graduation, dancers submitted a formal application to become accepted as an artist of the Imperial Theatres. Those who could not be accepted into the company as dancers were given other work, perhaps with the opera or in walk-on stage parts or as machinists.

Legat describes the large rehearsal hall next to the Theatre School, which was some fifty feet square and had the same rake as the stage of the Mariinsky Theatre. Mirrors were installed on one wall and *barres* on the other three, where portraits of the great dancers and ballet masters of the past were also hung. Boys and girls were strictly segregated and did not meet except for classes in ballroom dancing and double-work. Rehearsals and performances were closely supervised, and while waiting their turn during rehearsals, boys and girls had to stand against the wall on opposite sides of the room and were not allowed to speak to each other. Inevitably, attachments were formed. Legat relates that he, Sergei and the other boys were enamoured of girl students. In their day, Olga Preobrazhenskaya had the best grammar and spelling and she was called upon to rewrite their love letters.

At the age of seventy-eight, in 1895, Johansson introduced a *classe de perfectionnement* for the most dedicated and promising dancers who had already graduated into the company, and he taught this class for the next eight years until just before he died. (Then, as now, members of ballet companies took a daily class together to maintain their technique.) Among the dancers originally in Johansson's *classe de perfectionnement* were Varvara

Nikitina, Kschessinskaya, Julia Sedova, Preobrazhenskaya and Maria Petipa, as well as his daughter, Anna. Although the class was principally for women, Johansson also permitted the Legat brothers to attend. At that time, Gerdt taught the senior girls, while Cecchetti taught a "parallel" girls' class in the Italian style. Descriptions of Johansson's classes show that he was both revered and loved, and somewhat feared by his students. He watered the wooden floor in preparation and then sat near the mirror, his violin at the ready – Karsavina recalls that he held his violin across his knees, like a guitar (*Dancing Times*, July 1964). By the second half of the nineteenth century, not all dancing teachers accompanied their classes on their own violins, and some had a violinist to play for them. Earlier it had been almost universal and the Legat brothers' caricatures show both their father and Johansson with their instruments. (In her article on Anna Johansson for the *Dancing Times*, January 1965, Karsavina remembers the innovation introduced when Lubov Egorova suggested that the class contribute to engaging a pianist for their lessons. She says that they had a member of the *corps de ballet* who was an indifferent dancer but an excellent musician who was able to improvise – and who must have really understood what was needed for a ballet class.) Johansson's tunes were either his own or remembered from the Romantic ballets of his youth. Karsavina describes how he would demonstrate the steps with his hands and use the bow of his violin to point to a pupil to come forward for a correction. But she also remembers his "tough and sharp" spirit and his rich *répertoire* of Russian invectives, which contrasted with his frailty as an old man. His *enchaînements* were flowing but methodical, intricate and diverse, and required quick changes of direction and weight. Not only that, but Karsavina remembers that *adage* in the centre was done on *demi-pointe*, including *grands ronds de jambe en l'air* so his *classe de perfectionnement* was very demanding. He also used changes of tempo within an exercise to teach his students to react quickly, with the result that an even tempo then became easy, and he deliberately created puddles of water on the studio floor to teach them how to keep their balance.

Johansson never repeated a class believing, as did Legat after him, that such repetition dulled memory and versatility. The ultimate praise was for Johansson to say, "Now you may do that in public". Legat describes his class as a "fairyland of movement, with the severe but benevolent old sorcerer waving his magic violin wand and awaking to life our most secret and often unlooked-for artistic capacities". Kschessinskaya acknowledges that she owed her career, in large part, to Johansson and saw him not only as an excellent teacher but "an inspired creator" who strove to give meaning to every movement and to pass that meaning on to his students. Egorova describes him as a wonderful, if severe, teacher (interview with Pierre Tugal, *Dancing Times*, June 1952). But, because he hardly spoke in his classes and marked his *enchaînements* with his hands, students had to concentrate hard to understand what he wanted. For all his railings against Legat's traditionalism, Fokine venerated Johansson and considered those classes sacred, believing that Johansson was a "living museum of choreographic art". Nijinska was too young to take classes with him but she describes how he once came to watch a student class, dressed in an old-fashioned stiff collar and wide cravat, adding that the points of the red handkerchief that he used when he took snuff always showed from under the tails of his long coat. The Legat brothers had the special privilege of helping Johansson, by then in his eighties, up the three flights of stairs to the studio.

Petipa taught at the school for about nine years in the mid-1800s, but he must have continued with some classes after that, although perhaps not on a regular basis, since Shiryaev briefly describes how he used his students to try out his ideas. It was not until after he graduated that Shiryaev appreciated Petipa's mime classes, which, as a student, he found restricting since Petipa required his pupils to copy his gestures and expressions precisely. In contrast, Gerdt seems to have been an inspiring teacher. For Shiryaev, and others, he was not an outstanding pedagogue because he could not explain how to do a step, but he demonstrated brilliantly with grace and an elegant purity of line and position that had its roots in the French school of Johansson and Petipa. In the centre, his classes took on a magical quality as he taught *enchaînements* that were fragments of ballets no longer in the *répertoire*. Fatigue was forgotten as the students looked forward to the next class. In "Era of the Russian Ballet", Roslavleva notes that he took care to ensure that his male students maintained a masculine quality while the females had a softer quality and poise, particularly in their *ports de bras*. Gerdt also taught mime twice a week, demonstrating from ballets in the current *répertoire* as well as from those much older. Karsavina recalls how he folded a handkerchief to resemble a flower to teach his class how to hold a rose and to smell it.

Cecchetti's class for the female students is described by Karsavina as being in a "much softened" Italian style, although he was allowed to use his own teaching methods, but she gives only the example of the Italian style of slightly bent knees in *pointe* work as being not permitted in the school (*Dancing Times*, December 1927). Cecchetti stressed the importance of correct placement at the *barre*; Karsavina acknowledges that all good teachers know and accept the importance of placement, but that Cecchetti was particularly able to see where a correction needed to be made. A number of accounts refer to the prescribed structure of Cecchetti's classes but she describes it in detail. He concentrated on specific steps for each day of the week: Monday devoted to *assemblés*, Tuesday to *jetés*, Wednesday to *ronds de jambe sautés* and *pas de bourrées*, Thursday to *pirouettes*, and so on, though he varied the weekly agenda so as to cover all the steps. Cecchetti's approach was in complete contrast to Johansson's and Karsavina admits that she missed the variety of what she calls composed *enchaînements*. Indeed, in an interview with Pierre Tugal, Lubov Egorova goes so far as to say that Cecchetti's classes were monotonous (*Dancing Times*, June 1952), while Karsavina writes that she felt that his approach dulled the artistic response and did not foster visual memory. But she also describes how Cecchetti would sometimes surprise his class in which every exercise was doubled – sixty-four *tendus*, and thirty-two *grands battements*, ending the class, wickedly, with *entrechat six* from the preparation of a slow full *plié*. Clearly, he expected, and received, much from his female students (*Dancing Times*, December 1964).

Accounts of Ivanov's classes, on the other hand, suggest that his heart really was not in teaching. Vazem recalls that he was too gentle to enforce discipline and encourage his students to work and Vaganova remembers his indifference to his students (see Wiley's "A Century of Russian Ballet"), while, for Kschessinskaya, he seemed never to stop to make corrections and was simply fulfilling his duty. Like Johansson, he accompanied himself on his violin, which Kschessinskaya feels that he may have loved more than his pupils – implying that the musician in him preferred playing the instrument rather than teaching ballet.

∽

Nicolai's own career as a teacher started long before he was formally appointed at the Theatre School. As the eldest son, he was left in charge of his siblings when his father had to travel to Moscow, and, when Sergei was still in the school, Nicolai coached him tirelessly at the weekends when he was allowed home. Nicolai was appointed instructor to the junior class at the school in 1896. Fedor Lopukhov was one of Legat's earliest pupils in a class which included Adolf Bolm, Anatole Bourman, Leonid Leontiev and Alexander Matiatin. They started in Legat's beginners' class, where, as a teacher, he was himself also a beginner, and they remained in his class throughout their time at the school. As referenced in "The Legat Saga", Lopukhov describes how Legat saw every pupil as an individual, each with his or her own needs, while maintaining the integrity of the class as a whole. He goes on to describe how, as an artist, Legat had learned anatomy and how his teaching method was based on working and resting groups of muscles in turn, to follow stretches with relaxation, and to work without strain. In "The Tragedy of Nijinsky", Bourman describes how Legat would open wide the windows of the studio before his class to let in the fresh – and, in winter, the freezing air – and then close them a minute before class began. Within ten minutes the students were warm as Legat plucked the strings of his violin. In contrast to Johansson's severity, Nicolai brought his irrepressible sense of comedy to his classes which he made enjoyable and full of fun, his sketch book and pencil always to hand. Lopukhov notes that Legat's senior class included Fokine, Mikhail Obukhov, Alexander Chekrygin and Samuil Andrianov, each of whom benefitted from his teaching and who went on themselves to teach. When Shiryaev was appointed to teach character, Nicolai replaced him to take the senior boys' class.

Legat was in a position to recognise the early potential of Vaslav Nijinsky. At his audition for the Theatre School the young boy showed a spectacular leap upon which Legat urged that he should be admitted. Nijinsky went into the junior boys' class taught by Sergei (and where he soon became a favourite pupil), and then into Obukhov's class and finally into Nicolai's *classe de perfectionnement*. Romola Nijinsky says in her biography of her husband that Nicolai Legat was the only person able to penetrate Nijinsky's reserve and that his "untiring tutoring" developed into a regard that was mutual and lasted "ever after". In turn, Bourman, a close friend, notes that Nijinsky was fired with enthusiasm if Legat requested a particularly difficult step. Karsavina calls him the "Eighth Wonder of the World", hardly noticed until she saw him at the end of a boys' class, seeming to hold himself in the air as he jumped. Later of course, she and Nijinsky often danced together, but the first time was in a *pas de deux* from "Roxana" around 1906. Bourman tells of how, while still a student, Nijinsky was chosen to dance with Georgi Kyaksht, Obukhov and Nicolai Legat. The performance was a triumph, prompting Kschessinskaya to promise that he would be her partner in the following summer, and that the critics would recognise a new star.

From Johansson as well as Petipa and through his father, Nicolai was thoroughly imbued with the French style and this is what Gennady Albert recognises in Legat's precision and what he calls "clarity" and "rationality" in the connecting steps. Legat built on his own training and experience by working out the best preparation for a turn or jump. At the same time, he tried to maintain the energy and enthusiasm of his students with his lively music and witty jokes, but his classes were carefully planned so that each exercise was a preparation for the one to follow. He started teaching the *classe de perfectionnement* when Johansson retired not long before his death. According to his own account, this was on Johansson's recommendation to the director at the time, Vladimir Teliakovsky, although Karsavina's version of events is a little more complicated. While Legat continued to teach Johansson's class, Evgenia Sokolova was officially appointed by Teliakovsky to the position which Legat expected to hold, with the result that he campaigned among the dancers and some, including Karsavina, chose to remain with him (see *Dancing Times*, August 1964). (Karsavina was particularly torn, because, in befriending her, the Legat brothers invited her to join them for lunch between the morning class and the afternoon rehearsal.) Sokolova left after two years and gave private lessons in her house, at which time Legat was officially appointed in her place in 1904. The entry on Sokolova in the "Encyclopedia of Dance and Ballet" states that Johansson recommended her as his replacement, rather than Legat, who was nearly twenty years younger. In some light verse quoted in "The Legat Saga", Legat suggests that although she taught for many years, Sokolova was not a pedagogue and that her students did "not dance". Karsavina might not have agreed with this since, in the end, she did leave Legat's class to join Egorova and Pavlova at Sokolova's house on the outskirts of St Petersburg. Karsavina says that she felt she had learned all she could from Legat and especially needed the finish for her *pointe* work that she implies could only be given by a female teacher. But she says that Legat never forgave her for her defection. Later, Karsavina defected once more, this time to Cecchetti for the virtuosity of the Italian school. As we have seen, having also been a student of Johansson, Preobrazhenskaya regarded Cecchetti as her most important teacher, believing that the Italian influence enriched the Russian dancers without fundamentally changing them.

Legat was very conscious of the difference between assisting Johansson, as he had done for some time, and being responsible for the *classe de perfectionnement*. He says that Johansson supervised the transition, finally saying, "Good. You can go on". This would have been before he officially took over from Sokolova. Following Johansson's example, he would arrive a little before the start of the class at ten-thirty in the morning so that he could prepare the floor himself. Karsavina describes how teachers had different techniques for watering the floor for class or rehearsal – Legat used a rapid circular motion in contrast to others' pendulum motion or figures of eight (*Dancing Times*, December 1966). He wore a practice costume consisting of a white shirt, black tights and white ballet shoes. As the students entered the studio, he would greet each of them individually, as friends and colleagues, before striking a chord on Johansson's violin to start the class; the violin had been given to him by Johansson's daughter on his death. Mathilde Kschessinskaya positioned herself at the front of the class with Vera Trefilova, Tamara Karsavina, Lydia Kyasht, Julie Sedova, Agrippina Vaganova and Elsa Vil. The men – Michel Fokine, Adolf Bolm, Vaslav Nijinsky, Theodore Kozloff and Alexander Gavriloff – took their places behind the women. Legat says that Pavlova preferred to study privately with him, taking class on the Mariinsky stage before rehearsals.

While Legat had great regard for the technical accomplishments brought to St Petersburg by the Italians, he shared Johansson's view that they had allowed artistry and expression to become secondary to physical feats. He also shared Johansson's disapproval of set exercises, particularly in his *classe de perfectionnement*, so each of Legat's classes was different in contrast to Cecchetti's formulaic approach. Mary followed Legat in this respect and she never exactly repeated an *enchaînement*, let alone an entire class. Legat believed that the Italian school had great attributes which he and his Russian colleagues seized upon, but which were absorbed into the Russian school, while retaining the Russian subtlety and épaulement – giving it the *russkaya dusha*, or Russian soul. As he says in his memoir:

> We found that they had a school all their own, which was distinguished by remarkable dexterity and sensational brilliance. Their *tours*, their *pirouettes*, their *fouettés* were all superior to our own… Theirs was a school of *tours de force*; taste was sacrificed to effect and dexterity. But we Russians had not invited them to criticize them. We readily acknowledged their technical superiority, and promptly set about to imitate, adapt, and ultimately to excel their technique.
>
> From that moment onward we set ourselves the deliberate goal of learning the Italian tricks.

Famous among those tricks, of course, was the ability to turn thirty-two *fouettés*, a virtuoso feat, and a challenge even for modern dancers. It caused a sensation when the Italian ballerina, Pierina Legnani, first performed it for a St Petersburg audience in "Zolushka" on 5 December 1893. On that occasion, she was partnered by Gerdt and she generally appeared with him. But Legat was later called upon to replace an injured Gerdt and, from then on, he was her favoured partner. She was a few years older, but they worked together in the studio as she wished to learn Russian style and line, while Legat wished to master the Italian technique. (Legnani lived with Legat's great-aunt Sophia, so as well as partners, they became good friends.) Kschessinskaya struggled to learn the thirty-two *fouettés* from Cecchetti and from Legnani herself, but it was Legat who was able to observe Legnani's technique and then to pass it on to Kschessinskaya – "Tighten this muscle, and at every turn relax and contract it, making such and such a movement with the head." He says that, as a result of Kschessinskaya's success, he received a gift of a gold cigar case and a note of thanks from a "certain very exalted personage", possibly her lover, the tsarevitch. In her own memoir, Kschessinskaya does not acknowledge Legat's help, but from his account it is clear that she had been unsuccessful in learning the technique from Cecchetti and that he worked with her "systematically" until she had mastered it.

Legat went on to teach not only how to achieve thirty-two *fouettés* to Preobrazhenskaya, Trefilova, Vil and Vaganova (and later to his wife, Nadine Nicolaeva, and Alicia Markova, among others), but also to teach the men how to turn multiple *pirouettes*. It seems that an important aspect of the ability to turn, which the Italians had adopted but, until then, the Russians had not, was using the head to "spot", that is, moving the head around quickly during the turn to avoid dizziness and to give the turn a sharp, clean quality. The technique was immediately accepted by Johansson and Petipa. Much later, in his articles on the *pirouette* in the *Dancing Times* (August, September and November 1932), Legat recalls that a *pirouette* or a *tours en l'air* was not allowed to be a feat on its own but was blended into the setting and that "[d]exterity became the henchman of Beauty". He notes that the accomplished "pirouettists" were Laurent Novikoff, Sergei Legat, Fokine and Nijinsky, among others. A direct result of Legat's instruction was that, by the time of Legnani's retirement from the Mariinsky in 1901, Italian ballerinas would no longer be invited to dance in St Petersburg. Having overcome the challenge of the thirty-two *fouettés*, Kschessinskaya felt that she and her colleagues were more than able to hold their own and she used her considerable influence to request the Tsar to issue the appropriate order. While this certainly provided Kschessinskaya with less competition and more opportunities, the other dancers would also have benefitted.

In English sources, Johansson's daughter Anna is not referred to a great deal among the teachers at the Imperial school. She was nearly ten years older than Legat and, not surprisingly, seems also to have taught her classes in the manner of her father since she trained with him rather than at the school. She too showed great variety in the *enchaînements* of her *adages*, and the same must have applied to other exercises. Karsavina reiterates that this variety maintained both the interest and the mental agility of her students. But, while adhering to the classical tradition, Anna Johansson introduced what Karsavina refers to as "torsal" movements at the end of the class and which Karsavina believed greatly improved flexibility and strength in the back (see *Dancing Times*, January 1965). Anna Johansson performed for over twenty years and was a soloist in many of Petipa's ballets. For Karsavina, she was the best of all her teachers, using quiet authority to encourage her students rather than flamboyant histrionics; Nijinska also calls her a "great" teacher.

CHAPTER 9
NICOLAI AND SERGEI LEGAT – THE RISING STARS

One day the director informed me that it had been decided
to invite us to produce a new ballet "The Fairy Doll" at
the Hermitage Theatre of the Winter Palace for a special
performance at which the Tsar was to be present.

Nicolai Legat, "The Story of the Russian School".

As a student, Nicolai was supported by a scholarship that had been established under a legacy from Didelot. He studied both the piano and violin, and played the *balalaika*, a triangular three-stringed Russian instrument akin to a lute. While he took his academic work seriously, he could never resist the opportunity for a practical joke and his well-developed sense of humour was one of his outstanding qualities throughout his life. Students often performed with the company before graduation and Legat was no exception; his antics drew an ovation when he appeared as a monkey in "The Pharaoh's Daughter" with Virginia Zucchi. More unusually, after his graduation in April 1888 he was taken into the *corps de ballet* as a *coryphé* of the first rank. He was sufficiently well thought of to stand in for an indisposed Cecchetti in the following October when he danced "The Fisherman and the Pearl" *pas de deux* in "The King's Command". Although he was physically strong and athletic, Gregory chronicles Legat's frequent illnesses and injuries, implying that he played on these to his advantage, even while requests for leave were supported by doctors' certificates. However, St Petersburg, with its open sewers and damp climate, was known to be particularly unhealthy.

In "The Story of the Russian School" Legat lists the works, about sixty in all, in which he appeared, starting with those while still a student between about 1886 and 1888, and which were all by Petipa - "Daughter of the Snows", "The Pharaoh's Daughter", "Paquarette", "Mlada", "Roxana", "Night and Day", "The King's Orders" ("The King's Command"), "Zaraya" and "Deva Dunaya". Then, as a soloist or in the leading role, the list continues with ballets by Petipa and Ivanov, and Petipa's productions of Perrot's and Saint-Léon's works, moving on to include ballets by Legat himself, "The Fairy Doll" choreographed with Sergei, and then just one by Cecchetti, his revival of Perrot's "Catarina, ou La Fille du Bandit". Legat partnered all the great ballerinas; the Italians, Legnani and Carlotta Brianza, were among the earliest - Legnani in "Zoluchka" and "Sylvia", and Brianza in "Kalkabrino". But Maria Anderson and then Preobrazhenskaya, Kschessinskaya and Pavlova appear frequently in his list, and towards the end of his performing career, so does his third wife, Nadine Nicolaeva-Legat.

One of Legat's first leading parts was as Olivier in February 1891, when he partnered Brianza in the *première* of Petipa's "Kalkabrino". He went on to dance Franz in "Coppélia" and Colas in "La Fille mal gardée". In October 1894, he took Gerdt's place as Prince Charming in "Zoluchka" with Legnani. In the *première* of "Le Réveil de Flore" in 1894, he was Zephyr, the god of the west wind, while his brother Sergei was Mercury, Kschessinskaya danced the leading role of Flora and Anna Johansson was Aurora. He was given many character or demi-character roles that drew on his physical strength and skills as a partner, including the Genius in "The Enchanted Forest", the Phoenix Moth in "Les Caprices du papillon", Zephyr in "Le Talisman" and the Troubadour Béranger in "Raymonda". Having gained the rank of soloist in 1896, he was transferred to the Bolshoi Theatre in Moscow for two months. Gregory suggests that Kschessinskaya may have been responsible for arranging this as a way of thanking him, not only for his partnering but also for teaching her how to achieve the thirty-two *fouettés* which Legnani had made famous. Two roles were particularly noted for Legat's musicality and artistry in mime, Harlequin in "Les millions d'Arlequin" and Gringoire in "La Esmeralda". His assured partnering allowed him to be given the leading roles in the major ballets despite his rather stocky and muscular stature compared to the elegance of Gerdt and Johansson. Volynsky describes how Preobrazhenskaya seemed "like a light doll" in Legat's arms after he had caught her in a flying leap in "Coppélia" (see "Ballet's Magic Kingdom"). When Legat took over the role of Prince Siegfried in "Swan Lake" from

Gerdt he partnered the ballerina on his own in all variations, setting a new standard that has been followed ever since. Previously Gerdt and Alexander Oblakov performed a *pas de deux á trois* with Legnani in the *adagio* passage for violin and cello.

Many years later, Mary warned her students to bring their arms in when turning a *pirouette* with a partner because, as she told us, Legat had had his front teeth knocked out during a variation. It was amusing to discover his own account in his memoir. In a charity performance of his "Valse Caprice" at the Mikhailovsky Theatre, Preobrazhenskaya hit him in the face with her elbow. Characteristically, he finished the piece, including his solo, before spitting out blood and four teeth – at which Preobrazhenskaya fainted on the spot. In typical fashion, Legat treats the mishap as a joke at his own expense, concluding that, when he took out his dentures, he could better amuse young children. On another occasion, he tore his Achilles tendon at the beginning of a *pas de deux* with Claudia Kulichevskaya in "The Pharaoh's Daughter". He does not relate if fines were imposed but he was on crutches for three months and could not perform for six.

Legat's younger brother, Sergei, graduated from the Theatre School in 1894 and was quickly promoted to *coryphé*. His first major role was Acis in Ivanov's "Acis and Galatea" and he, rather than Nicolai, was seen as Gerdt's successor for his noble bearing as he partnered Lubov Roslavleva. Sergei had success as Jean de Brienne in "Raymonda" and was given leading parts in "Javotte", "The Stream" and "The Magic Mirror", and others followed. He gained the rank of *premier danseur* in 1903. Karsavina wrote an interesting sketch of the brothers in her article on "My Partners at the Maryinsky" for the *Dancing Times* (December 1966). Nicolai was a true *danseur noble*, working tremendously hard to improve his elevation by attaching weights to his legs, which, however, she felt had a detrimental effect on his *pirouettes*, although his performances on stage were "fine and effortless". As some of his photographs suggest, Sergei was also on the stocky side, but very good-looking. In their folio of caricatures, the brothers make fun of his cupid-bow mouth and long eyelashes. Karsavina remembers him as the most cheerful and friendly person she had ever met. She called him the "blue-eyed boy" of the company, always good-natured and loved by everyone. They became friends as well as colleagues and she often sat with the brothers while waiting during rehearsals. Her working relationship with Sergei was clearly more relaxed than with Nicolai, who may simply have been teasing her when he kept up a stream of whispered comments while dancing Siegfried to her Odette in "Swan Lake", but it undermined her confidence.

Despite the six-year difference in their ages, the brothers' already-close relationship became even closer as they worked alongside each other in the company. Together they continually improved their strength and technique, and perfected daring lifts, but also enjoyed time at the athletic club of Count Ribopierre, skiing, skating and horseback riding and playing practical jokes on their fellow dancers. As dashing young men, Nicolai and Sergei found regular girlfriends within the company. Nicolai took up with Olga Tchumakova, a character dancer in the *corps de ballet* with whom he had a common-law relationship for the next ten or more years, while Sergei had an equally serious liaison with Petipa's daughter Maria, who was nearly twenty years his senior, and twelve years older even than Nicolai. The brothers formed a *balalaika* orchestra with their brother-in-law Ivan de Lazari, and enjoyed regular dinners with friends, followed by billiards into the small hours. Some of these dinners were organised by Drigo, and included Petipa, the composer Alexander Glazunov and the watercolourist Richard Bergholz.

A little later, Bergholz was instrumental in encouraging the brothers to publish their album of caricatures. They would have been instructed in art at the Theatre School and both were fond of drawing, although their father did not like them to take time from their dancing. Anatole Bourman recalls that Legat's pencil and sketchbook were always to hand. In his memoir, Legat says that the idea of drawing caricatures came almost as a whim, with Sergei first trying to capture Nicolai and then Nicolai his brother, and being pleased with the results. Given Nicolai's playful sense of humour, inevitably they turned their attention to their colleagues in the theatre. Having shown a few sketches at the Opera, the bass singer Fyodor Stravinsky (father of the composer Igor) encouraged them to publish a collection and promised to be the first subscriber. Their album, "Русскій балетъ въ каррикатурахъ", or "The Russian Ballet in Caricatures", was published between 1902 and 1905 and contained ninety-four coloured lithographs in a white leather binding lettered in gold. Priced at the relatively high sum of twenty-five roubles, it sold out rapidly. One copy was presented to Tsar Nicolas II. Plans to publish a second edition suffered a setback when the publisher printed around forty copies but then absconded with both money and pictures, never to be seen again. They started once more with a new publisher and must have been successful, although Legat notes that they lost a significant amount of money overall. The brothers regularly exhibited at the Imperial Society of Water Colour Artists and were made honorary members.

As the nineteenth century drew to a close, Nicolai and Sergei added choreography to their work as dancers and teachers. Nicolai had great admiration for Petipa's ballets and he saw what are now the great classics come to the stage. He went on to work closely with Petipa, creating the debut variations for his daughter Lubov and then for Karsavina. Petipa had been fearful of choreographing a piece for his own daughter and Gerdt was similarly nervous of choreographing for his goddaughter, Karsavina. There is no reason to believe that Legat was exaggerating when he says, "I set many *pas de deux* for [Petipa] that passed under his name" and that Petipa would say in his broken Russian, "Da, ya vizh ti mozh karasha komposi", or "Yes, I see you composed well". Petipa's strength was in choreography for his female dancers and the *corps de ballet* while both Johansson and Legat contributed many male variations to Petipa's ballets, as did Shiryaev, although without official recognition. Legat broke with tradition by using waltzes for *pas de deux* that allowed faster and freer movement than the usual slow adagio pieces. At first, they were regarded as daring, even risky, but quickly became popular.

An important, although abortive opportunity came in 1901 when the brothers were to choreograph the ballet "Sylvia", on which the artist Léon Bakst and Diaghilev would collaborate and in which Preobrazhenskaya would dance the title role. Diaghilev and his close friends in the editorial group of the journal *Mir iskusstva* (*World of Art*) developed the concept and Diaghilev won the approval of the then director, Prince Serge Volkonsky. It would have been the Legats' first major work had Diaghilev not been dismissed suddenly from his post as assistant to Volkonsky during Volkonsky's short tenure as director. According to Prince Peter Lieven in "The Birth of the Ballets-Russes", upper management would not accept that an important production should be entrusted to Diaghilev as a junior assistant, and Volkonsky was forced to ask Diaghilev to stop work. Diaghilev protested but the result of heated discussions and the withdrawal by the tsar of his initial support was Diaghilev's summary discharge and, with it, no opportunity for future employment in any official capacity. With Diaghilev's departure, however, "Sylvia", as choreographed by the Legats, went no further. Lieven does not discuss the Legats' position, and nor does Alexandre Benois, who was an important member of Diaghilev's circle. Some histories of the ballet do not mention that they were the original choreographers for this staging of "Sylvia", and it is not clear why they were not permitted to continue since the dispute was between Diaghilev and the management of the theatre which may have wished to separate Diaghilev's work entirely from the production planned for the following season. In the event, Ivanov started work on the ballet but he was taken ill in November 1901, and responsibility was assumed by Gerdt on Ivanov's death shortly afterwards. Nicolai went on to choreograph the mime scenes for Preobrazhenskaya in the Ivanov–Gerdt version and Sergei danced the male lead of the simple shepherd, Aminta.

After the tribulations around "Sylvia", Nicolai and Sergei enjoyed great success in 1903 with their production of "The Fairy Doll", or "Feya Kukol" in Russian, in collaboration with Bakst. Based on Josef Bayer's "Die Puppenfee", they added music by Tchaikovsky, Anatoly Liadov, Anton Rubinstein, Drigo and an American composer Louis Moreau Gottschalk. In "Reminiscences of the Russian Ballet", Benois describes how the idea for the ballet was Bakst's, inspired by his childhood memories of the toy shops of the St Petersburg Arcade (or Gostiny Dvor), and of the Palm Week fair in the sixth week of Lent (also known as Verba or willow week in Russia, where pussy willow was substituted for palm branches). The ballet was set in a toy shop and Kschessinskaya recalls that the interior looked onto Nevsky prospekt with the people of St Petersburg walking past in the dress of 1830. The ballet, though light and amusing, was seen by Benois as capturing the lost paradise of childhood. He also regards this work as a masterpiece by Bakst for which the artist was inspired by Benois's own collection of toys, the wooden soldiers in particular. It is a charming period piece made the more interesting by Bakst's costume designs, which were among his earliest. The colour palette is soft compared to many of his exotic costumes designed for the Ballets Russes a few years later but evokes the affluence of St Petersburg's well-to-do families seventy years before. Nijinska adds that, as well as designing the costumes, Bakst designed and applied the make=up for the dolls. (A costume designed by Bakst for "The Fairy Doll" was later used for the male dancer in the "Moonlight Vision" scene in Fokine's "Chopiniana".)

The brothers had been asked to choreograph "The Fairy Doll" for a special performance at the Hermitage Theatre of the Winter Palace to be attended by the tsar on 7 February 1903. The tsar then chose it for a performance at the Mariinsky on 16 February when his children were to be taken to the ballet for the first time. ("La Flûte magique" with Pavlova and "Paquita" with Kschessinskaya were also on the programme.) In the performance at the Mariinsky, Kschessinskaya danced the title part of the Fairy Doll. Variations were danced by Olga Preobrazhenskaya (the Baby Doll), Alfred Bekefi and Alexander Shiryaev (a Negro and Negress), Olga Tchumakova (the Little French Doll), Agrippina Vaganova (the Chinese Doll), Vera Trefilova (the Japanese Doll), Anna Pavlova (the Spanish Doll), Maria Petipa (the Russian Doll) and Elena Makarova (the Tyrolean Doll). The two Negro Dolls did a tap dance and circus tricks to Gottschalk's music in a comedic interpretation of the then-accepted view of black culture. (In "Alexander Shiryaev: Master of Movement", Birgit Beumers notes that Shiryaev made a paper animated film of a cakewalk for two women and a man in the early 1900s and the Legats may have been similarly taken with the dance, which at the time was quite novel.) Gerdt appeared as the Chief Assistant and Stanislav Gillert as the Manager. In the first performance, Sergei and Nicolai were the two Pierrots but at the Mariinsky Fokine danced with Sergei since Nicolai was on crutches after an accident that must have occurred between the two performances and may have been when he tore his Achilles tendon. Tamara Karsavina, Lydia Kyasht, Evgenia Lopukhova and Elena Poliakova were Lace Dolls, in pantalettes and with bows and curls in their hair. Shiryaev's wife, Natalia Matveeva, was one of the Porcelain Dolls and Evgenia Eduardova was cast as the Lady's Maid. Alexander Schouvaloff specifically references the design for the Lady's Maid for Eduardova and includes in his book, "The Art of the Ballets Russes", a copy of the design that was one of a set of twelve postcards published for the Red Cross in 1904. "The Fairy Doll" was immediately popular and remained in the *répertoire* for many years, although Petipa himself did not care for it. Mary would have learned about "The Fairy Doll" from Legat himself, and perhaps from Eduardova and Poliakova as well. Almost certainly, it was the inspiration for her own "Land of Toys", choreographed over fifty years later.

Short fragments of "The Fairy Doll" that are contemporary with the original choreography are preserved in films taken by Shiryaev. Barely a decade after the cinematograph was invented in the 1880s, he proposed to the directorate of the Imperial Theatres that film could be used to record choreography – but was told that a still photographic record was sufficient. Possibly having seen how Petipa worked with paper dolls, he experimented with the use of drawings on strips of paper and puppets made with *papier mâché* on wire, recording the images or figures with stop-motion photography. His stop-motion films date from between about 1906 and 1909 and the intriguing details of his work and the story of how his films were rediscovered and preserved are documented in "Alexander Shiryaev: Master of Movement". Beumers writes that a comedy dance called "Artist Pierrots" includes the *pas de trois* from "The Fairy Doll" as a dance for the two Pierrots and Columbine. She suggests too that Shiryaev captured his own style of dancing, and that the film of his puppets accurately reflects how a variation was actually danced since the sequence of Columbine's *fouettés* in "Shutka Arlekina" ("Harlequin's Jest"), a shortened version of "Les millions d'Arlequin", is shown to the left as Preobrazhenskaya performed them. Viktor Bocharov's documentary of 2003, "A Belated Premiere" (available in four parts online), shows some of Shiryaev's rediscovered and restored film footage, including part of the *pas de trois*. Neither Legat nor Preobrazhenskaya mention Shiryaev's films but they must surely have known about them. (In "A Belated Premiere", there is also a stop-motion sequence using puppets of the fakirs' dance in "La Bayadère" which is entirely recognisable.) The choreographic notation for "The Fairy Doll" is included in the Sergeyev Collection of the Harvard Theatre Collection and was among the notations brought out of Russia by Nicolai Sergeyev after the revolution of 1917.

In 1914, Ivan Clustine restaged "The Fairy Doll" for the American tour of Pavlova's company, for which the costumes were redesigned and the story was set in Moscow. Pavlova continued to use Clustine's version through the 1920s, presenting it at Covent Garden in 1923 and in Germany in 1927, including at the Hamburg Volksoper in March when Kathleen Crofton, later Mary's friend and colleague in London, was a Small Doll. Much better known is the adaptation of the story by Léonide Massine for his "La Boutique fantasque" to music by Rossini and arranged by Respighi for the Ballets Russes in 1919. The set and costumes were designed by André Derain since Diaghilev rejected designs put forward by Bakst, possibly because they drew on his original designs for the Mariinsky while Diaghilev was looking for a more modern approach. As well as being performed by the Vaganova Academy, a version of the Legat choreography for the *pas de trois* for the Fairy Doll and Pierrots is danced by Les Ballets Trockadero de Monte Carlo.

The final years of both Petipa and Ivanov were marked by ill health and in 1892, when neither was able to conduct rehearsals, Ivan Vsevolozhsky appointed Cecchetti to the position of second ballet master. Then, on Vsevolozhsky's appointment as director of the Hermitage Museum in July 1899, Volkonsky took over as director of the theatre but his tenure was cut short and he was replaced by Vladimir Teliakovsky in 1901. (Volkonsky's position became untenable when he fined Kschessinskaya for failing to wear "hoops" or panniers in her costume for "La Camargo". She demanded that the fine be rescinded, essentially appealing to the tsar, her former lover.) In his memoir, Petipa recalls the years between 1881 and 1899, under the directorship of Vsevolozhsky, as particularly happy and productive. Vsevolozhsky also designed costumes for ballet and opera, a collaboration which Petipa enjoyed and valued. In contrast, as his health was failing and, despite Petipa's numerous successes, Teliakovsky actively undermined Petipa's position. In "Alexander Shiryaev: Master of Movement", Robinson suggests that Teliakovsky may not have been as callous as Petipa's and Shiryaev's memoirs indicate, and that he saw the Mariinsky needed to be infused with new thinking. At the same time, however, Robinson points out that Teliakovsky was quite ruthless in his determination to get rid of Petipa. Teliakovsky also replaced the *régisseur* Nikolai Aistov by Nicolai Sergeyev, without informing Petipa.

In February 1903, Petipa was given notice that he would be retired on 1 September, although he could remain employed by the Imperial Theatres, without a contract and at his current salary, which would be paid for life. The pretext may have been the failure of "The Magic Mirror", which had had its *première* shortly before. Fokine writes that he believed Petipa remained in full command of his talents, contrary to the statements of "his enemies". In spite of this, Petipa continued to choreograph and to work with the dancers of the company, including coaching Pavlova in "Giselle" and for her debut in "Paquita", in addition to choreographing new variations for "Le Roi Candaule". His final work, and Drigo's last full-length ballet score, "La Romance d'un Bouton de rose et d'un Papillon", was scheduled to open at the Hermitage Theatre on 23 January 1904. The performance was cancelled by Teliakovsky on less than two weeks' notice ostensibly by reason of the outbreak of the war between Russia and Japan. For Petipa, however, this was the final insult and he seldom returned to the theatre or the ballet school, though he did prepare a variation for Preobrazhenskaya from "La danseuse en voyage".

Born within barely a year of each other, Johansson and Petipa grew old together, with Johansson teasing that Petipa could not leap up the stairs as quickly as he could at the age of seventy-five. Johansson died a few years before Petipa, on 12 December 1903, indirectly as a result of the death of his wife. Legat describes how, in his grief, Johansson went at night into the room where her body was lying to touch her face once more. Coming from the room he hit his head on the doorpost and suffered a stroke. He could not speak and died within a month. On hearing the news, Petipa was in rehearsal and, typical of their shared dry humour, Legat remembers that on hearing the news he simply remarked, "Ah? We must die once". More sympathetically, Petipa's diary refers to the death of "my old friend". Like members of the Legat family who had also come from Sweden, Johansson is buried in the Smolenskoe Lutheran Cemetery. To Legat's lasting regret, Johansson's violin, given to him by Anna Johansson, was destroyed when he returned to Petrograd in 1919. Petipa remained in St Petersburg until 1907 when, on the recommendation of his doctors, he moved with his family to the Black Sea coast. He died there, at Gurzuf, on 4 July 1910 but is buried in St Petersburg at the Alexander Nevsky Monastery.

Much younger than Johansson and Petipa, Cecchetti had nearly thirty years of his career still before him. He was offered the position of director of the Imperial School of Ballet in Warsaw in 1902 and reluctantly moved to Poland, largely because of his own difficulties with the new management at the Mariinsky. Apparently, Mme Cecchetti did not want to move and confided to Karsavina that her husband's hot temper meant that he did not stay in one place for long. In Warsaw, Cecchetti invited Russian artists as guests, including Vera Trefilova, Julie Sedova, Preobrazhenskaya and Kschessinskaya, and mounted one of his own ballets as well as managing new opera productions. However, violence and social unrest had spread to the city from St Petersburg, and anti-Russian feelings ran high. The fact that he and Giuseppina spoke Russian rather than Polish did not help matters and they moved back to Italy, settling in Turin. But the Italy that they came back to was not the Italy of thirty years before and, in 1906, Cecchetti returned to St Petersburg, where he opened a private ballet school on Peterhof prospekt. Four years later, Diaghilev brought him into the Ballets Russes as character dancer and ballet master though he continued to teach at his school. With the outbreak of war in 1914, however, he and Giuseppina closed the school and continued to tour with Diaghilev. September 1918 found them in London, where they settled for a few years.

⁓

The Legat brothers' star rose during what is known as Russia's Silver Age. The twenty to thirty years starting roughly in the 1890s was a brilliant and creative period in Russian art and culture that was also coloured by social and political change. According to Murray Frame in "The St. Petersburg Imperial Theaters: Stage and State in Revolutionary Russia 1900–1920", Nicolai Legat had become the most influential figure in the Mariinsky after Kschessinskaya. Legat acknowledges that a few of the dancers did achieve positions in which they could "practically dictate" to the director what they would or would not do, and in which ballets they would or would not appear. But Legat's influence was borne of his experience and his value to the company, and was rather different to the political power wielded by Kschessinskaya by virtue of her connections with the Imperial family. However, the success of "The Fairy Doll" took place as the theatre lost first Ivanov, then Johansson and Petipa, as well as Cecchetti, while the Mariinsky Theatre itself was by no means insulated from far-reaching external events starting with the political and social unrest which led to the revolution of 1905.

CHAPTER 10
WINDS OF CHANGE

...my inseparable companion was my younger brother
Serge, who, had he not died a tragic death at an early age,
would surely have become one of the greatest dancers of
all time.

Nicolai Legat, "The Story of the Russian School".

St Petersburg celebrated the two-hundredth year of its founding by
Peter the Great in May 1903. The city had expanded rapidly over the
previous decades with people from across Russia, mostly peasants, drawn
to employment in its many factories and businesses. But the social and
economic divide between the workers and the prosperous industrialists and
court of the tsar deepened, giving rise to political tensions that the tsar was
unable to relieve. In July 1904, the interior minister was assassinated and by
November unrest had spread throughout the country. This led to a strike
at the Putilov engineering works in December followed by other strikes in
the city. On "Bloody Sunday", 9 January 1905, Imperial soldiers fired on
unarmed demonstrators marching to the Winter Palace to petition the tsar.
This event marked the beginning of the 1905 revolution and, that evening,
Olga Preobrazhenskaya's sold-out benefit performance of "Les Caprices du
papillon" was performed to a theatre that was only half-full.

As the year progressed, the dancers of the Mariinsky struggled to reconcile
their loyalty to the institution that supported their art and livelihoods with
the political and social changes taking place in the outside world. Some of
them organised their own strike at the time of the general strike in October
1905. Twelve delegates, led by Pyotr Mikhailov and including Fokine,

Pavlova, Karsavina, Preobrazhenskaya, Kschessinskaya's brother Josef, Fedor Lopukhov and Sergei Legat, were chosen to put forward their claims for more autonomy in the theatre, and for the reinstatement of Petipa, Shiryaev and the Legats' friend Bekefi. Shiryaev held the position of *répétiteur*, or coach, and had been forced to resign when he refused Teliakovsky's request to make changes to Petipa's works. Teliakovsky had also forced out Bekefi. The delegates' action was regarded as a breach of discipline and all those in the company who wished to remain loyal were required to sign a declaration to that effect. Karsavina notes that the majority elected to sign, effectively cutting loose the delegates who they had chosen to represent them. (According to Roslavleva in "Era of the Russian Ballet", Gerdt withdrew his signature, so he must have been in sympathy with the delegation, at least initially.) A political caricature of the time, reproduced in Roslavleva's book, shows Sergeyev, who was Teliakovsky's informant within the company, waving the declaration in the face of the dancers while Preobrazhenskaya is spanked and Teliakovsky watches from a baby's highchair. He claimed that it was the least talented dancers who were among the petitioners – a view that was hardly applicable to recognised artists like Preobrazhenskaya and Sergei Legat, although others were less well established in their careers. Much as Mona Inglesby, founder of International Ballet, writes later with affection for Sergeyev when he was the company's ballet master in England in the 1940s, at this stage of his life he seems to have been domineering and self-serving in his position as *régisseur*. In very few words, Shiryaev portrays a servile opportunist, while Gregory notes that he had been able to secure annual increases to his salary and was paid a significant sum, illegally, to mount Petipa's "Le Roi Candaule" while locking him out of the theatre as the choreographer sought a royalty for his work. Kschessinskaya was not in St Petersburg through the autumn of 1905 and did not have to declare her position directly, which almost certainly would have been contrary to that of her brother. He was dismissed for his part in the strike, but later she successfully requested that he be reinstated, although this did not occur until 1914.

Sergei Legat came under intense pressure to sign the declaration from his common-law wife, Maria Petipa, who strongly favoured the monarchy. But, conflicted by his loyalty to his friends and their ideals, he committed suicide by slitting his throat with a razor on the night of 18 October and dying the next morning. Karsavina relates that he questioned Maria whether, in the eyes of God, it was the lesser evil to kill her or to kill himself.

Gregory elaborates further – having been drinking and roaming the streets that night, Sergei returned home to the frightened Maria, who locked him in another room and went to bed. According to Petipa, he went so far as to bite her. She found him bleeding to death and by the time Nicolai arrived he was dead, the razor still in his hand. Without naming her, Nicolai blames Sergei's intense infatuation with Maria and her pressure on him to sign the declaration. In "Theatre Street", Karsavina describes how the group of delegates was at Fokine's flat when he answered a knock at the door and that, shocked and sobbing, he broke the news of Sergei's death. Nijinska (in "Early Memoirs") remembers that students of the school were not allowed to attend Sergei's funeral on 21 October and that only one representative of the directorate was present. She adds that many of the dancers saw Sergei as a martyr to their cause, while Roslavleva notes that Pavlova made a point of arranging and rearranging the red ribbons on a wreath which read, "To the first victim at the dawn of freedom of art."

Gregory quotes Diaghilev, who placed the blame squarely on the management of the Imperial Theatres through its failure to listen to the dancers' delegation and by demanding the declaration of loyalty. In "Diaghileff, His Artistic and Private Life", Arnold Haskell and Walter Novel note that Diaghilev encouraged the dancers' requests for more autonomy, although this was less because he actively supported their aspirations and more that he hoped it would lead to Teliakovsky's removal. (Gregory also quotes Diaghilev referring to another, unnamed individual having a mental breakdown.) While she was among the chosen delegates, Karsavina had some difficulty reconciling her own loyalty to the court and the fervour of some of her colleagues, Fokine in particular. In contrast to Karsavina's and others' memoirs, it is interesting that Fokine's does not mention the events of October 1905 at all, possibly because he felt that they had no relevance to his development as a teacher and choreographer, but possibly because he deeply regretted what transpired.

For Karsavina, the company came together to mourn Sergei and, with time, the rifts were healed. But, for Nicolai, Sergei's death was a loss from which, almost certainly, he never fully recovered. Sergei was just thirty and Nicolai was nearly thirty-six. They had worked together in class and in rehearsal, they had enjoyed success with "The Fairy Doll" and they had published their album of caricatures. They were inseparable companions, although, as the elder brother, Nicolai was naturally the leader. But Sergei could not resolve the conflict between his devotion to Maria and the friends he had aligned himself with and, perhaps for the first and only time in their lives, the brothers were themselves divided since the more conservative Nicolai sided with those who favoured the status quo. While he blamed Sergei's passion for Maria, inevitably Nicolai would have felt himself at least partly responsible for Sergei's suicide – whether because he was unsuccessful in his arguments, or because he had left Sergei to make his own decision, or because he failed to stop Sergei's drunken wandering through the streets. If Sergei had lived, the brothers would have reconciled their differences, and perhaps Nicolai would have been less reactionary and more accepting of the inevitable changes of the twentieth century. As it was, he saw the time when they worked together as the "most brilliant period" of his career. Nicolai took his position very seriously, seeing himself as responsible for preserving the teaching of Johansson and the traditions of Petipa. But, without Sergei's leavening influence, the burden of this responsibility would have weighed heavily in face of personalities like Fokine and Diaghilev and their supporters.

✌

The period of social unrest that led to Sergei's death was also a time of artistic ferment and Fokine especially was eager to experiment with new dance forms, including that of the American dancer Isadora Duncan, whose free-spirited choreography was already captivating audiences in Europe. She first performed in St Petersburg in December 1904. Her return early in 1905 coincided with the funeral procession for the victims of "Bloody Sunday" and her emotional and powerful performances created a stir among the public, as they had elsewhere. In her memoir, "My Life", Duncan notes that Kschessinskaya herself invited her to one of her performances, and a few days later she was invited by Pavlova to a performance of "Giselle". She seems to have appreciated the artistry of both performances but saw the studio of the school where she was taken to observe a class as a "torture chamber" and anathema to her own thinking. Kschessinskaya had earlier attended a performance by Duncan in Vienna and considered her a "mistress" of her art. It is tempting, however, to think that Kschessinskaya realised Duncan posed no threat to her own position and saw an opportunity to show herself as forward thinking and ready to support Fokine's efforts. According to Gregory, and not surprisingly, Legat was unimpressed with Duncan's dancing, which he considered unstructured and with no underlying technique, while Fokine believes she expressed emotion more freely than was possible in traditional ballet forms encumbered with stiff and heavy costumes. Although this may be the most obvious example of the differences between Legat and Fokine, the latter had been thinking for some time of how classical ballet should be reformed to fully integrate music, painting and *art plastique* (flowing movements of the whole body), and to strip away ornate costumes and stylised mime. Fokine revered Johansson but he was particularly dismissive of Legat, who he regarded as a slave to tradition, unable to sympathise with the younger man's questioning and his search for new ways to find expression in dance. It is Shiryaev rather than Legat who Fokine credits with improving his technique to the point that he was able to take leading parts in performances of the school. Gennady Albert notes, however, that Fokine's view of Legat as a teacher was "unfair" and, further, that Fokine had essentially lost sight of the fundamental strengths of the Russian school. Fokine's apparent disavowal of the training that provided the foundation for his later work extended also to Ivanov. Karsavina goes a little further, suggesting that Ivanov brought in the use of arms and shoulders that foreshadowed Fokine (*Dancing Times*, September 1966).

Fokine was appointed ballet master to the Theatre School in 1902 and one of his first works was his own version of "Acis and Galatea", staged for the student graduation performance in 1905. He was not allowed to have the nymphs dance in sandals, though he was permitted to give them tunics rather than *tutus*. He went on to create "The Swan" (later "The Dying Swan") for Pavlova later in the year and the ballet "Eunice", in which Kschessinskaya danced the title role in its first performance in February 1907. She seems to have been more enthusiastic than either Volynsky or Nijinska about this new work which caused heated debate among audiences, critics and dancers because of its absence of fixed poses and references to Duncan's style. Fokine's first major work for the Mariinsky was "Le Pavillon d'Armide", which finally opened in November 1907 after five years in the making. The concept of Benois and the composer Nikolai Tcherepnin was to bring to life on the stage the Gobelin tapestries described in the French poet Théophile Gautier's novella "Omphale". Importantly, it fired Diaghilev with excitement. But, while "Le Pavillon d'Armide" was not a great success in St Petersburg, it was one of Nijinsky's first major roles, dancing with Pavlova, who stepped in at the last minute to replace Kschessinskaya. In "Reminiscences of the Russian Ballet", Benois says that Kschessinskaya gave no reason for her refusal to perform the role of Armida but he suspected that she was attempting to humour the Directorate and to halt the production. A little more directly, Nijinska suggests that she had begun to have doubts about the success of the ballet and did not want to risk being associated with it. As famous as "The Dying Swan", Fokine's lasting "Chopiniana" (later "Les Sylphides") was first performed in 1907. Fokine created the "Prelude" in "Chopiniana" for Preobrazhenskaya and made particular use of her balance and her projection of the ethereal quality he was looking for. He recalls that Pavlova gave the impression of flight as she jumped, while Karsavina portrayed intense romanticism.

Shortly after Sergei's death, Legat was appointed second ballet master, although unofficially he had become head of the company since Petipa officially held his position as first ballet master until his death in 1910. His responsibilities included the production of new, full-length ballets, of which his first was "Puss in Boots" ("Kot v sapogakh"), which opened in 1906. The cast included Trefilova, Preobrazhenskaya, Egorova, Kyasht and Karsavina, with Andrianov and Bolm taking the male leads, but it was not a success and had few performances. The following year, Legat staged a revival of Petipa's "The Seasons". The critic Valerian Svetlov was not impressed, although the audience had been enthusiastic to see both Glazunov, the composer, and Petipa attending the performance. Next came "The Blood Red Flower" (also known as "The Scarlet Flower" or "The Purple Flower"), with music by Thomas de Hartmann and designs by Konstantin Korovine, in December 1907. An extravaganza in the Petipa mould, the first cast included Pavlova, Preobrazhenskaya and Trefilova, with Fokine, Bolm and Kyasht joining Gerdt in the male leads. It was evidently more successful than "Puss in Boots". The dance historian and critic Cyril Beaumont includes it in his "Complete Book of Ballets" and suggests that the story was inspired by "Beauty and the Beast". Like "Puss in Boots", it failed to win critical acclaim. Fundamentally, however, Legat may well have been better able to choreograph shorter *divertissements* and *pas de deux* than the full-length spectacles which were expected of him, and it was unfortunate that he was choreographing the longer works at a time when the old order of Petipa was being challenged by Fokine. But in contrast to Petipa's successful early collaborations with Pugni, and then with Minkus and Drigo, Legat seems also have been particularly unlucky in not having a composer with whom he could develop a close working relationship.

∽

Towards the end of the nineteenth century, Russian dancers had increasing opportunities to take engagements abroad, particularly in the summer, when there were no performances in the theatre. Legat was among those who regularly danced in the major cities of Europe; he had already been to Warsaw in 1895 with Kschessinskaya, her father and Bekefi. In the summer of 1907, he appeared with Trefilova at the Palais du Trocadéro and the Opéra Comique in Paris, where, according to Gregory, they were offered a lucrative contract in the United States but which Legat turned down, partly because he was too committed in St Petersburg. The following year he danced with Kschessinskaya at the Paris Opera (in place of Nijinsky, who was ill) and at the beginning of 1909 he accompanied her to Warsaw to dance "La Fille mal gardée". Legat joined the second tour of the Imperial Russian Ballet of St Petersburg organised by Fazer in May of the same year, replacing Bolm as Pavlova's partner and ballet master. A group of twenty-nine dancers from the Mariinsky, including Eduardova and Poliakova (as we have already seen), as well as Egorova, Shiryaev, Matveeva, Sergeyev and Vil and also Olga Tchumakova, visited Berlin, Leipzig, Prague and Vienna. Back in St Petersburg, Legat was given two *pas de deux* classes to teach together with an increase in salary and, in March, he was awarded the Order of St Stanislav in recognition of his artistic work.

At the same time, Diaghilev was laying the foundations for the Ballets Russes. His relationship to Mary is indirect, however. She did not dance for him, and neither did Ana or Oskar. They were outside his orbit and too young to have joined his Ballets Russes, although all three of them studied with or worked with dancers who had been in his company and were influenced by his productions. Diaghilev's *Mir iskusstva* was the nucleus for a group of artists, including Benois and Bakst, which believed that ballet was particularly suited to their ideals. As a result, ballet became central to their debate on artistic reform and innovation. It is interesting that Diaghilev and Legat were only two years apart in age – Diaghilev so ready to challenge convention while Legat clung to tradition in spite of his innate humour and sense of fun. Benois worked in the theatre and collaborated with Diaghilev until the outbreak of the First World War. Bakst is well known for his designs for the Ballets Russes but he designed Petipa's "Le Coeur de la Marquise" for the Hermitage Theatre as early as 1902, as well as, of course, the Legats' "The Fairy Doll". After the revolution of 1905, and in need of an occupation that would support his recently impoverished family, Diaghilev's first major success beyond *Mir iskusstva* was his exhibition of historical portraits at the Tauride Palace, which was followed by an exhibition of Russian paintings in Paris in 1906 at the Salon d'Automne. That foray into the West led to concerts of Russian music at the Paris Opera in 1907, and a production of the opera "Boris Godunov" in 1908. He may not have intended to take both ballet and opera to Paris in 1909, but withdrawal of financial support from the tsar resulted in a change of direction. It was less expensive to stage ballet than opera and Diaghilev brought a large group of dancers to the Théâtre du Châtelet. The season was a great success and the Ballets Russes was formed in the following year.

After taking Bolm's place as ballet master on the second of the tours organised by Fazer, Legat joined another group that performed in Paris in the summer of 1909. This tour included Olga Tchumakova's younger sister Antonina, a contemporary of Nijinska and Gerdt's daughter Elizaveta and who graduated into the Mariinsky company in 1908. Nijinska relates that her brother courted Antonina in the summer of 1906, while Bourman notes that Nijinsky had written her name on a misted windowpane in their classroom. The romance between Nijinsky and Antonina, and their being able to dance together in ballroom and character lessons, ended abruptly, however, when Nijinska was caught with a letter from her brother that she was to deliver to Antonina. She goes on to say that Antonina did not appear particularly upset. She was spending her free time with her sister and Legat and lived with them in the summer of 1906. She may already have fallen in love with him since she began to extol Legat's artistry and his teaching while disparaging both Nijinsky and Fokine. Nijinsky, on the other hand, may have been more hurt since he started to avoid Legat's classes, with the excuse that they were boring. By then, Legat must already have ended his common-law relationship with Olga and, as the feelings between him and Antonina grew, he sought permission from Alexander Krupensky, administrator of the office of the directorate of the St Petersburg theatres, to marry her. The ceremony took place while they were on tour in Paris, at the Russian Embassy Church of the Holy Trinity on 1 July 1909.

On his return home, Legat started work on a revival of Petipa's "Le Talisman", for which Drigo reorchestrated his original score. Performed to celebrate the thirteenth wedding anniversary of Tsar Nicolas II and Empress Alexandra Feodorovna, Legat's version remained in the *répertoire* of the Mariinsky until 1917. Preobrazhenskaya selected the work to mark her twentieth anniversary with the company in November 1909. She chose Legat as her partner and when asked, many years later, who was her favourite partner, Preobrazhenskaya answered, "above all", that it was Legat, who was a "marvellous dancer" (*Dancing Times*, April 1952). Taking over Preobrazhenskaya's role in "Le Talisman", Kschessinskaya says that Legat composed some beautiful dances that were always greeted with enthusiastic ovations. Nijinska, on the other hand, younger and more critical of the work in general, saw it as an anachronism, calling it "that awful old ballet".

Having enjoyed a long tour through central Europe with Pavlova in the spring of 1910, Legat joined Julia Sedova and Fedor Lopukhov at the Sarah Bernhardt Theatre in Paris that summer. He then returned to St Petersburg to work on a revival of Petipa's "Bluebeard" for the fiftieth anniversary of Gerdt's debut with the Imperial Theatre. The following year he produced the dance variations for Modest Mussorgsky's opera "Khovanshchina" and, later in the year, received a three-year contract for services as first ballet master (the title having passed to him on Petipa's death) and as principal dancer, with a bonus if he appeared in more than thirty performances in any one year. However, in what should have been a period of professional and financial security, the growing acclaim of the Ballets Russes and the personal success of Kschessinskaya with Nijinsky in "The Sleeping Beauty", "Swan Lake", "Le Pavillon d'Armide" and "Le Carnaval" in London, but without Legat as her customary partner, weighed on him, as did Fokine's growing reputation. Indeed, Kschessinskaya was determined to dance with Nijinsky, seeing the advantages of having her name associated with his. It was a particularly sore point that she had chosen him as her partner in "La Bayadère" in Moscow as far back as 1907 since it included the *pas de deux* that Legat was reluctant to pass on to the younger dancer. The announcement in January 1908 of Kschessinskaya's engagement at the Paris Opera with Nijinsky had been another snub.

But within the Mariinsky itself two factions had emerged – the "Imperialisty", Legat among them, were traditionalists, while the "Diaghilevsty-Fokinisty" embraced the future and were somewhat critical of Legat's – to them – less-than-appealing choreography. However, in reference to the 1911 and 1912 seasons of Pavlova and Mikhail Mordkin at the Palace Theatre in London, Jane Pritchard, curator of dance at the Victoria and

Albert Museum in London, writing in "Anna Pavlova, Twentieth Century Ballerina", links Legat with Fokine in this period as being among the most forward-looking of the Russian choreographers. Karsavina also notes that he and Sergei broadened the scope of *pas de deux* and *adagio* work (*Dancing Times*, August 1964) as they introduced daring lifts and the use of waltzes for *pas de deux*. But, as Fokine began to compete directly with Legat, the antipathy between them grew as his other partners, Preobrazhenskaya, Egorova, Trefilova and Pavlova, as well as Kschessinskaya, looked for opportunities to dance with Nijinsky in Fokine's choreography. Perhaps because of the tension, Legat became subject to repeated illness and the benefit performance for his twenty-fifth anniversary had to be postponed twice.

Legat's marriage to Antonina did not provide a lasting, happy home life to balance the stresses in the theatre, however. Their daughter Maria was born not long after they were married, sometime in 1910, but he says they lived together for only around two years. By 1913, Legat had become enamoured of Nadine (Nadezhda) Alexandrovna Briger, daughter of the director of the Royal Naval College in St Petersburg and a former student at the Theatre School. She was born on 25 May 1889, a little older than Antonina, but still over twenty years Legat's junior. (This date is provided in her death record but the year 1895 is recorded on her gravestone.) According to a passage quoted by Gregory in "The Legat Saga" from Legat's unpublished memoir, he explained to Nadine that Antonina had become fat and lazy, that he only wanted beautiful dancers in his ballets, and, moreover, that Antonina had tricked him into marriage when he was drunk. Legat's brief marriage to Antonina and then his liaison with Nadine suggest a man reluctant to accept middle age while still struggling to come to terms with his brother's suicide, Fokine's ascendancy and the prospect of the end of his performing career with the Mariinsky. His twenty-fifth anniversary benefit gala took place on 9 February 1914 with a performance of "La Esmeralda" in which he danced the role of Gringoire with Kschessinskaya as Esmeralda. Paul Dukes was able to get a standing place in the theatre from Teliakovsky. His description in the foreword to Legat's memoir of the "elite of Russian nobility" glittering with jewels, the orchestra under Drigo, and the principal dancers, Kschessinskaya in the title role, Gerdt as Frolo, Vassily Stoukolkin as Quasimodo and, finally, Legat as Gringoire, captures the excitement of the evening. Legat's appearance in the first act brought the performance to a halt as the entire audience rose to its feet. He was given the title Honoured Artist (or His Majesty's Soloist) of the Imperial Theatres and presented by the tsar with a gold cigarette case embellished with the Imperial coat of arms in enamel and diamonds. Although his formal employment with the Mariinsky Theatre had come to an end, he could not have foreseen that this would be his last performance on the Mariinsky stage. Not only was it Legat's last performance at the Mariinsky, it was also the last time that Kschessinskaya performed in front of the tsar, and the only time that he saw his former mistress in her favourite role. Nor could anyone have foreseen that it would be the last time the tsar attended a performance there. The evening marked the end of an era for Legat; less directly, it marked the end of an era for St Petersburg and for the country as well, just months before Archduke Franz Ferdinand was assassinated in Sarajevo in June 1914, precipitating declarations of war against Russia, first by Germany and then by Austria-Hungary.

CHAPTER 11
LEGAT'S JOURNEY FROM PETROGRAD TO LONDON

*Perhaps, had I been able to see twelve years ahead, and
had caught a vision of myself fleeing from the Bolsheviks with
little but the clothes on my back...*

Nicolai Legat, "The Story of the Russian School".

Shortly after receiving the money due to him from his benefit performance
in February 1914, Legat was granted permission to go abroad. Away from
the vigilance of Nadine's family, the lovers were free to indulge their mutual
infatuation and enjoy the acclaim of both critics and audiences. Writing from
Italy in May, Legat requested an extension of two weeks and on 1 August he
wrote again from Paris, asking for a further extension of up to a year. (As he was
writing, he may not have known that Germany declared war on Russia on the
same day but he would have been very aware of the threat of hostilities.) Behind
this was the fact that he had secured engagements for himself and Nadine. She
performed under the name Nadine Nicolaeva and was known more formally as
Nadine Nicolaeva-Legat. Nicolaeva writes of how they came to England, saying
that they were engaged at the Paris Opera and that Legat had received offers
from London although she was reluctant to go even further from home. (See
Ballet, January–February 1951 and "The Legat Story".) Events overtook them,
however, as Germany declared war on France on 3 August and they were able to
reach London just as war was declared in Britain on the following day.

Legat and Nicolaeva appeared in various reviews in London, the provinces
and Scotland before engagements at the Savoy and Alhambra Theatres at the
end of the year. "The Passing Show", a review at the Palace Theatre followed

and they danced "The Khan's Vision" at the London Coliseum in February 1915, as well as in other revues and music hall. But they, or rather Nicolaeva, took exception to less-than-enthusiastic comments on her elevation (the height of her jumps) by "Sitter Out" of the *Dancing Times*, P.J.S. Richardson. A letter was written in Legat's name, extolling Nicolaeva's technique and asking not only that it be published but with an offer of payment that was not well received. In "The Legat Saga", John Gregory points out that Legat himself was incapable of writing such a letter in English, while Nicolaeva's own English was fluent, though she maintains that she spoke very little in those days (see her articles for *Ballet* on "How I Came to England".) The spat with "Sitter Out" and Legat's antipathy towards the new works of Diaghilev's Ballets Russes did little to endear them to the English ballet world. (Gregory describes how "Sitter Out" elicited Legat's criticism of Diaghilev without Legat knowing that he was being baited.) Nicolaeva may have come to realise that their prospects in London were limited and she longed to return to Russia to fulfil her ambition of becoming a ballerina with the Mariinsky. The opportunity came while on tour a little later in the year when the Russian consul in Hull advised that, under wartime conditions, their only hope would be to sail on a fishing boat across the North Sea to Norway. Legat reluctantly agreed to the hazardous journey, which Nicolaeva says was in the pilot boat for a minesweeper. Having landed at Bergen, they made their way slowly to Stockholm and Helsinki, then to Riga, and finally to Petrograd, earning what they could by performing as they went.

But Petrograd in wartime and under threat of revolution was very different to the St Petersburg they remembered and any thought that Legat could regain his former position with the Mariinsky, let alone Nicolaeva's dream of dancing with the company, had to be abandoned. She took daily class with Legat and volunteered with the Red Cross at the naval hospital. Gregory suggests that her nursing work was undertaken partly to mollify her parents, who were justifiably upset that she was living with a middle-aged man who was not even divorced from his second wife. (Nicolaeva's obituary in the *Dancing Times* of January 1971 states that she and Legat were married in 1917, although Gregory notes that Legat was not finally divorced from Antonina until 1919.) Nursing was an area in which dancers could contribute to the war effort. With their greater financial resources and influence, Kschessinskaya and Preobrazhenskaya both founded hospitals for the wounded; Kschessinskaya's was in a large apartment overlooking the Kamennoostrovsky prospekt, while Preobrazhenskaya's was located in the large apartment building that she owned at 68 Fontanka River Embankment. Legat taught at the private school of Madame Moskalyeva, where Preobrazhenskaya was also teaching and, with Bekefi and Nicolaeva, he put on ballets at the Narodny Dom, including "The Rose of Margita", "The White Lily", "Cleopatra" and "Walpurgis Night". He worked with the young musician and conductor Samuil Samosud to train an orchestra for the Moskalyeva school with the idea of forming a company to showcase Nicolaeva's technique. Like Legat, Preobrazhenskaya had also celebrated her twenty-fifth anniversary with the Mariinsky in 1914, but she continued to appear as a guest artist, as well as touring. She taught at the Theatre School and, from 1917, at Akim Volynsky's School of Russian Ballet, as did Legat a little later.

As the months and then the years passed, revolution within Russia added to the daily miseries of war. Gregory quotes passages from Legat's notebook describing the events of February and March 1917 – gunfire in the streets, the abdication of the tsar, looting and arson. For Karsavina, the desolation of the empty streets and ruined buildings lent the city a "new tragic beauty". Kschessinskaya's mansion was taken over by the Bolsheviks and Lenin addressed the crowds from the balcony. Nicolaeva's family left Petrograd as soon as they could, taking with them her daughter Anna from a previous relationship, and made their way to the safety of London. Nicolaeva and Legat continued to stage ballets and *divertissements* and were able to tour under the auspices of the new government, which wished to introduce ballet and other artistic forms to the workers, even though, as Karsavina observes, they were all, dancers and audience alike, close to starvation. Life became increasingly difficult as Nicolaeva and Legat struggled to find a place in the new order, but they were able to settle for a time in Moscow, where he was appointed to teach the principal dancers of the Bolshoi company. After some negotiation, Nicolaeva was accepted into the company, though her life was not made easy by the resentment of the senior ballerinas. In the summer, Legat and Nicolaeva performed at open-air concerts and were often paid with food because money was universally short. In the end, her ambition to teach at the Bolshoi school was impossible to achieve.

Over the winter of 1918–1919, Nicolaeva had become ill with a form of tuberculosis and, while she had been allowed to go to a sanatorium in the Caucasus, her health remained poor. She and Legat returned to Petrograd to find their house occupied by a Cossack who not only would not let them take away any of their possessions but, out of sheer malice, broke Johansson's violin over his knee. Vera Volkova, who was later known for having Erik Bruhn, Rudolf Nureyev and Margot Fonteyn among her students, may have studied with Legat at Volynsky's school and then took classes with him in London. Describing her own return to Petrograd in January 1920, she saw the city a drab grey, the streets full of rubbish, the few people clearly ill and malnourished. The desperation is captured in one of Legat's caricatures which shows him with Nicolaeva in 1921, thin and in rags, Nicolaeva dragging her feet behind him and seeing her reflection in the worn fabric of his jacket, but with their "honours" listed wryly alongside – Nicolaeva's "Order of the Night-Pot" next to Legat's "Cavalier of the French Academy of Dance". (See "The Legat Saga".)

A staunch supporter of Legat, Volynsky tried to come to their rescue, bringing him into his ballet school as a teacher. (Nicolaeva also taught at the school when Alexander Pushkin was one of her students.) While outspoken in his criticism of the teaching at the Theatre School, which had been renamed the Academic Theatre School, or State Choreographic Technical School, in 1917, Volynsky advocated the return of Legat as the only ballet master able to lead the company, which had similarly been renamed the State Academic Theatre for Opera and Ballet, or GATOB. (The company was not named after the Bolshevik revolutionary Sergei Kirov until 1935.) Legat was also critical of the teaching at the Theatre School and he supported the merger of Volynsky's school with the State School. Meanwhile, Nicolaeva's health continued to be a concern. Finally, in 1922, she was granted six months leave of absence, to be accompanied by Legat, and they seized their chance to join her family. The majority of Legat's colleagues and contemporaries had already left Petrograd. Ironically, just as Legat and Nicolaeva departed, it was announced that he had been elected to membership of the Supreme Choreographic Council of the Petrograd Academic Theatres. Volynsky writes that they were mistaken in their pursuit of money, the "yellow demon", in Europe, possibly foreseeing that, without Legat's support, his own position was weakened. He became isolated both from the theatre and the State School and died not long afterwards, in 1926.

Legat and Nicolaeva made their way to Berlin through Latvia, Lithuania and Sweden. If Legat and Nicolaeva performed in Berlin and were welcomed by the Russian *émigré* community, surely they must have met Eduardova as well.

They went on to Paris, where they planned to settle, but Kschessinskaya and Trefilova begged Legat not to compete with them for pupils. Kschessinskaya had her own, if limited, financial resources but other teachers were dependent on students from Russian *émigré* families who, themselves, could barely afford to pay for lessons. So they moved on again, to London. But, if Legat's former colleagues and students had implored him not to compete with them in Paris, London was hardly less crowded with dancers and former dancers who had arrived some years earlier. Pavlova had moved into Ivy House in Golders Green in 1912; Seraphina Astafieva settled in London in 1914 and established her studio at the Pheasantry in the King's Road in 1916; Kyasht had left Russia for the last time in 1917 and ran her own school until she founded a touring company; and Karsavina had left Russia with her English husband in 1918. They were all much younger and had embarked on teaching careers while still performing. Cecchetti had also come to London in 1918. He set up a studio in Maiden Lane before establishing his Academy of Dancing at 160 Shaftesbury Avenue, which was hung with pictures of his pupils, colleagues and friends, including Karsavina, Trefilova, Pavlova and Nijinsky. To mark the fiftieth anniversary of his first performance, he appeared with the Ballets Russes as Carabosse in "The Sleeping Princess" at the Alhambra Theatre on 5 January 1922. He was championed by Cyril Beaumont and the Polish dancer Stanislas Idzikowski, with the result that "A Manual of the Theory and Practice of Classical Theatrical Dancing" was published by Beaumont later in the year. Since Beaumont also initiated the founding of the Cecchetti Society, Legat may well have been relieved to see his friend return to Italy in 1924 when he was appointed director of the school at La Scala in Milan.

Another friend and former pupil (perhaps from the days when Legat was in Moscow), Laurent Novikoff had set up a studio in the garden of his house at 13 Blomfield Road in Maida Vale. Legat and Nicolaeva gave classes there and lived with him when they first arrived in England. Novikoff was born in Moscow in 1888 and studied with Vasily Tikhomirov at the Bolshoi school, graduating into the company in 1906. He danced with the Ballets Russes in the 1909 season, including in "Prince Igor" in May at the Théâtre du Châtelet, and then toured with Pavlova between 1911 and 1914. (There is a photograph of him in costume for "Raymonda" in the *Dancing Times* of December 1928, with the caption stating only that the occasion was the opening of the Théâtre des Champs-Elysées in 1912.) Presumably, he stayed in Europe during the war years and would have married his wife, Elizabeth, also a dancer, around this time. He danced again with the Ballets Russes in 1919–1921 and rejoined Pavlova between 1921 and 1928. Novikoff ran his studio in Maida Vale until 1929, when he emigrated to the United States where he was ballet master at the Chicago Opera between 1929 and 1933 and had his own studio in the Lyon & Healy Building, 64 East Jackson Boulevard. He was ballet master for the Metropolitan Opera in New York between 1941 and 1945, when he opened a ballet school at New Buffalo, Michigan. He died there in June 1956. Importantly, and to Legat's great pleasure, Novikoff had his own copy of the album of caricatures made with Sergei and allowed Legat to have them all reproduced, essentially replacing what had been lost in the revolution. Novikoff's own copy, a gift of his estate, is held at the New York Public Library and has the transcribed inscription in the catalogue, "*Ot odnogo iz avtorov etikh karrikatur, N. Legata, milomu Lavrush Novikovu, na pamiat' obo mikh. N. Legat. 1930 13 Mai London*", translated as "From one of the authors of these caricatures, N. Legat, to dear Lavrush Novikov, to remember me by N. Legat. May 13, 1930, London".

Again, writing in the January–February 1951 issue of *Ballet*, Nicolaeva says that she and Legat set up a studio in Swiss Cottage as early as 1915, at the "Eire" Arms (Eyre Arms), on the suggestion of Pavlova, who came with Kyasht to take classes. John Gregory notes that a studio in Swiss Cottage was set up in 1923, and, since Anton Dolin refers to the studio in Swiss Cottage as a "small drill hall" with a bad floor, and would have been in his teens, the studio at the Eyre Arms may have been established when Legat and Nicolaeva returned to England in the early 1920s. Dolin's advanced training was with Astafieva but, not long before he joined the Ballets Russes, she had recommended that he work further with Legat, who taught him *pas de deux* over several "wonderful" months. This included the *adagios* from "Swan Lake" and "The Nutcracker", which he rehearsed with Nicolaeva. For class he says Legat played his improvised tunes, each one "more charming" than the last. Alicia Markova also went to the Swiss Cottage studio, walking from Hampstead to save the bus fare so that she could take private lessons with him. A little later, Legat moved the studio to a basement in Percy Street off Tottenham Court Road. Nicolaeva goes on to say that in 1924 they made their home at Golders Green and established a studio in Cricklewood. They moved the studio again, to Poland Street off Oxford Street, then to a church hall off Portland Place and, once again, to Regent House in Fitzroy Square. The interior of one of those studios is shown in a caricature from 1924 reproduced in "The Legat Saga" and captioned "Nicolaeva Taking Her

| *Nicolaeva taking class, caricature by Nicolai Legat, courtesy of The Legat Foundation*

Lesson from Legat". Wearing a jacket and tie, he is seated at an upright piano while Nicolaeva is swinging from a *barre*. The walls are hung with what can just be made out to be a selection of the caricatures made with Sergei.

As before the war, Legat and Nicolaeva secured various engagements in London. Legat was retained by the London Palladium in October 1923, to produce ballet numbers for what Dolin calls a group of "Russian Art dancers", in which he appeared, with Nicolaeva and Dolin (as Nicolaeva's partner), and a twelve-year old Markova. (Nicolaeva refers to them as "The Moscow Art Dancers".) Markova recalls that Legat had come to Astafieva's studio to look for dancers and that she and Dolin were among those chosen. Legat arranged Pavlova's solo, "The Dragonfly", for her. (See Dolin's "Alicia Markova, Her Life and Art" and Markova's "Markova Remembers".) Legat and Nicolaeva appeared in the Sunshine Matinée charity performance in December 1923 in "La Poupée", which "Sitter Out" refers to as their well-known piece, for an old "pundit" and a Doll (in this context, the pundit seems to be modelled on Dr Coppélius), and they danced a *pavanne* for the Mi-Careme Ball in 1924. Lydia Lopokova, a former student at the Theatre School and younger sister of Evgenia and Fedor, enlisted Legat to choreograph a dance for herself and Idzikowski in a programme for which the impresario Oswald Stoll had engaged her for a short season over the spring of 1924 at the London Coliseum. "Soldier and Grisette", to music by Alexandre Lecocq, was a humorous love story set in nineteenth-century Paris in which Legat evidently showed off the dancers' speed and elevation, and their comic acting abilities. In the summer, Legat provided the choreography for Arnold Bennett's play with Edward Knoblock, "London Life", at the Drury Lane Theatre (see Wearing, "The London Stage 1920–1929: A Calendar of Productions, Performers, and Personnel"). Early in 1925, he and Nicolaeva appeared as Dr Coppélius and Coppélia in a *pas de deux* from the ballet at the Coliseum, followed by an appearance at the Manchester Hippodrome, and then back to the Alhambra in London. This merited a photograph of him on the front cover of the February issue of the *Dancing Times*. In April 1925, Legat worked again with Lopokova and Idzikowski, choreographing "The Postman" to a Beethoven piano sonata arranged for orchestra. It was another light-hearted story, this time about a lady's maid who, regretting having posted a letter to her lover, waits for the postman to collect the mail so that she can take it back again. A highlight must have been Lopokova riding off the stage on the postman's bicycle with the letter between her teeth. Both dancers had to learn how to ride a bicycle and Legat must have delighted in the comic opportunities offered by the story. By then, Lopokova was very much part of the Bloomsbury group through her relationship with the economist John Maynard Keynes, and the backcloth and costumes were designed by the painter Duncan Grant. In October of the same year, Legat appeared with the Ballets Russes as the Showman or Charlatan in "Petrushka" at the Coliseum with Lopokova as the Ballerina, Léon Woizikowski as Petrushka and Nicolas Zvereff as the Moor. *The Times* (30 October 1925) was enthusiastic except that it was noted that the orchestra was under-rehearsed and struggled with Stravinsky's score. The critic praised the dancers and noted Legat's admirable mime, but particularly saw Woizikowski as a worthy Petrushka – showing "all the heart-break of the semi-human, inarticulate being". The *Dancing Times* (December 1925) reported that Legat filled his role with "considerable distinction" and included a photograph of the principal dancers in their costumes.

⁂

Meanwhile, Cecchetti's departure from the Ballets Russes in 1924 to go to La Scala left Diaghilev in need of a ballet master for the company and a teacher for his new star and *protégé* Serge Lifar. He turned to Legat, who, despite misgivings, yielded to Diaghilev's well-known persuasiveness. Nicolaeva was engaged as a soloist and, with performances for Legat, who took over Cecchetti's roles, including the Showman in "Petrushka" and the Shopkeeper in "La Boutique fantasque", the prospect of secure work for them both, with a season at the Coliseum, would have been attractive. However, George Balanchine had been brought into the company as choreographer and Legat found both Lifar and Balanchine lacking experience. Not surprisingly, the company was not wholly enthusiastic to have Legat as their ballet master. The dancers did not respond well to the more relaxed atmosphere of Legat's classes and the demands of a new one every day. In her memoir, the English dancer Lydia Sokolova (Hilda Munnings) says that, although his classes were more fun, it was impossible for him to make the corrections necessary for a large company, while accompanying the class on the piano as well as teaching. But Alexandra Danilova recalls that the company did not like Cecchetti's classes because he did not warm them up sufficiently at the *barre* and because his routines were set to specific days of the week. Lubov Tchernicheva, wife of Diaghilev's *régisseur* Serge Grigoriev was more enthusiastic and believed that the company benefitted from Legat's teaching. As always, and for a variety of reasons, the dancers had their personal preferences.

Even allowing for a degree of exaggeration on Lifar's part, he and Legat appear to have had a good working relationship given Lifar's description of an audition requested by Bronislava Nijinska for the male lead in her ballet "Roméo et Juliette". Lifar was indignant but had to agree. He recalls that Legat arrived first and tried to allay his apprehension, and they were then joined by Diaghilev, his assistant Boris Kochno, Pavel Koribout, a cousin of Diaghilev, and finally Nijinska. Legat directed the audition from the piano, starting with relatively easy *enchaînements,* which he then made more difficult. Lifar says he had never danced so well and turned twelve *pirouettes*. Diaghilev was delighted, while Nijinska was "*visiblement confondu*". Lifar's book about his time with Diaghilev, "A l'aube de mon destin chez Diaghilew", sheds a little light on this period. In August and September 1925, Legat and Nicolaeva travelled through Italy with Diaghilev and Lifar while Legat continued to work with the young dancer in Florence, Rome and Naples. In October, the company started a two-month season at the Coliseum in London, followed by engagements in Berlin and Monte Carlo, and then preparations for the Paris and London seasons. Legat's relationship with Diaghilev was prone to disagreement and was short-lived, however. If Legat had joined the Ballets Russes with greater appreciation for the work of Diaghilev and for the ballets of choreographers like Balanchine and Nijinska, his time might have been less unhappy. (In his recollections, in verse, of some of the people he knew and worked with, as set out in Gregory's "The Legat Saga", he somewhat cryptically observes of Balanchine that he would always live as if he were a bachelor, while of Nijinska he simply says "sad".) But this was when ballets like Nijinska's "Le Train bleu" and Balanchine's "L'enfant et les sortilèges" were mounted, neither of which is likely to have appealed to him, although the *répertoire* did also include works by Petipa. But Gregory references Vladimir Koshevnikoff, who believed that Nicolaeva's demands for status within the company caused difficulties for both Balanchine and Diaghilev, while Markova felt that Legat did not relish the prospect of touring and wished to be more settled. Nicolaeva herself writes that Legat was not prepared to appear in Diaghilev's new ballets and "decided to leave" the company. According to Grigoriev, the final rift came when Diaghilev blamed him for failing to improve Lifar's *pirouettes*, to which Legat took great exception, as well he might, even given some embellishment in Lifar's account of his audition for "Roméo et Juliette". Legat resigned in July 1926 and his place was taken by Tchernicheva.

Cecchetti continued to dance with the company and his last performance was as the Charlatan in "Petrushka" at La Scala at the age of seventy-seven. The death of his wife Giuseppina not long afterwards, in October 1927, was a great loss – they had been married for nearly fifty years and had been partners onstage for even longer. He went on teaching at La Scala, but just a year later he collapsed during his morning class on 12 November 1928 and sank unconscious to his chair. He died early the next day at the age of seventy-eight.

❧

Remaining in Paris, Legat and Nicolaeva established their Haute École de Ballet at 5 rue des Petites Écuries off the Faubourg Saint-Denis. Classes were offered in classical, character, operatic and modern stage dance, as well as a "class of perfection" for advanced students. Legat also taught at the Salle Wacker, while Nicolaeva found engagements to support her parents and siblings, and the education of her daughter Anna, then aged about sixteen, in London. Links were maintained with the dance world in England since

Legat's photograph appeared on the front cover of the *Dancing Times* for June 1926 and his "life story" was given inside. The magazine also published photographs of Nicolaeva and Serge Renoff, noting that they had toured in Denmark, Germany and Algeria in 1927 before a season at the Apollo Theatre in Paris. Nicolaeva and Renoff then joined Ida Rubinstein's company, which performed in Paris and on tour in 1928 and 1929.

It was in the middle of 1927 that the Estonian sculptor and painter Auguste Albo came to Paris. In return for ballet lessons, he sculpted the bronze bust of Legat that later stood on a wooden column at the entrance to the studio at 46 Colet Gardens and is now held in the Legat archive at the Royal Ballet School. Another visitor in Paris was Paul Dukes, who had called on Legat at the Fitzroy House studio and came to Paris eager to study with him. According to Gregory, Dukes had a bet with a colleague that he could become a professional ballet dancer and sought out Legat in order to achieve that ambition. But Dukes had known Legat in St Petersburg, and probably Nicolaeva as well. Born in 1889, Dukes went to Russia at the age of twenty to study music with Albert Coates, an Anglo-Russian conductor, and became assistant conductor himself with the Mariinsky opera company. Shortly after the start of the First World War, he worked unofficially for the British Foreign Office and joined the Anglo-Russian Commission, a propaganda organisation. Drawn to the attention of Mansfield Cumming, known as 'C', who ran the Russian office of the Secret Service Bureau, the forerunner of the Secret Intelligence Service, or MI6, Dukes was summoned back to London and briefed by Cumming on his new assignment, the task of rebuilding the British intelligence network within Russia. Having been trained in the use of codes and secret inks, Dukes returned to Russia and over the next two years, as agent 'ST 25', proved himself a master of disguise in the classic tradition of espionage, passing himself off as a Serbian business man, a shabby Ukrainian, a member of the Cheka (All-Russian Extraordinary Commission for Combating Counter-Revolution and Sabotage) and even joining the Bolshevik party. On his return to London, he was knighted by King George V. He published a series of memoirs between 1922 and 1950: "Red Dusk and the Morrow: Adventures and Investigations in Red Russia"; "The Story of "ST 25": Adventure and Romance in the Secret Intelligence Service in Red Russia"; "An Epic of the Gestapo"; and "The Unending Quest: Autobiographical Sketches". Dukes's colleagues in the intelligence service included Sidney Reilly (known as the "Ace of Spies") and Arthur Ransome, then a journalist in Russia for the *Daily News* and who later wrote the "Swallows and Amazons" books for children. Dukes did not go on to a peacetime career in intelligence, although in 1939 he was asked to investigate the death of a Czechoslovak industrialist, which he describes in "An Epic of the Gestapo". Instead, he became a special correspondent for *The Times* but was most interested in pursuing his studies in yoga and the philosophies of George Gurdjieff and Pyotr Ouspensky. (Nicolaeva may have known of Gurdieff and Ouspensky in St Petersburg but under Dukes's guidance she was particularly drawn to their theories.)

When Dukes arrived in Paris, Nicolaeva was attracted to him as a possible partner for the gymnastic dance acts that she was developing for music-hall performances. On his part, he seems to have been able to draw a fine distinction between his relationship with Legat and his relationship with Nicolaeva, since Gregory suggests that Dukes and Nicolaeva quickly became lovers. Perhaps the skills he used as a spy were brought into play to reassure Legat that he was a friend and not a rival; perhaps Legat was conscious of the fact that he was well into middle age and had already accepted that Nicolaeva was determined to maintain her performing career, but without him. Legat, Dukes and Albo devised a spectacular *pas de trois* for Nicolaeva, Dukes (who appeared on stage as Dukaine) and Renoff. Dukes composed the score and Albo designed the sets and costumes for the number, which was billed as "Le Jardin exotique". It contained the acrobatic lifts which Legat accepted were needed to attract engagements. However, at its first performance in Liège, the orchestra refused to play Dukes's music, his score was abandoned and a medley of pieces was pulled together at the last minute. The dance was reset and retitled "Dreams of Delight" but was not a success, although Dukes maintained his faith in its potential. Finally, in 1929, the trio was offered a contract to tour in England in a variety review called "Beauty on Parade" in which the number was renamed again, to "Revels of Flame and Smoke"; the music was composed by Legat's friend Vladimir Launitz and the roles of the three dancers were modified to suit. Launitz had been the conductor for several companies and toured with Pavlova, the successor companies to the Ballets Russes, the Dandré-Levitoff Russian Ballet and the Anglo-Polish Ballet.

Gregory stresses Dukes's sincerity in his support for Legat in building up his studio and Nicolaeva's opportunities for performances. Dukes actively looked for ways to get Legat's name more widely known. He certainly translated Legat's articles in the *Dancing Times* on the "Boyar Dance" and

"Folk Dancing in Russia", which appeared in November and December 1927, followed by "Polanaise [sic] and Mazurka" in April 1928, and, as "P.D.", he wrote "Nicolas Legat and the Class of Perfection" for the February 1930 issue.

CHAPTER 12
THE STUDIO AT 46 COLET GARDENS

---

*Thus, through all my years of study with Monsieur Legat I
collected a library of written lessons, which have been a
continuous inspiration and divine guidance to me...*
Cleo Nordi, "Heritage of a Ballet Master: Nicolas Legat".

After Diaghilev's death in 1929, and with the future of Russian ballet
in Europe in doubt, Legat followed Nicolaeva back to England.
They lived first at 3 The Ridge, Holders Hill Avenue in Hendon, where
Nicolaeva's brother's family had settled, though she was often away on
tour. ("The Ridge" seems no longer to exist but may have been near the
present Ridge Close.) In a letter in the collection of the late Dawn Tudor,
Legat says (in translation) that he was occupied with "starting work in
the studio, mostly writing my memoirs and gardening, and painting (not
art), the house." Until this point, gardening and house painting can hardly
have been familiar activities but he seems to have embraced them with his
usual energy and good humour. In those days, there was a small Russian
community in Fulham and around Barons Court, and at the end of 1930
Nicolaeva found the premises for a permanent studio at Colet House, 46
Colet Gardens. The first advertisement appeared in the January 1931 edition
of the *Dancing Times* in which Legat listed his credentials as Soloist of His
Majesty the Tsar, Maître de Ballet of the Imperial Theatres of Petrograd and
Moscow, Director of the Class of Perfection of the Imperial Ballet School,
Officier de l'Academie des Beaux Arts de France and Vice President of the
Imperial Society of Teachers of Dancing. (If correct, this latter position
cannot have lasted long since there is no mention of it elsewhere.) In

March, the advertisement offered operatic dance, choreography and mime, and a variety of character dances.

Students and dancers who studied with Legat in Colet Gardens ranged from those in their teens – Alan Carter, Margot Fonteyn, Alicia Markova, Moira Shearer and Michael Somes – to stars like Anna Pavlova, Alexandra Danilova and Léonide Massine with the Ballets Russes, and dancers who were already established in their careers, including Anton Dolin, André Eglevsky and Serge Lifar, as well as Mary, Ana Roje and Oskar Harmoš. Many came back to him for classes whenever time and circumstances allowed. Markova recalls how she took a class with him in the morning and then danced Papillon to his Pantaloon in "Le Carnaval" the same evening, as well as the fact that he helped to make her *fouettés* secure, for which she remained thankful for the rest of her life. A little later, Eglevsky left the Ballets Russes de Monte Carlo, sacrificing his salary and position as a soloist, in order to train continuously with him. To compile an exhaustive list of everyone who studied with Legat in London would be almost impossible, but those who contributed to "Heritage of a Ballet Master", written by Eglevsky and John Gregory, shed light on the man and his classes – Frederick Ashton, Alan Carter, Anton Dolin, Barbara Gregory, Patrick Hall, Dorothy Lysaght, Grania Guiness, Alicia Markova, Léonide Massine, Cleo Nordi, Michael Somes, Jack Spurgeon and Wendy Toye, as well as Mary herself. Many express gratitude for what Legat taught them. Guiness and Massine particularly comment that he had not received the recognition he deserved in England. Others can be identified from the programmes for performances of the studio and various articles and memoirs, notably Pearl Argyle, Phyllis Bedells, June Brae, Joy Camden, Kathleen Crofton, Agnes de Mille, Ninette de Valois, Rupert Doone, Frederic Franklin, Robert Helpmann, Mona Inglesby, Keith Lester, Pamela May, Kyra Nijinsky, Harold Turner, Vera Volkova, Nesta Williams (later Nesta Toumine) and Vera Zorina. As well as becoming well known as dancers, many of them became teachers and a number of them established schools which were affiliated with various bodies, like the Association of Russian Ballet, and which were set up specifically to foster teaching in the Russian classical tradition.

Colet House offered domestic space as well as several large studios. Built in the mid-1880s, it was constructed a year or so earlier than the adjoining row of eight artists' studios known as St Paul's Studios and is believed to have been designed by Sir Coutts Lindsay. Colet House and St Paul's Studios are built of red brick and, while red sandstone was extensively used for the facade of Colet House, intricate details on the studios are in white terracotta. All were designed with large, arched north-facing windows overlooking the street. As work was being completed to provide living quarters, Legat lodged with Mrs Viatkin at number 1 Colet Gardens and must have continued to live there, at least when Nicolaeva was not in London, since Mary remembers those happy evenings when Oskar Harmoš cooked steaks and artichokes with *sauce hollandaise*. Colet House is symmetrical but the present wide central staircase, rising from the lobby opposite the front door, was installed after Legat's death, replacing two staircases at the back of the building. Two large studios open from each side of the lobby. Reception rooms and what would have been used as bedrooms are located on each floor towards the rear. Ana Roje lived in the house herself, probably in the last years of Legat's life, but her bedroom was a large cupboard on one of the landings. Behind the house are two small gardens protected from the surface level platforms of Barons Court Underground station by a high brick wall. Balconies, reached by French doors located at either end of the main studio on the top floor, open onto what is now Talgarth Road and are separated by full-length windows. In the interview, Mary mentions very large windows looking onto the street and in those days a substantial glazed structure opened off the upper studio and would have dated from when the building was used by artists such as Frank Brangwyn and Edward Burne-Jones. Balconies at the rear of the house look onto the gardens.

The upper studio is at least as large as those at the Theatre School in St Petersburg. The ceiling is high, open to the arched timbered roof of the main part of the building, and the floor is made of wide wooden planks – although not varnished as they are today, since, as in St Petersburg, the floor was watered carefully before class. In a note in the *Dancing Times* of April 1935, the studio was considered to be one of the "finest" in London (it measures seventy-five feet by thirty-three feet). The writer commented that with Legat looking so well it was difficult to imagine that he had started his career at the Mariinsky Theatre forty years previously. Seeing Legat's caricatures displayed on the walls, the writer notes also that, had he not become a dancer, "a small fortune" could have been made as a caricaturist. A photograph in "The Legat Saga" shows the caricatures propped up along the top of the dado and at the western end of the studio there were many photographs as well as the full-sized copy of the poster with Serov's drawing of Pavlova used for the 1909 season of the Ballets Russes. A stage was built for performances and Alan Carter recalls that a row of tip-up theatre seats had been installed for visitors. (Mary remembers seating for about one hundred people.) But the great room was heated only by a single anthracite stove – apparently at the opposite end to the piano. In "Recollections of Legat" (a compilation of memories of students of the Legat School which was established by Nicolaeva after Legat's death), Joy Camden notes that the costumes for Pavlova's company were stored in the basement, where the men's changing room was located. Some of the costumes were used in performances of the studio and, in her memoir, Anna Lendrum describes her delight at wearing Pavlova's costume for the Sugar Plum Fairy. (At the time of writing, reminiscences by Alan Carter of Legat and the studio are available in an interview with Norman Frizzel in 2008 and posted online in 2013.)

A general "class of perfection" was offered daily from noon to 1pm, classes for children on Monday, Wednesday and Friday evenings with private lessons and production of character and ballet dances by arrangement. An advertisement from the *Dancing Times* of February 1932 announced that a branch studio had opened at 4c Langford Place in St John's Wood, adding that "Old Ballroom Dances now in fashion" would be taught. Kathleen Crofton was to have run the Langford Place studio but, despite the advertisements and a prospectus, the venture never materialised.

Among the mix of well-known and aspiring dancers, Mona Inglesby, who went on to found the International Ballet Company, remembers an "electric atmosphere" when the dancers of the Ballets Russes de Monte Carlo were in London, all changing in the same dressing room, and how Alexandra Danilova, great as she was, had no airs or affectation. Others, like Frederic Franklin, were intimidated rather than exhilarated by the presence of the Russian stars, as well as by the fact that Legat's English never progressed beyond a few basic, heavily accented words. The names of steps were given in equally heavily accented French and only demonstrated by marking with his hands. That he taught his classes while accompanying himself on the piano posed something of a barrier, particularly for the younger English dancers at the beginning of their careers. Those who persevered were rewarded, not only with his teaching but with his sense of fun, though his jokes could be sharp and penetrating, as Mary remembers, and often at the expense of those who could not understand Russian. Others, including Inglesby, recall how he improvised his accompaniment with amusing and attractive tunes, and marvelled that he could play, while spotting every fault, his eyes bright in "a kind but tough face". Pearl Argyle (who danced with Marie Rambert's Ballet Club and with the Ninette de Valois's Vic-Wells company) describes how the dancers would gather around the piano (a grand piano in her recollection) to learn the next *enchaînement* which Legat demonstrated with his "beautiful hands" on the top of the piano, finishing with his arms and head in the final position. The piano was covered with a cloth to prevent sweating dancers leaning directly on it and often had a vase of flowers bought from the shop on the bridge just outside Barons Court station. Legat only occasionally got up to demonstrate what he wanted, or if he was particularly displeased. For Argyle, it was the way he used his own music to encourage his students really to dance that made him different; his *enchaînements* were dances rather than exercises and difficult movements were approached easily so that they could be mastered naturally. She also describes, as others have done, how he was able to correct a position or show how a muscle was held so that difficulty with a *pirouette*, for example, would amazingly vanish. For her, Legat was always alive and inspiring, did not complain, though his health was not always good, and had "the spirit of eternal youth" (see her appreciation in the *Dancing Times*, March 1937). Carter remembers that Legat explained how balance could be achieved by using the weight of the body, how strain should be avoided, and how he emphasised that all steps and *enchaînements* should be done equally on both right and left sides.

Many of the dancers writing in "Heritage of a Ballet Master" comment on Legat's use of épaulement, and how it improved not only the line of a position but the balance as well. Carter notes that it brought lightness to even "gargantuan" dancers. Camden writes, too, in "Recollections of Legat", that not even Legat's contemporaries teaching in Paris taught this valuable "science of control". While, in his introduction to the film of a Legat class, Eglevsky says that Legat looked for three qualities in his dancers – precision, discipline and brilliance – he was also patient, saying "leetle by leetle" to encourage his students to overcome setbacks. The majority were trying to make a living in the theatre, so not all were able to work with him for more than a few months, but among those who sought him out was the film actress Merle Oberon, who he coached for her dances in the role of Tonita in "The Private Life of Don Juan". Legat's vivacity and sense of fun is captured in footage taken during a visit of what appears to be a group of dancers with the Ballets Russes de Monte Carlo to the studio in Colet Gardens and available on the website of the Legat Foundation.

Students and professional dancers alike absorbed what they could and many acknowledge their debt to him in their own memoirs and in their contributions to "Heritage of a Ballet Master". Cleo Nordi, then nearly eighty, says in "Heritage of a Ballet Master" that she believed she was the oldest of Legat's pupils still alive and continuing to teach his method:

> His method used every muscle of the body in an harmonious, logical way, in perfect sychronisation. He taught the dancer to execute with ease the technical demands of steps, big and small, in simple and in complicated combinations, embracing the whole range of existing movement... The essence of the teachings of Nicolas Legat are so profound, so intelligent, so ingenious. To teach his way is nearly impossible.

Nordi studied with Legat in Petrograd as well as in London, where she and Mary would have known each other through the Federation of Russian Classical Ballet, although she does not come directly into Mary's story. She was born Cleopatra Helenius in Kronstadt in January 1898 and was a student of Legat in the days when he accompanied himself on the violin, possibly before Johansson's violin was lost in the revolution. She also trained in Paris with Preobrazhenskaya, Egorova and Trefilova, and danced with the Paris Opera for two years before joining Pavlova in 1926, remaining in the company until Pavlova's death. She worked again with Legat in London and wrote down his lessons, which were "a continuous inspiration and divine guidance to me since the time I started to teach". Cleo Nordi was the stage name that she used in Pavlova's company, and probably before that. When she died, in March 1983, the writer in the "Off Stage!" section of the *Dancing Times* of June, 1983 suggests that it was Legat who called her "Nordi", meaning "from the north"; it may well have been his nickname for her, dating from her studies in Petrograd. (The *Dancing Times* published a short obituary in May 1983.) Photographs show that she favoured a ballerina hair style, parted and draped over the ears, and then drawn into a bun at the nape of the neck, as for "Les Sylphides" or "Giselle", like Kathleen Crofton, whom she would have known well. Nordi taught at her own studio in Scarsdale Villas, South Kensington, for twenty-five years. She took a position in 1964 at the Folkwang Hochschule in Essen under the directorship of Kurt Jooss, which lasted for four years. On her return, she continued to teach when in her seventies from a studio at 10 Queens Gate Mews.

Although Legat regularly taught character, which Mary must have enjoyed and appreciated, there are very few references to these classes, let alone any descriptions. Joy Camden simply says that they were "beautiful". (See "Recollections of Legat".)

Legat's bald head was part of his personality. It had been a feature for most of his life and would have been striking to those who had not met him before. His caricatures with Sergei show that his hair was thinning even in his early thirties and Legat's nephew, Andrew Briger, recalls that he was sometimes allowed to polish his uncle's head with a soft cloth kept especially for the purpose. In this way, he used his physical attributes to entertain children, and writes that many of them laughed at the faces he pulled when he took out his false teeth. A self-caricature, *sans* teeth, in "The Legat Saga" captures his delight in being amusing at his own expense. Carter observes that Legat had dealt with his baldness by adopting "the 'Yul Brynner' hair cut", but in the days of his last illness he shaved neither his head nor his face.

Mary and her friends Ana and Oskar, shared the experience of the performances of Legat's studio as well as his classes. One of the most elaborate of these was at the New Scala Theatre in Charlotte Street on 19 December 1934. Legat choreographed twenty-eight numbers for a cast that included Pearl Argyle, André Eglevsky, Nijinsky's daughter Kyra, Cleo Nordi and Ana Roje as principals, with Alan Carter and Grania Guiness, among others. The programme included a variation from "Le Pavillon d'Armide", which suggests, perhaps, that Legat was more supportive of Fokine's choreography than Fokine's antipathy towards him would indicate – or perhaps that Legat simply used Tcherepnin's music. In another performance, on 2 July 1935, dancers in addition to Ana and Oskar included Kathleen Crofton, Alan Carter, Joy Camden and Kyra Nijinsky. (Crofton was seen as having great promise by "Sitter Out" in the *Dancing Times* of February 1936. She had already toured with Pavlova's company in the 1920s and appeared in a special season of Nijinska's ballets with de Basil's Ballets Russes in Monte Carlo in 1934.) Mary, Ana and Oskar appeared together in at least one performance at the studio, on 24 May 1936, when the three of them danced in a "Nocturne" for eight dancers to music by César Cui. (Anna Northcote, later a fellow examiner with Mary at the Society of Russian Style Ballet Schools, was another of the dancers.) Oskar was the only male and the title suggests that the piece was similar to "Les Sylphides". Mary and Oskar danced a *pas de deux*, "In the Night", to music by Artur Rubenstein, followed by a solo for Ana, "Valse", to music by Anton Arensky. The final piece, Mussorgsky's "Night on a Bald Mountain", brought the cast together. The notes describe a Russian legend in which Satan appears to a group of witches as they hold a Black Mass. Again, as the lone male, Oskar must have danced the role of Satan presaging his later appearances as Death in "The Green Table" when he joined the Ballets Jooss, and the Devil in "The Devil in the Village" in Zagreb. Vladimir Launitz, who by then lived nearby in Comeragh Road, played for other performances of the studio, including the ballet "The Pagoda of Schwezayan", for an evening of ballet on 3 June 1937 at the Studio Theatre. They may well have planned the programme together before Legat's death.

The large studio in Colet House was used on Sundays by the White Russian *balalaika* group with whom Legat played. Carter remembers that the room sometimes seemed like an "exotic museum" of musical instruments, with *balalaikas* of all shapes and sizes propped up against the walls. It was also used for performances and events by other groups. On 29 October 1933, Legat and the Russian organisation, Obshchestvo Severyan, or North Russian Association, arranged for Pavlova's husband Victor Dandré to speak on Russian arts outside Russia and a tribute to Pavlova was given by M.B. Braykevitch. Following the presentations, short variations were danced by Cleo Nordi, Alexandra Danilova, André Eglevsky, Harcourt Algeranoff and Léon Woizikowski. A Carnival Dance was hosted by the association on 29 December 1934 and the New Dance Group presented works by Stanley Judson and Molly Lake in October, 1935.

While Paul Dukes was assisting Legat, his older brother Ashley, critic, playwright, and husband of Marie Rambert, was helping to promote the Ballet Club founded by the two of them with Arnold Haskell, who was by then well known as a dance critic, writer and historian. Based at the Mercury Theatre in Ladbroke Road, where Rambert also had her studio, the members attended Sunday night performances on a subscription basis. There was little direct contact between Legat and Rambert. Indeed, some dancers, including Mona Inglesby, write of Rambert's anger when they decided to take classes with Legat, while Gregory notes that it would be hard to see Ashley and Paul Dukes collaborating on any undertaking. Ninette de Valois, who formed the Vic-Wells Ballet in 1931, did attend some of Legat's classes and danced in his choreography for the Camargo Society, and he drew at least one caricature of her. But their personalities were so different that it is difficult to imagine that they could have become colleagues, let alone good friends.

The Camargo Society was founded in 1930 shortly after the Ballets Russes had been disbanded following Diaghilev's death. Its objective was to maintain interest in ballet in Britain by producing several works per year and on a scale that could not then be attempted by Ballet Club and the Vic-Wells Ballet. Led by Haskell and P.J.S. Richardson, the committee included Lydia Lopokova as choreographic adviser, her husband John Maynard Keynes as treasurer and the composer Constant Lambert as conductor. It is interesting that, in an article to record the origins of the society in October 1950, the *Dancing Times* chose to reproduce Legat's caricature of "The Unholy Trinity" of the founders, Haskell, Richardson and Edwin Evans. In her biography of Lopokova, "Bloomsbury Ballerina", Judith Mackrell sees her as the unlikely de facto leader of the society so it may well have been Lopokova who brought Legat into the group. The first performances were given at the Cambridge Theatre in October 1930. Legat choreographed the "Variations and Coda" to music by Mikhail Glinka in which de Valois and Dolin danced a *pas de deux*, and the entire company performed the *coda*. For performances in January 1931, also at the Cambridge Theatre, Legat choreographed "Le Roi s'amuse" to music by Léo Delibes, and his "Straussiana" closed the programme at the Apollo Theatre in the following month. Thereafter, however, the organisers leant towards contemporary works by Frederick Ashton, de Valois and Rambert, rather than on Legat's more traditional choreography, and his work was not included in later programmes. At the same time, Legat may well have found himself uncomfortable collaborating with a much younger group eager to forge new traditions for ballet in Britain. The Camargo Society was short-lived, having overreached itself with a four-week season at the Savoy Theatre in 1932 when Olga Spessivtseva danced in shortened versions of "Giselle" and "Swan Lake". The debts were cleared through two gala performances at the Royal Opera House in June 1933, when Lopokova, Dolin and Markova danced to full houses. In its time, it was seen as having filled the void between the demise of the Ballets Russes and the establishment of de Valois's and Rambert's companies on a sustainable basis. Legat's work with the Camargo Society may have been his last direct involvement with public performances that were not associated with his studio or his students.

His liaison with Nicolaeva notwithstanding, Dukes had deep admiration for Legat and must have encouraged him to write his memoir as well as looking for opportunities to promote him as he was settling in London. As "P.D.", he wrote the article "Nicolas Legat and the Class of Perfection", for the February 1930 issue of the *Dancing Times* and in the following year, the magazine published articles based on extracts from Legat's memoir, including "Whence Came the 'Russian' School?" in February and "The Making of a Dancer and Ballet Master, Pages from the Memoir of Nicolas Legat" in the following month. Having translated the memoir, Dukes wrote the foreword and, in his capacity as chairman of the British-Continental Press, ensured its publication in 1932 as "The Story of the Russian School". (The last page lists seven books on dancers already published by the press, including Trefilova, Pavlova, Karsavina and Dolin, as well as four in preparation, of which one was a volume of Legat's caricatures titled "Legat s'amuse" and which must never have been completed.) Further articles on "The Secret of the Pirouette" were published in the *Dancing Times* in August, September and November 1932, suggesting that Dukes genuinely felt that Legat's experience as a teacher and performer should be better known. Before going into the technicalities of the *pirouette*, Legat recounts how even experienced dancers might suddenly find their ability to turn vanish unaccountably, and gives the example of how, when Cecchetti made his debut at the Mariinsky Theatre, he "missed his stroke and collapsed" but then went on to execute six or seven turns without music, just to show the audience that he could do it. He goes on to say that the record of fourteen turns was held by his brother Sergei at his final examination. In December, 1932, "Limbering the Limbs for Practice" was accompanied by Legat's own sketches as well as photographs. (This and Legat's later articles must also have been translated by Dukes.) In these articles, and in the recollections of his students, it is Legat's understanding of the principles of the body's movement that sets him apart – he knew that when the body is in an optimum position, the muscles make the least effort to execute a step.

Legat's last article for the *Dancing Times*, "What is 'Élan' in Dancing?", was published in February 1937, almost at the time of this death. It must have been written in 1936, before his last illness. The subject is fitting since *élan* was what Legat looked for in his students and tried to impart to them. He explores the relationship between *élan*, or spirit, or fire and technique, noting that, if the body is held correctly, the way is paved for *élan* to be expressed – the spirit is "emancipated". He also ponders on the question of why English dancers did not seem to have the *élan* of their Russian counterparts, concluding that some who had been taught by Russians did, indeed, show this "flame of inspiration" but that perhaps the quality was not yet fully understood and fostered in what he reluctantly called the English school. Legat is also keen to point out the importance of exercises for strength to supplement ballet training and relates how his own strength was based on his use of athletics and acrobatics, allowing him to lift the heaviest of partners with ease. (In his memoir, he describes how, when working with Gerdt on a *pas de deux* for himself and Alexandra Vinogradova, she was afraid to leap into a fish dive, to which Gerdt responded by throwing himself into Legat's arms.) For women, he draws on Nicolaeva's experience of the benefits of gymnastics and head stands to dispel fatigue and strain. Legat writes that he believed physical strength in a male dancer at least reduced the appearance of effeminacy. Perhaps in making such a comment he refers to what he observed in the Ballets Russes while avoiding any comparison with the Mariinsky of the late nineteenth and early twentieth centuries.

෴

Legat's obituary appeared in *The Times* on 25 January 1937, the day after his death, and almost certainly was written by Dukes. An obituary in the *Dancing Times* appeared in April. Pearl Argyle had written her own appreciation of Legat's life for the March issue because she felt compelled to express her thoughts about the "great man" with whom she studied for three years. For her, Legat's greatest gift as a teacher was his ability to convey what he wanted from his pupils through his music. This gift was inherited from his father and Johansson and in that respect alone, Legat's death was a "tragic loss".

Legat's poor English may well have contributed to the fact that his experience was not drawn upon directly when the teaching of ballet in England was being formalised and English companies were founded. Considerable effort was being made towards establishing an organisation which would foster standards among dancing schools in Britain, with Eduardo Espinosa, Haskell, Richardson and Beaumont leading the way. (Beaumont's efforts to ensure that Cecchetti's methods were codified did not extend to Legat.) But, in his sixties, Legat may simply have not had the energy, or even the interest, to become closely involved with people whose plans and ideals he did not share, preferring to spend his time teaching and with students like Mary and Ana and Oskar, and playing the *balalaika* with his Russian friends.

Gregory writes of Legat in the later years in London as lonely and homesick, hating the damp and foggy English winters, and Carter also remembers him as sad in his old age, despite the humour which he brought to his classes. His wife appeared infrequently and like a tornado to disrupt them. But, disruption or not, Nicolaeva's income from her touring underpinned the studio and she was also driven by the need to support her parents, daughter and other family members. A happier portrait was written by Legat's nephew, "G.S.", in the introduction to Nicolaeva's "Ballet Education" in which he describes a man with an irrepressible and wicked sense of humour, who was always cheerful even under the most depressing circumstances. Nicolaeva also remembers his humour and cheer in even the most difficult times in their lives and through the most desperate events.

CHAPTER 13
NADINE NICOLAEVA AND THE LEGAT SCHOOL

I taught the *fouettés* to Vera Trefilova, Vil, Vaganova; later to Nicolaeva and many others."

Nicolai Legat, "The Story of the Russian School".

After Legat's death, Nicolaeva continued to run the studio and to stage performances. She edited and published a series of ten of his classes, written by the "incomparable master", offering them through the *Dancing Times* in June 1937 at five shillings for one class or two guineas for the set. These days, *barre* and *pointe* work are so widely used that it is interesting to see that "bar work" and "toe work" were the accepted terms as used in the description. An advertisement for "Legat's School of Ballet Dancing" on the same page, with Nicolaeva's name in brackets, offered a "speedy special method" of teaching *fouettés*. In 1938, she published a series of six articles in the *Dancing Times* on Russian dances (plus one on costumes), building on the three less detailed pieces written by Legat in 1927 and 1928 (see *Dancing Times*, January through September 1938). It seems a little surprising that she would have promoted character dances rather than ballet but it is possible that they had already been drafted to follow Legat's article on *élan* in dancing, and Nicolaeva then edited and presented them herself. In the middle of the year, she moved the studio from Colet House to St Matthew's Hall in Milson Road, just north of the Hammersmith Road. Her interest in other forms of movement is evident from an advertisement for the new premises which notes that classes in physical culture and acrobatics would be held on an open-air roof terrace.

Dukes arranged for Legat's memoir to be republished in 1939 as "Ballet Russe, Memoirs of Nicolas Legat". He expanded his original foreword to acknowledge Legat's death and to credit Nicolaeva with bearing the torch for the school of Christian Johansson. He prefaces the book with a dedicatory poem written by John Masefield, "To Nicolas Legat with my thanks". The poem is autographed by Masefield and dated 2 July 1939 and would have been commissioned especially by Dukes as an expression of his appreciation to Legat. Masefield was Britain's Poet Laureate from 1930 until his death in 1967 and had a more than passing interest in ballet since a collection of poems, "Tribute to Ballet", with illustrations by Edward Seago, had been published the year before. Masefield had visited the studio and asked Nicolaeva to arrange some ballets for the Oxford Festival in 1938. "Ballet Russe" includes a number of photographs and Legat's own tribute to Pavlova, and the selection of caricatures is reproduced in colour. Some years later, in 1947, Masefield provided another dedicatory poem, this time for Nicolaeva's book, "Ballet Education". The preface is by Dukes and, as noted at the end of the last chapter, her nephew "G.S." wrote the introduction. In her own prefatory note, Nicolaeva says that the book was long-planned and that she had hoped to produce it in collaboration with Legat but demands of work for them both had made it impossible. Most of the technical material came from Legat's notebooks that she elaborated upon. In 1945, she established a quarterly magazine, *The Ballet*, which was published through the Russian Ballet League. It was then published as *Ballet* until the critic Richard Buckle established prior claim to the title, having founded his own magazine of the same name in 1939. Nicolaeva modified the title of her journal to *Ballet World* in 1948; in all, it ran from 1945 to 1950. Nicolaeva's second book, "Preparation for Ballet", was published in 1953, again with a foreword by Dukes, setting out Nicolaeva's approach to teaching ballet under modern conditions and including a section on a practical approach to yoga. In this respect, she would have been among the first teachers to actively promote yoga to support ballet training, anticipating the Pilates and other techniques that are widely used today.

In July 1938, Nicolaeva hosted a reception to announce the formation of the institution which became the Russian Ballet Association. Members of the Russian Imperial family attended the reception at which *divertissements* were performed by Nicolaeva's students. The association was founded by Nicolaeva, Kyasht, Flora Fairbairn and Catherine Weguelin under the patronage of the Grand Duchess Xenia of Russia, sister of Tsar Nicolas II, and the Grand Duke Andrei Vladimirovitch, Kschessinskaya's husband. Supporters included Kschessinskaya, Preobrazhenskaya, Kyasht, Dolin and Anatole Oboukoff (soloist in the Ballets Russes companies and nephew of Legat's colleague in the Mariinsky company, Mikhail Obukhov, who had died in 1914). Examinations were announced in the *Dancing Times* in September, to be held in the following November. The Cecchetti Society had already been established in England in 1922 and, in "Recollections of Legat", it is noted that Nicolaeva had discussed the formation of a Russian association with her husband before his death. A post-war prospectus reproduced in "Recollections of Legat" lists members of the technical committee as Nicolaeva with Ana Roje and Oskar Harmoš, Dolin, Kyasht, Markova, Nordi, Valentin Prorwitsch and Weguelin; Dukes was the honorary treasurer.

At the urging of her students and their parents, Nicolaeva was persuaded to establish a boarding school for ballet training. At first it was set up in a house on the Essex coast in Mersea Island but in 1939 she moved to First House at Seer Green in Buckinghamshire, just east of Beaconsfield, where it became the first residential ballet school in Britain. Following the war, the school was relocated to Warberry House in Tunbridge Wells, Kent and then to a larger house, Finchcocks, in Goudhurst in 1960. Ten years later, the school moved to St Joseph's College at Mark Cross and, in 1975, the Legat School of Dance was recognised by the Department of Education and Science. In 1989, the school became part of Wadhurst College in East Sussex. Following the merge of Wadhurst College with Micklefield School (later a branch of Bellerby's College), the school became part of St Bede's School at Upper Dicker near Eastbourne as the Legat School of Contemporary Ballet and Dance within the Senior School.

Gregory does not mention any ongoing contact between Legat and Nijinsky in "The Legat Saga", and nor does Romola Nijinsky in her biography of her husband, but their daughter Kyra was a student at the Colet Gardens studio and close ties were maintained after Legat's death when Romola often brought Nijinsky to the Legat School. In her book, "Dance to the Challenge", Nicolaeva's student Jill Lhotka (then Jill Morse) describes how she danced the "Ribbon" *pas de deux* from "Coppélia" with Alan Carter for Nijinsky in an attempt to bring him out of the withdrawn state of his insanity. She also notes that Nijinsky and Vera Volkova were godparents to John and Barbara Gregory's daughter Paula and that the christening took place in November 1949 in the studio at Warberry House. Romola enlisted Nicolaeva's help to translate Nijinsky's notebooks for his system of dance notation and she gave her husband's costumes to Nicolaeva before leaving for the United States in 1950. A poignant note in the *Daily Mirror* of 20 June 1951 reports that all that remained of Nijinsky's personal belongings were stored in a battered packing case near the entrance to the school at Warberry House, close to where Albo's bronze bust of Legat then stood.

☙

When Nicolaeva moved out of Colet House, Pyotr Ouspensky took over the building as the centre for his work in London and founded the forerunner of today's Study Society, the owners since 1957. Given Nicolaeva's interest in Ouspensky's philosophies, they must have continued to be in contact in the second half of the 1920s and through the 1930s. During the Second World War, Colet House was requisitioned and occupied by the Admiralty. (A member of the Study Society, Kenneth Dunjohn, writing in the spring 2014 newsletter of the Hammersmith and Fulham Historic Buildings Group, provides the amusing anecdote that senior Royal Navy officers "played" with wooden boats in a large water tank set up in one of the studios.) Colet House was returned to the Study Society after the war. Some years after Ouspensky's death in 1947, it was leased to the Sadler's Wells School (predecessor to the Royal Ballet School), which had moved next door into what then became 155 Talgarth Road. As well as leasing the building, Ninette de Valois also participated in discussion groups of the society.

A plaque to honour Nicolai Legat was installed on the front of Colet House at the end of 2012 under the Historic Plaques scheme of the Hammersmith and Fulham Historic Buildings Group. It was formally unveiled on 9 April 2013, just over seventy-six years after his death. Around fifty dancers, teachers and former students of the Legat pedagogic system were welcomed by Clive Hicks of the Study Society. Special guests were Tatiana Legat, Legat's granddaughter from his marriage to Antonina, and Dame Monica Mason, who had recently retired as artistic director of the Royal Ballet. The group was too large to remain outside on the pavement next to the heavy traffic in Talgarth Road, and speeches by Angela Dixon of the Historic Buildings Group, Councillor Belinda Donovan the Mayor of Hammersmith and Fulham, and I were given on the landing at the top of the stairs, outside the large upper studio. Hicks spoke on the history of Colet House and gave a tour of the studios, reception rooms and the little enclosed gardens behind the building. The group was later taken by Anna Meadmore, curator of the Royal Ballet School's Special Collections, to look at materials in the Legat archive which had recently been donated by Mimi Legat and which were on display at the premises of the school in Floral Street.

CHAPTER 14
WARTIME IN EUROPE

I spent it all in Yugoslavia – the war... Everybody was... very happy to have lived during the war and to being alive after the war. Because it was a very difficult war, I am sure.

Maria Zybina, interview with Patricia Deane-Gray.

In the mid- and late 1930s Mary, Ana and Oskar had various performing engagements, although not always together and details are sparse. Mary divided her time between England and the company in Belgrade, while, among other tours, Ana and Oskar visited England, Scotland and Germany with the Ballet Russe de Paris. In Germany, performances included one at the Nymphenburg Palace and another, under the auspices of the "Russischen Ballets aus London" on 29 July 1936, at Garmisch-Partenkirchen. That programme included "Les Sylphides" with Ana and Nesta Williams (using her stage name, Maslova) among the soloists, "Kaukasische Suite" in which Oskar was a soloist with Margaret Severn, "Spectre de la Rose" for Ana and Anton Vujanitsch (Vujanić), "Bolero" in which Oskar danced and, finally, "The Polovtsian Dances" in which both Ana and Oskar were among the soloists. Legat's friend Vladimir Launitz was the conductor.

After Legat's death, Ana and Oskar remained in London for a few months to help Nicolaeva run the studio. Ana taught classical ballet and Oskar taught character, *pas de deux*, acting and make-up. Oskar also danced with Pino and Pia Mlakar and Olga Orlova in "The Devil in the Village" when it opened in Zagreb in April 1937 and, even then, may have been given the title role. In June, Ana won the first prize for classical dance and third prize for character dance at the International Theatre Dance Competition in Paris, part of the

Exposition Internationale des Arts et Techniques dans la Vie Moderne. The character piece was "Dalmatian Girl", choreographed to Tijardović's music. Towards the end of the same year, she was back in Zagreb when she and Oskar staged an evening of dance which presented choreography by Legat, as well as their own, at the National Theatre in November, and they would have secured other engagements as well. For the spring/summer season of 1938, Ana was invited by Massine to join Colonel de Basil's successor to Diaghilev's Ballets Russes both as a dancer and as ballet mistress. Fellow Yugoslavs Mia Slavenska and Igor Youskevitch were soloists in the company, as were several others who she would have known from Legat's studio – Alexandra Danilova, Alicia Markova, Anton Dolin and Frederic Franklin. New productions for that season included "Gâité Parisienne", "Seventh Symphony" and "Nobilissima Visione" ("St Francis"). De Basil's "Season of Russian Ballet" opened in June at Covent Garden as Educational Ballets Ltd, Massine's departure to join René Blum and the dispute over Massine's rights to his works resulted in the "ballet war" in London between the two rival successor companies to Diaghilev's Ballets Russes, with Educational Ballets appearing at Covent Garden and René Blum's Ballet Russe de Monte Carlo at the Drury Lane Theatre. (Blum's company, existing in 1936–1938, used "Ballet Russe" in the singular.) The impasse between the two companies was finally resolved when the impresario Sol Hurok suggested that they cease to compete: Educational Ballets would tour in Australia and New Zealand, but as the Original Ballet Russe, while the Ballet Russe de Monte Carlo would tour in North America.

Ana remained with de Basil in the erstwhile Covent Garden Russian Ballet, predecessor to the Original Ballet Russe, and went on the tour to Australia and New Zealand as ballet mistress for about a year from the summer of 1938. The company sailed from Tilbury on P&O's RMS *Maloja* and, having landed in Adelaide, they went on to the Theatre Royal in Melbourne, where it presented programmes of "Les Sylphides", "Aurora", "Swan Lake", "Symphonie Fantastique", "Prince Igor", "Petrushka" and "The Gods Go A-Begging". By the end of October, rehearsals started on "Protée", which was performed over three days before the company moved on to Sydney. They sailed for New Zealand at the beginning of February 1939 but returned to Melbourne in March for performances at His Majesty's Theatre, and to the Theatre Royal in Adelaide. (An archive of material on the de Basil company is held at the National Library of Australia.) At the end of April, the company sailed for London, where they opened on 19 June at Covent Garden. There is brief mention of Ana in the letters of a young Canadian dancer Rosemary Deveson that were published as "Dancing for de Basil". The first dates from 29 August 1938, in which Deveson clearly enjoyed her first class with Ana, writing that she had a very good line and would be giving classes while the company was in Australia. Later, however, on 7 November, she complained that she could not do well in Ana's classes because the *enchaînements* were uncomfortable due to Cecchetti's tradition. This comment is quite clearly expressed and contrasts Ana's morning classes with Tatiana Riabouchinskaya's, although it is strange that Deveson made an incorrect reference to Cecchetti and had previously found Ana's *enchaînements* to be uncomplicated and similar to those given by June Roper, her teacher in Vancouver.

While Ana was dancing with de Basil's companies, Oskar was invited to join the Ballets Jooss in August 1938, following his performance in "Die Gesöpfche des Prometheus" ("The Creatures of Prometheus") in Munich. Oskar had seen the company perform in Zagreb in April 1937 and was drawn to Jooss's work. Born in 1901 in Germany, Jooss studied with Rudolf Laban and danced in the Tanzbühne Laban but left the company in 1924 to form the Neue Tanzbühne at Münster with dancers Sigurd Leeder and Aino Siimola and the composer Fritz Cohen. In 1928, Jooss and Leeder founded the Folkwang Tanztheater in Essen but left Germany in 1934. Jooss moved to England, where he founded the Ballets Jooss and established the Jooss-Leeder School at Dartington Hall in Devon, which also became the home base for the company. There, Oskar rehearsed with the company as three new ballets were choreographed – "A Spring Tale", "Chronica" and "The Prodigal Son" – and then toured England in 1939. A notice in the December 1938 issue of the *Dancing Times* lists him among the dancers for performances of "Chronica", "A Spring Tale", "The Seven Heroes", "The Green Table", "A Ball in Old Vienna", "The Big City", "Pavanne" and "Crossroads". Engagements in the first half of the year were in Stratford on Avon, Oxford, Cambridge, Edinburgh, Glasgow, Newcastle, Liverpool and Bournemouth, to be followed by a season in London in May and June. Oskar danced the roles of the Old Soldier, Death and the Standard Bearer in Jooss's most famous ballet, "The Green Table". But the company was contracted to go on tour to North and South America at the end of the year and his time with Jooss was cut short by the prospect of war in Europe. Much later, advertisements for Ana and Oskar's school at Primošten in Croatia note that he was a "soloist of the Jooss ballet".

Mary, Ana and Oskar were all in England in the summer of 1939 and realised that they should get back to Yugoslavia while it was still possible. At that point, war in the rest of Europe seemed increasingly inevitable, although Yugoslavia was still neutral and remained so until the bombing of Belgrade in April 1941 plunged it into civil conflict and occupation by Italy and Germany. Mary describes how she provided the means for the three friends to make the journey home:

> I had a car [her father's] which had German registration and we passed from England, you know, through Germany, to see my mother, who was then a widow as well… just before the war was declared. Ana, Oskar and I, we are going in that German car to Yugoslavia. They wanted to get back, and I could never have got back if I hadn't Oskar and Ana with me because they, with their Yugoslav passports, could get petrol. I, with my British passport, had to hide my[self]. So, we had a very adventurous trip. But we got in just before the war started at the end of August.

As she says, it was an adventurous trip, with Mary doing most of the driving, but with Oskar taking over as they bought petrol and with Ana supporting him as a passenger. Mary must have hidden under blankets and clothes, or even in the boot of the car, when they were crossing borders. (Much later, Jill Lhotka recalls in "Dance to the Challenge" that, in even the early 1950s, Oskar may not have had a driver's licence, and suggests he was not a particularly good driver.) They must have reached Yugoslavia with weeks, if not days, to spare before the outbreak of war in Europe on 3 September.

Mary had met Germano Jakasha when he was studying engineering at the university in Belgrade in the late 1930s. Just a year younger than Mary – his birthday was 22 May 1911 – he had first gone to university in Vienna but, believing he was being distracted by the bright lights of the city, his family brought him back home to Split and then sent him to Belgrade. They may not have realised that the lights of Belgrade also burned brightly at that time, so the punishment may not have been very harsh, even allowing for Germano being a Croat in a Serbian city. By the late 1930s, however, Mary had already opened a ballet school in Split. Hers was the second in the city; the first had been opened by Mila Katić in the early 1930s and both schools staged ballet performances, but on an amateur rather than a professional basis. This may have been on Ana's suggestion since Germano would not have planned to live permanently in Serbia. Whether through the legation or by coincidence, he had already been brought into Mary's group in Belgrade since a letter of reference written by Colonel Robert Lethbridge in 1947 states that in 1940 and 1941 Germano was engaged in work of a "highly confidential nature" in support of the Allied war effort. At that time, Lethbridge was a member of the legation staff, but it is hardly surprising that no details on what either of them were doing have come to light. Mary and Germano were married in a civil ceremony in Split, on 3 April 1942.

Belgrade had been home and the centre of Mary's working life for over ten years and she had been joined by her younger sister, Kitty. Her brother Slavchik may well have visited in the early 1930s too and family documents show that he had a permit to work in Serbia in 1935–1936. Sadly, he became ill while in Belgrade, possibly with diphtheria, but fell and hit his head while going to the bathroom at night, and died at the age of only thirty-three, in 1936. His gravestone is in the Russian Cemetery (the New Cemetery) in Belgrade. Although she was then unmarried, Kitty had a daughter, Dikica, from a relationship with a Russian named Nicolas, or Kolya. But Dikica also died when she was very young. Against Mary's advice, Kitty had allowed the child to go to a summer camp when she was obviously still suffering from an infection, again possibly diphtheria. She was only seven and did not survive. So, shortly after separating from Hugh, in the space of just a few years, Mary lost her brother and her father, and her only niece.

More happily, sometime after Dikica's death Kitty met and married the actor Viktor Starčić. Viktor was born in 1901 in Ruse, now in Bulgaria, but his father was from Istria in the northern Adriatic and his mother was French. The family moved frequently since Viktor's father was involved in the building of railways, possibly as an engineer. Apparently, Viktor had relatively little formal education as his father followed the available work in Turkey, Greece, Romania and Serbia. At the age of eighteen, he started working as an amateur actor in the town of Gornji Milanovac in central Serbia but was able to join the theatre in Sarajevo, where his *répertoire* increased and, between 1925 and 1930, he worked in Split, Zagreb and Novi

Sad, and with the Belgrade Opera. He and Kitty may have met while he was working with the opera company, but in the 1930s he worked at the National Theatre in Belgrade and, in 1938, established the Belgrade Arts Theatre with a group of fellow artists. Wartime found him in Novi Sad and Rijeka, but he returned to Belgrade and became a permanent member of the Yugoslav Drama Theatre until 1948. From 1949, he was a professor of acting at the Theatre Academy in Belgrade. He was particularly known for his expressive voice, subtle portrayal of character and dramatic presence.

✑

As well as running her school in Split, Mary remained connected to the theatre in Belgrade and went on tour with the company to Germany. She recalls:

> I stayed all that time in Yugoslavia. And there was the theatre, theatre from Belgrade… We went once to Frankfurt, the whole company, and I was in the "Ero" there. Yes, and I was dancing in "Ero" with a British passport, just around the corner. Actually, I got ill there because they gave us many tins, tinned food, yes and I had a tin poisoning… I came back very ill.

Mary is clear that it was the Belgrade company which took "Ero the Joker" to Frankfurt, although the opera originated in Zagreb. Since the National Theatre was heavily bombed in April 1941, and Mary and Germano had moved to Split, this tour may have taken place before the occupation of Yugoslavia by Germany. The opera was first performed outside Yugoslavia in Brno, Czechoslovakia, in 1936. Even apart from the tin poisoning, which may have resulted from a poorly sealed or damaged tin, that tour must have been another adventure. Presumably, the company travelled as a group from Yugoslavia and individual passports were not scrutinised so that it was possible for Mary to avoid revealing her British citizenship.

Meanwhile, Ana and Oskar had married on 18 February 1940 and settled at first in Zagreb. They established a studio and taught classes in their flat where one of their first students was Nenad Lhotka, son of Fran Lhotka, composer of "The Devil in the Village". Soon afterwards, however, they were invited by Tijardović to manage ballet and opera performances in Split. He had returned there from Zagreb in the 1930s to direct what became the Croatian National Theatre, which occupied the Italianate theatre built in 1893. As in Zagreb and Belgrade, ballet had been presented in Split by foreign companies but until Tijardović's return there had been no regular ballet programmes.

But this creative period in Split was cut short as the country was carved up between Germany, Italy, Bulgaria and Hungary, while Croatia was controlled by Ante Pavelić and the fascist Ustaša movement. Italian forces occupied Split from April 1941 and parts of Dalmatia, including Split, were annexed a month later as Italy was given control of the southern third of Slovenia, access to the Adriatic south of Rijeka, the islands of the northern Adriatic, the strip of coastline as far as Montenegro and Kosovo. An independent State of Croatia was created comprising Croatia, Bosnia, Herzegovina and part of Serbia. Nominally a monarchy and Italian protectorate, the territory was divided between Germany and Italy but the ambitions of Pavelić and the Ustaša were nationalistic and extreme, to the extent of eliminating Serbs, Jews, Roma and non-Catholics within their borders. Two rival guerilla factions then emerged outside the state of Croatia: the Četniks, mostly Serbian and loyal to the exiled King Peter of Yugoslavia and his government under the leadership of Draža Mihailović; and the Communist partisans under the control of Josip Broz (shortly to become universally known as Tito), born in Croatia and as yet hardly recognised outside Yugoslavia and Russia. The region was plunged into chaos as people tried to move to relative safety to escape the incoming armies and rejoin families elsewhere.

At first, it was possible for Mary to join Ana and Oskar in some of their performances, including a series of ballet "afternoons" in April 1941 for which they jointly choreographed the pieces. These were called ballet afternoons because performances started at five o'clock. Among the dancers, Mary is listed as "Marija Zibina". A programme for 29 April, given in Ana's biography, lists "Poziv na Ples" ("Invitation to the Dance"), a piece called "Čežna" ("Longing") to Chopin, "Asirski Ples" ("Assyrian Dance") to Tijardović, a *trepak* by Tchaikovsky (a Cossack dance, possibly based on the *trepak* in "The Nutcracker") and "Svatovac" by Zajc and Baranović. On that occasion, Mary performed in "Invitation to the Dance" and "Longing". But then it became a question of how to live and work under the occupation. Ana and Oskar moved back to Zagreb while Mary and Germano remained in Split. All theatrical productions in Split were suspended for the duration of the war, although for a short period in 1943 the theatre reopened under the partisans, only to close again as German troops retook the city. A short biographical note in the *Dancing Times* (September 1958) says that Mary trained the dancers of the company in her own home in the pretty area of Bačvice to the south of the old part of the town because, as she says in the interview:

> I took over the theatre from Ana and Oskar in Split, but it was shut. So, during that war I had the pupils, the ballerinas there, teaching them at the school. But I was obliged to close the school because the Yugoslavs said, "No, because the Italians will try and bring their children here to your school and that would not be any good for us." People could meet there and so on.

As well as teaching, Mary put her languages to good use working as a translator for the British consulate in Split. Mary and Germano's daughter Tamara Antonieta was born at home on 10 January 1943 and Mary lost no time registering the birth with the consulate. Tamara's nickname, used within the family, was given her by Ana. Tamara has letters written by Mary in Split to her sister Kitty in Belgrade in 1941, 1943 and 1944, each of them wishing Kitty well for her name day on 7 December. They are written in German, which was the language Mary used as she was growing up and may also have served to get the letters through the German censors since they are marked with blue crayon. Mary writes to Kitty as Katok and Katüscha, and signs herself Zapinky. Not surprisingly, given the censorship, she sends affectionate messages to Kitty and includes only mundane comments about her lodgers.

Under Italian occupation, the Governorate of Dalmatia was established with Zadar as its capital. A process of Italianisation was initiated that included the opening of Italian schools and public works and modernisation programmes in Split, with Italian nationals being brought in to fill administrative positions. Despite the long period of rule from Venice, the population was generally opposed to Italian control, resistance by the Croat population was particularly strong and Split became a centre of anti-fascist sentiment. There was violence in the streets and food was rationed and scarce. By August 1943, however, most of the administrative personnel had returned to Italy and the Governorate of Dalmatia was transferred to Croatia following the Italian surrender to the Allies in September of the same year. The partisans gained control of Split in the second half of the month but were quickly driven out by German forces. Resistance continued as large numbers of people joined the partisans, including the entire Hadjuk football team. The town was bombed in 1943 and 1944, by the Allies as well as the Germans, but the partisans finally took control at the end of October, 1944 and it was made the provisional capital of Croatia. The profile of Mary in *Dance and Dancers* (October 1957) notes that she was interned by German forces in Split, possibly until the partisans liberated the city. Of course, she held her British passport and would have been classed as an enemy alien. (Internment may not have meant imprisonment, but she would have had to report regularly to the authorities.) Germano was imprisoned for about three months after being informed on for trying to sell some jewellery, but the two incidents are unrelated. He also served in the Yugoslav army in 1944 and 1946. In the interview, the tone of Mary's short sentence "Because it was a very difficult war, I am sure" expresses heartfelt relief that she and her family survived, but allows the listener to imagine the depths of despair that they must often have felt.

Tijardović returned to Split after its final liberation by the partisans and revitalised its theatrical scene as the Narodnooslobodilačko kazalište Dalmatija (National Liberation Theatre of Dalmatia). The war in Europe ended at last on 8 May 1945. On 1 July, the theatre was finally reinstated as the Croatian National Theatre and, shortly afterwards, Mary became principal ballet mistress. The archives of the theatre in Split record several pieces of Mary's choreography in 1945 and 1946, including "*Šišmiš*" ("The Bat", which may have been based on a piece by Margarita Froman) in August 1945, "Zemlja smješka" ("Land of Smiles") in December, and various *divertissements*. There is almost no information on Mary's students at this time, but soloist Franje Jelinčić worked with her in Split and was also a student of Ana and Oskar, as was Franjo Horvat.

Ana and Oskar's invitation back to Zagreb at the beginning of the war arose because the management of the theatre had become dissatisfied with the leadership of Margarita Froman and wished to improve the standing of the ballet company, although the dissatisfaction may have been politically motivated since she was not Croatian. On 27 June 1941, Ana and Oskar staged "Invitation to the Dance", "Noć na pustoj gori" ("A Night on a Bald Mountain", which may have been based on Legat's choreography) and a piece called "Život" ("The Life") to the music of Tchaikovsky's Fifth

Symphony. Other candidates were considered to run the ballet company, including several who had established careers outside Yugoslavia – Anton Vujanić, Mia Slavenska, Pino and Pia Mlakar (at that time directors of the ballet company in Munich), and Mercedes Goritz Pavelić among them – but only Pavelić and Ana and Oskar presented their choreography to the theatre management. The performance directed by Ana and Oskar was well received and they were jointly appointed heads of the ballet company and principal dancers under Dušan Žanko, the general manager, and Stanislav Stražnicki, director of the opera.

They choreographed for the opera as well as mounting ballets and in January 1942 they again staged "Invitation to the Dance" and "The Life" and also "The Dying Swan" for Ana. In April the following year, Oskar mounted "The Devil in the Village", once more taking the title role himself. The two lovers Yela and Mirko were danced by Ana and Nenad Lhotka, who had joined the company shortly after Ana and Oskar were engaged as directors. Olga Orlova was the Devil's wife. In the following month, the company took "Ero the Joker", "The Devil in the Village" and the opera, "Nikola Šubić Zrinjski" (about the eponymous sixteenth-century hero) to Vienna, where the composer Richard Strauss attended the performances. Since both Croatia and Serbia were under German control, it was possible to travel to Germany and Austria.

Shortly afterwards, however, their contract as directors expired and was not renewed, and from then on Ana and Oskar performed only as guest artists. Oskar went to Berlin, where he had been invited to teach by Rudolf Kölling, director of the Deutsche Oper (German Opera) and the ballet school. Almost immediately the school was evacuated to the Sudetenland, near the border with Czechoslovakia. Ana joined him there and they continued to teach until the school closed. They then moved to Vienna, where the Volksoper Wein was still giving performances and where they may have hoped to teach and to perform but, with the bombing of the city in 1944, they finally returned to Zagreb in the autumn. In her scholarly biography of Tito, Phyllis Auty tantalisingly states that among the visitors to his headquarters in the mountains at Drvar around May 1944 were "some dancers from the Zagreb ballet". It is tempting to think that Ana may have been among them because her brother, Tonči, was within Tito's inner cadre and she may have joined Oskar in Germany a little later in the year. After the war, when they were reinstated as directors in Zagreb, Oskar was questioned by the Court of Honour of the theatre regarding his work during the war.

Although he was suspended for three months, he returned to the theatre before the term of the suspension had been completed. Ana, on the other hand, was not suspended on the strength of the fact that all three of her brothers, Jakov and Bogumil as well as Tonči, had been partisans.

Elena Poliakova and Margarita Froman lived through the war in Yugoslavia but, unlike Kirsanova, did not remain there for the rest of their lives. Poliakova taught for a time in Austria before moving to Santiago, Chile, in 1949. There, she worked with Vadim Sulima who had opened a studio training dancers who then formed the Ballet Clasico Nacional. (Dates are conflicting as to whether she left Belgrade in 1940 or 1949, although, given the reference to her appointment as ballet mistress at the Ballet Nacional Chileno directed by Ernst Utoff in 1952, the latter may be correct.) In 1958, she became the ballet mistress for Ballet Municipal. She was awarded the Gold Medal of the City of Santiago in December 1971, and for its presentation wore the badge of the Mariinsky Theatre School that she had received on graduation. Poliakova died on 25 July 1972 and is buried in the Russian Cemetery outside the city. The library and archive of Claire Robilant was named in her honour and is housed at the Municipal Theatre of Santiago; papers relevant to Poliakova are also held at the Jerome Robbins Dance Division of the New York Public Library. The Elena Poliakova National Ballet Competition (Concurso de Danza Elena Poliakova) was established in Chile in 1990.

Margarita Froman continued to direct and choreograph for opera but her last major ballet was "Romeo and Juliet" in 1948. She accompanied the tour of the Yugoslav National Opera and Ballet to London in 1955 but then moved to the United States from Yugoslavia and settled in New London, Connecticut. Her brother Max and his wife Olga, who was a pianist and choreographer, had reached the United States earlier, around 1949. Ten years before, he had been invited to the National Theatre in Bratislava, where he met Olga and where he worked until the end of the war, bringing "The Gingerbread Heart" and "Imbrik with a Nose" to the stage there, as well as some of the Diaghilev ballets. Anticipating the Communist takeover, Max and Olga left Czechoslovakia in 1945 and spent four years in a displaced persons' camp in Munich. Max's former colleague from the Ballets Russes, Anatole Bourman, helped them reach the United States. (He had immigrated to America in 1922.) Around 1954, Max and Olga opened the Froman Professional School of Ballet in New London. Margarita taught there and also at the Connecticut School of Music, the Hartford Conservatory and the

University of Connecticut. She died on 24 March 1970 in Boston. An archive of Margarita Froman's papers is held at the University of Connecticut, Thomas J. Dodd Research Center.

Kirsanova remained in Belgrade and was the director and choreographer for the National Theatre until 1951. She went on to study archaeology in the late 1960s, gained a master's degree and worked on archaeological digs in the Middle East, and also appeared in the film "Nešto izmedju" ("Something in Between") in 1982. She died in the city in 1989 at the age of ninety-one.

CHAPTER 15
FRIENDS AND INTELLIGENCE AGENTS

*Still there is the excuse that I can't mention a word about
what I am doing at present.*

Duane Tyrrel (Bill) Hudson, letter to his parents, 8 December 1944, Imperial War
Museum reference 12691.

Although Mary and Hugh had gone their separate ways before the war,
a number of friends from Belgrade remained life-long. Among those
who were not directly connected with the theatre or ballet were Katherine
Mason's parents, her aunt and uncle, Helen and Charles Parsons, and a
young South African mining engineer Bill Hudson. Katherine's father,
William Morgan, met her Russian mother, Tamara Abaciev, in Belgrade and
they were married there in 1938, while Tamara's sister Helen had married
Charles Parsons in Belgrade in 1932. In the Russian Orthodox ceremony
for Katherine's parents, Bill Hudson held the crown over William Morgan's
head and Charles Parsons gave her mother away. The Abacievs came from
the Caucasus region of Russia and, through the efforts of General Pyotr
Wrangel, who had led anti-Bolshevik forces in southern Russia, they reached
Kikinda in northern Serbia, just inside the border with Romania, in the
early 1920s. Katherine's grandmother set up a school there but by the end
of the decade they had moved to Belgrade ,where her mother attended the
university and her grandfather helped to set up the Ruski Dom, or Russian
House, in Králice Natalije.

Mary also knew Zora, the Montenegrin second wife of Ernest Bunker,
an accountant at the British-owned mining operation at Trepča. They were
close friends of the Morgans and Zora was godmother to Katherine. Another

mutual friend, Trevor Glanville, had visited the country many times in the previous decade, first as an accountant for Price Waterhouse & Co., and he was appointed as the British vice consul in Zagreb from 1940 to provide diplomatic cover for his more covert activities. He and his Russian wife, Zlata Mionchinsky, were married in Zagreb. Colonel Robert Lethbridge was a member of the legation staff for whom Germano worked in 1940 and 1941 on matters of a "highly confidential" nature. Mary would have known Christine Granville (Krystyna Skarbek), a Polish resistance agent and good friend of Helen Parsons. (She came to Belgrade early in 1941, en route to Istanbul, and, among her other activities, was liaison officer to Hudson's mission to Poland at the end of 1944. See Clare Mulley's biography, "The Spy Who Loved".) In the 1930s and before the invasion of April 1941, but very aware of the likelihood of war, Mary's diverse circle enjoyed the social life of Belgrade. Photographs show them stylish and good-looking, wearing elegant casual clothes and shoes on trips into the countryside or to the coast, and in evening dress enjoying dinners in restaurants and nightclubs which may well have included the White Russian Kasbek club.

MI6, the British external security service, and the British Special Operations Executive were particularly active in the Balkans. Well before 1941, a number of expatriates were recruited to liaise with local groups sympathetic to the Allies, to disrupt the flow of supplies to Germany and, in the event of invasion, to provide a core of people able to assist resistance movements. Mary's friends were obvious candidates for SOE and its precursor organisation, known as Section D ("D" for destruction), which was set up to carry out undercover and sabotage work, and for other intelligence-related activities. They were multilingual and had detailed knowledge of local geography, customs and culture, and several of them also had first-hand knowledge of Yugoslavia's strategically important mining industry. Short profiles of many of these agents, including Trevor Glanville, Bill Hudson and William Morgan, are provided in Malcolm Atkin's "Section D for Destruction: Forerunner of SOE".

After the war, the Morgans, the Parsons and Mary and Germano all came to live in the London suburb of Beckenham in Kent. A small Russian community was already established there and it was where William Morgan had grown up. Glanville and his family lived nearby in Dulwich. Hudson returned to South Africa after the war but kept a flat in London and was a frequent visitor. Christine Granville helped to entertain Katherine's cousin, Donne Parsons, in London before they moved to Beckenham. Colonel

Lethbridge retired with his family to Bix in Oxfordshire and where Donne spent school holidays when Helen and Charles were abroad. Among this group of friends, however, only Mary and Germano and Bill Hudson remained in Yugoslavia after the German invasion, although they may have had little contact with each other until after the war was over. Mary's younger sister Kitty was with her husband Viktor Starčić in Belgrade. Her older sister Tatiana was in London with her husband Robert and, because of his business activities in the Balkans and eastern Europe, they were very much part of the group in Belgrade before the war. Despite those business interests, and unlike many of Mary's friends, Robert seems not to have been involved in any intelligence work.

William Morgan trained as an accountant and, before the war, worked in the Belgrade office of the French-controlled Société Française des mines de Bor in Serbia, which was set up with a French investor group by Georg Weifert, the same industrialist and philanthropist who had established hospitals in Belgrade. Morgan had worked and travelled extensively in northern and eastern Europe, was fluent in German and French, and spoke good Serbo-Croat. Through Julius Hanau, a South African businessman (and arms dealer by some accounts) who ran SOE activities in Yugoslavia, he was taken on as an employee by the accounting firm of Binder, Hamlyn & Co. in Budapest, but with half of his salary being paid by the Ministry of Economic Warfare, the ministry under which SOE operated. To all outward appearances, however, he was simply a chartered accountant. He worked for a short time in Belgrade on cyphers and codes, and his contacts within Serbia would have provided information on local conditions and support for sabotage operations.

Glanville combined his official positions as an accountant and vice consul with his enthusiasm for steam trains and butterflies, which provided additional cover for his propaganda and sabotage work. Also fluent in Serbo-Croat, Russian, German and French, he joined Section D in October 1939. Commissioned in the army with the rank of captain in March 1941, he was a liaison officer with the Yugoslav secret service when Germany invaded in April. Codenamed Nero, but also known as Sancho, Jim or Buster (the Morgans knew him as Jim), Glanville brought the news of German intelligence commando activities in the Balkans to London. Glanville's suggestion that undercover commando work would be a worthwhile undertaking was initially dismissed by SOE and MI6, though Ian Rankin notes in his history of the 30 Assault Unit that Lieutenant Commander Ian Fleming and John

Godfrey thought otherwise. Later, of course, Fleming created James Bond, Agent 007, based on several SOE agents including Hudson, and Granville is said to have inspired the female character of Vesper Lynd in Fleming's first book featuring Bond, "Casino Royale", which was published in 1953 and is set partly in Montenegro.

In the mid-1930s, Bill Hudson had gone to Yugoslavia to manage the Zajača antimony mine and then to manage other base metal operations. By the time he was recruited into Section D at the outbreak of war, he had a working knowledge of Russian and spoke French, German and Serbo-Croat. Early in 1940, he was posted to Zagreb to collaborate with Glanville with a view to taking over from him. He was assigned to carry out sabotage against shipping along the Dalmatian coast and in the first half of 1941 he carried out sabotage in Greece and Turkey. Hudson went on to serve in SOE Force 399 as a liaison officer in Yugoslavia from 1941 to 1944, staying within the country for longer than any other liaison officer. Although he is unlikely to have been the only agent to go into the field with minimal or no training, particularly those who were recruited outside Britain, as it was, he says, "they pitchforked me into the country with no preparation whatsoever" (BBC documentary "The Sword and the Shield").

Charles Parsons and Ernest Bunker did not work for SOE directly. Parsons was born in 1892 and, like Hugh Pearse, was awarded the Military Cross in the First World War. As a lieutenant with the Royal Engineers, he was in charge of a group laying cable under heavy fire. Then, after a short spell with the Auxiliary Division of the Royal Irish Constabulary in the early 1920s, he went via the United States to work in the mining industry in Mexico. At some point, he came to Belgrade, where he met and married Helen Abaciev. During the Second War he was first in the Intelligence Corps, which worked with SOE, but in October 1942 he resigned his commission as second lieutenant (presumably in order to travel as a civilian) and by January the following year he was on his way to the United States. The passenger list gives his occupation as mining engineer and his last permanent address as Veliki, Yugoslavia. (Since *veliki* simply means big, either the place name was incorrectly transcribed or he deliberately provided incomplete information.) By then, he may already have been working for or with the Consolidated Pneumatic Tool Company and was visiting the Chicago head office on war-related business. Charles's younger sister Joyce also worked for SOE from early in the war and may have been posted to the Far East since, somewhat later, there is a record of her returning to England by sea from Rangoon in 1953, with her occupation given as a civil servant in Bangkok.

Ernest Bunker, who had gone to Serbia in 1934 to run the accounting team at the Trepča lead-zinc mine of Selection Trust Ltd, spent the war working for the Ministry of Economic Warfare on the procurement of key metals and minerals from neutral countries. Selection Trust was founded by an American businessman, Alfred Chester Beatty, who, in 1927, had the opportunity to develop the lead, zinc and silver resources of southern Serbia. The Trepča mine opened three years later and became one of the largest in Europe. It was, of course, of interest to the Yugoslav government and, to the Germans, anxious to maintain supplies of metals, as well as to the British because of the ownership structure, although the concentrates were sold to smelters in Europe. From September 1939, agreements negotiated through the minister at the legation in Belgrade gave the Yugoslav government the right to seventy per cent of its output. (In his autobiography, "Burning Bright", Bunker's colleague Edward Wharton-Tigar notes that much of the Yugoslav portion would have been destined for Germany since arms could only be procured from Germany through a barter agreement for metal raw materials.) As events unfolded, however, Yugoslavia also made plans, which were never carried out, to sabotage the mine and its related facilities. Wharton-Tigar comments that explosive from the mine was placed in rail cars carrying concentrates to Germany, with predictable results once the concentrates reached the smelter, while Atkin reports that another idea was to drill holes in the bottom of the rail cars so that the concentrate would leak out en route – in practice, this was not successful, however, since the holes became clogged. Beatty suggested some of his own, more general, sabotage ideas to Major Laurence Grand, who had immediate charge of SOE. In his memoir, "Baker Street Irregular", Bickham Sweet-Escott, the liaison officer between Beatty and Grand, felt that some of his sabotage schemes were not entirely practical, since they reminded him of the White Knight's imaginative but highly impractical ideas in Lewis Carroll's "Through the Looking-Glass", although he notes that Beatty's extensive contacts were of great assistance.

Even several years before the declaration of war and invasion of Yugoslavia, the legation in Belgrade was engaged in trying to support the country's neutrality. Yugoslavia's position on critical supply routes meant that it was of interest to both Germany and the Allies, and the British government became increasingly concerned about the crucial importance of the country's mining industry during the 1930s. Serbia and Croatia were major producers of copper, bauxite, antimony, zinc and lead. Yugoslavia lay on the road, rail and river routes from western and central Europe to Greece and the Aegean, and between Europe and the Black Sea; chromite was imported to Germany via Yugoslavia from Turkey, and oil and grain from Romania. It became clear to British military intelligence that an undercover guerilla operation was essential, elsewhere in Europe as well as in Yugoslavia. SOE was formally set up in July 1940 and was disbanded after the war, in January 1946. It combined the sections of MI6 that dealt with sabotage (Section D), intelligence in uniform (R) and propaganda (also known as EH after its headquarters, Electra House, or CS, after its Foreign Office head, Sir Campbell Stuart). At first, SOE was housed at 2 Caxton Street in London and, for a short time, in St Ermin's Hotel nearby. The website for the hotel states that Winston Churchill's famous instruction to Hugh Dalton, the Minister of Economic Warfare, to "set Europe ablaze" was issued there, at a meeting of the founders of SOE in 1940. In October 1940, SOE headquarters were transferred to 64 Baker Street. Agents could not tell even their closest family members that they worked for SOE and could say only that they were employed by the Ministry of Economic Warfare, or some other relevant ministry. (Sweet-Escott says that he found the advised "Statistical Research Department of the War Office" unconvincing.) Outside the offices and training centres, agents were not to acknowledge each other at all.

SOE was set up in a hurry and, in the early days, its senior personnel had little direct knowledge of the ways in which its agents were to carry out their tasks and were too gentlemanly themselves to operate in the covert, underhand manner that the situation required. MI6 held that SOE was amateurish and, indeed, some SOE agents admitted as much – Alexander Glen recounts that they were immensely keen, if amateur, but that the Germans were keen and amateurish to the same extent. (See "Forgotten Voices of the Secret War. An Inside History of Special Operations During the Second World War" by modern war historian Roderick Bailey for oral testimonies of SOE agents.) SOE historian M.R.D. Foot points out, however, that despite its senior ranks coming overwhelmingly from well-known public schools and the older universities, SOE was able to recruit agents from a very wide range of social and political backgrounds, and their common bond was a determination that the Allies should win the war. (According to Peter Matthews in "House of Spies", it was Guy Burgess, then an MI6 officer, who proposed that training be set up for potential agents, an effort in which his Cambridge undergraduate friend Kim Philby assisted. Later, of course, and unrelated to this story, it was Philby and Burgess who, as Communist agents, defected to the Soviet Union.) Foot describes the rigours of SOE training, which generally started with a two- to three-week course (usually in an English country house) including physical fitness, map reading and work with pistols and submachine guns. Candidates who completed the initial course then went to Scotland for what was essentially paramilitary training near Arisaig in western Inverness. This covered the use of small arms, explosive demolition and sabotage, intensive map reading and ambush techniques. Only after these two courses had been successfully completed were the candidates brought back to country houses near Beaulieu in Hampshire and finally told that they were to work undercover in enemy territory. This last stage gave training in intelligence and coding and coping with interrogation. Parachute training, wireless operation and advanced coding took place afterwards in other locations.

The regional headquarters of SOE that come into this story were in Cairo, where a branch of the Foreign Office had been established in the 1914–1918 war, and at Monopoli near Bari on the Adriatic coast of Italy from the autumn of 1943. (Oversight of Balkan activities was moved from Budapest to Cairo in 1940.) Sweet-Escott notes that in the early days, in 1940, the Balkan section of SOE was the only part of the organisation that was fully operational. In Belgrade, the initial activities of Section D and SOE were controlled by Julius Hanau. Codenamed Caesar, Hanau was an agent for MI6 in Yugoslavia before being appointed to run SOE's operations in the country, organising resistance and sabotage efforts in the Balkans. Charismatic and capable, he was awarded the Distinguished Service Order and was made an Officer of the Order of the British Empire for his services; he had already been awarded the Order of the White Eagle by the King of Serbia in 1919. Early in the war in Europe, Hanau was responsible for the recruitment of Hudson and, probably Glanville, as well as Morgan and Stewart (Bill) Bailey, who was in charge of the concentrator at the Trepča mine. Bailey was brought on as Hanau's deputy but became responsible for Section D in Yugoslavia in mid-1940. Since Hanau had been identified by the Germans as a British agent, he was brought back to London prior to the invasion in 1941 and was given responsibility for SOE activities in West Africa. He was sent to Cairo to plan operations in the Balkans but had suffered from malaria earlier in the year and died of a heart attack in May 1943.

ℭℊↄ

By 1941, Yugoslavia had been fully unified for just over twenty years. Hitler's actions, and the actions of those who resisted him, were shaped by the lack of historical unity, and by the previous domination by the Venetians, Austria-Hungary and the Ottomans over different parts of the country that dated back several hundred years. The Kingdom of the Serbs, Croats and Slovenes was established at the end of 1918 and then became the Kingdom of Yugoslavia in 1929 under Alexander I Karađjorđjević. It principally encompassed the Kingdoms of Serbia and Montenegro, and the areas of Dalmatia, Slovenia, Croatia-Slavonia, Bosnia, Herzegovina and Vojvodina which previously were part of the Austro-Hungarian Empire. But unification as a kingdom did not reconcile the different outlooks of the three main ethnic groups. The Serbs saw it as the means of uniting Serbs beyond the borders of Serbia itself, essentially as an extension of the Principality of Serbia that was finally won from the Ottomans in 1867, and of the Kingdom of Serbia established in 1882 under Milan I Obrenović. For the Croats and the Slovenes, the founding of the Kingdom of Yugoslavia provided independence from Italian or Austro-Hungarian rule. But Serb dominance was resented and protested, particularly by Croat nationalists. King Alexander I was assassinated in Marseille in 1934 by a Bulgarian who may have acted with Croat separatist support. The result was that his eldest son, Peter, was only eleven when he succeeded his father and Yugoslavia was ruled by the regent Prince Paul until Peter was declared to have come of age in 1941.

As Hitler extended his reach across Europe in the second half of the 1930s, Yugoslavia struggled to develop a foreign policy that would preserve its neutrality. The situation came to a head in March 1941, when, against the wishes of Prince Peter and his advisers, Prince Paul brought Yugoslavia into the Tripartite Pact between Germany, Italy and Japan. Popular reaction was immediate and resulted in a coup against Prince Paul. Prince Peter was declared to be of age six months before his eighteenth birthday and installed as King Peter II on 27 March. Hitler's reaction was swift and harsh. He ordered that Yugoslavia should be invaded and Belgrade singled out for aerial attack. Warnings were not believed and Belgrade, virtually undefended, was bombed on 6 April, Serbian Orthodox Easter Sunday. A simultaneous land invasion resulted in Yugoslavia's surrender on 17 April. King Peter and his government had left the country after the invasion and finally arrived in London in June. Although the timing of Hitler's invasion may not have been planned, control of its territory and resources certainly was because of its position on important trade routes.

Katherine Mason's mother, William Morgan's wife, had already left Belgrade by train and was in Istanbul by March 1941, and other women connected with the legation and SOE were preparing to leave the city. On 13 March 1941, just weeks before the bombing of Belgrade, Morgan wrote to his wife that "Sweetie" Sweet-Escott, Colonel Lethbridge, Charles Parsons and Mary and Germano were all still in the city. "Sweetie" must refer to Sweet-Escott's sister, Louisa or "Lutie", since she was in Belgrade, but Sweet-Escott himself was not, and she left for Athens shortly afterwards. Morgan predicted that Yugoslavia would not fight, but that the country "will soon be occupied peacefully" by the Germans, at which point the legation staff would be evacuated. Morgan was arrested shortly after the German invasion but was repatriated to England, where he was interviewed in London in July for continued employment with SOE. (Sweet-Escott held a number of senior positions in SOE and was responsible for recruiting his sister into Section D as a secretary as early as 1940.)

For British expatriates in the interior of Yugoslavia, including the staff of the legation and employees of the Trepča mine, the invasion prompted a difficult journey to the Adriatic coast with the objective of evacuation to Greece, if not directly to England. While Katherine Mason's mother had already reached Budapest, her cousin, Donne Parsons, remembered how he left Belgrade for Bulgaria by train with his mother, Helen, and their grandmother. The train was attacked by machine guns near the border, perhaps near Dimitrovgrad, but they went on to Istanbul, where they endured bombing. From there, they made their way to Cairo and the Parsons went on from Port Said to London. Writing to Katherine's mother from on board RMS *Empress of Russia* at Freetown, Liberia, in July 1942, Helen says that they had met Trevor Glanville's wife Zlata in Cape Town (probably she was travelling on another ship) and asks if there was any news of Christine Granville and the "Russian crowd". She adds that Donne was making friends with soldiers on board who plied him with sweets. Louisa Sweet-Escott was evacuated from Belgrade to Athens and arrived in Cairo in April or May 1941. Her brother notes that she might have held some sort of record for the burning of SOE files ahead of advancing forces no fewer than three times – in Belgrade, Athens and Cairo.

The journey to the Adriatic of the Britons remaining in Yugoslavia is described in Wharton-Tigar's autobiography, "Burning Bright", as well as in an unpublished internal corporate history, "Trepča, A History of the Trepča Mines in Yugoslavia" (a copy of which was kindly provided by a fellow geologist in Toronto), by Basil Davidson in "Partisan Picture" and in "Balkan Exit" by Flavia Kingscote. (In one of the strange coincidences which have occurred during this research and writing, I was astonished to discover that Kingscote was the first wife of a family friend, the archaeologist Hamo Sassoon; they were married at the beginning of 1946 but she died before the end of the year.) Mary and Germano knew the legation staff and many of the SOE officers, as well as their friends Bunker and Glanville, who made their way to the coast hoping to be evacuated. Presumably, Colonel Lethbridge also travelled with the legation group. A mining engineer by training, he was a second lieutenant in the Royal Army Ordnance Corps in 1939 and was promoted to colonel in 1945.

The legation staff, led by the minister, Ronald Ian Campbell, other Britons and a few non-Yugoslavs also had to work out their best evacuation route and left Belgrade on 11 April. Some of the British staff who had wives and children at the Trepča mine had left the country at the end of 1940, but the majority decided to stay on. Their somewhat muted confidence in the future evaporated as German troops invaded southern Yugoslavia from Bulgaria, and German aircraft flew overhead. The Yugoslav army took over the mine and, on 8 April, advised that all remaining staff should leave immediately.

Starting from Trepča in northern Kosovo, the only possible route to avoid German troops was over the mountains of Montenegro to the Dalmatian coast – first north through Lešak and Raška and then south-west to Novi Pazar and Cetinje. Two of the American cars owned by Selection Trust were released from army control to provide transport. However, twelve passengers, including Bunker and Wharton-Tigar, and two of the company's Yugoslav drivers had to fit into the vehicles, along with a forty-five-gallon drum of petrol on each of the back seats, so that luggage had to be kept to an absolute minimum. In that remote and sparsely populated area there were few signs of war, although the cars were stopped a few times for questioning by Yugoslav soldiers. The hazards of narrow, rough roads and remaining winter snow meant that two nights had to be spent at small inns before the party reached Cetinje, the capital of Montenegro, early on the third morning. Above the coastal town of Kotor, the road drops steeply from Mount Lovćen towards the coast in a series of tight hairpin bends which offer dramatic scenery and views of the Adriatic. Wharton-Tigar's description brought back vivid memories of driving the same road on a family holiday in 1967 and it was easy to appreciate that spirits of the Trepča party began to rise as they descended, in spite of the cramped discomfort of the cars. The group continued on to Dubrovnik, where there was a British consulate, but moved back to Kotor after a single night in reasonable comfort since the consul warned of considerable anti-British feeling in the town.

Kingscote describes the difficulties of finding her own route against a background of rumours and incomplete information on where German and Italian forces were gathering. She had travelled by train from Zagreb to Sarajevo, intending to find other Britons in Skopje and thinking that she would be able to offer her services as an interpreter or in a field hospital. She arrived in Sarajevo the morning after the convoy of cars carrying the legation staff, with their diplomatic plates and Union Jacks, had come in from Belgrade. After three days of driving, the condition of the vehicles showed how difficult their journey had been – they were covered in mud, windows had been broken and one large American-made Nash had its front door tied back to the hinges with string. The main hotel, the Europa, was full of English, Greek and French people, all struggling to find rooms. Kingscote learned that Skopje was already in German hands and that, like everyone else, she would have to try to reach the Croatian coast. She discovered that the legation party expected to be met at Kotor by a British destroyer which would take them to Greece and that Campbell and most of his staff were staying at Ilidža about five miles from Sarajevo on one of the roads to the Adriatic. The head of the British Council in Zagreb, who Kingscote knew from her work there, secured a place for her in the convoy of British cars, in the Nash with its front door still held on with string, warning that space would be cramped and that only minimal luggage could be taken. The route was debated since a mountainous but fairly direct road passed through Croatia but was likely to be in the hands of hostile Ustaša. The alternative was a longer road avoiding Croatia but which would mean crossing the high mountains of the Sandžak of Novi Pazar and Montenegro to Cetinje. After several false starts, the cars finally left Sarajevo and at Ilidža the party learned that the Montenegrin route was the only possible one, which meant driving back through Sarajevo. By that time, Kingscote had taken the wheel of the Nash since the exhausted driver refused to go further. From earlier travels, she knew the roads, but had never driven on them. It was Sunday, 13 April. The morning was clear and cloudless. Sarajevo was subjected to bombing that was almost as severe as on Belgrade the previous Sunday, but out at Ilidža the convoy had missed the worst of the first onslaught and drove through silent streets past gutted houses and through dense smoke. A second wave of bombing followed, just as all the cars gathered on the other side of the town. Once on their way, the convoy spread out. Progress was hampered by the road being cratered by mines and with military patrols at every bridge. Slowly, part of the convoy reached Cetinje. There, knowing the coast and Kotor were within reach, and with food and comfortable beds available, spirits rose, as they had for the Trepča party which arrived a few days ahead of the legation staff.

The next day, however, it was learned that the surrender of Yugoslavia had been negotiated and King Peter and his government had flown to England on the previous afternoon. Then it was a question of racing for the coast ahead of German or Italian forces. At Kotor, Kingscote and her companions learned that the British group was assembling at Perast and that the minister and most of the legation and SOE staff had already arrived. Campbell had been able to maintain contact with the outside world by means of a wireless transmitter so that, on 15 April, two Sunderland flying boats landed on the Bay of Kotor and took off a few British nationals and a number of Europeans believed to be in particular danger from the Germans. A destroyer was to be sent to the entrance of the gulf to pick up the remaining hundred or so Britons who made their way further down the coast to where two small boats had been arranged to ferry them out to the larger ship. After a few hours, as light was dawning, they had no choice but to return to land at Herceg Novi on Kotor Bay since the destroyer never appeared. Kingscote, still with the legation group, notes that the possibility of sailing on to Greece was considered but abandoned since the boats were overloaded, and had no food or water and little fuel. Campbell reluctantly cast the wireless transmitter overboard as the party returned to Herceg Novi. At that point, Wharton-Tigar, tempted to make a dash for the mountains, was dissuaded by Bunker, who reminded him that the Trepča party was now under the protection of the British legation, while a sole British refugee would stand little chance if picked up by pro-German or pro-Italian locals. Wharton-Tigar describes Bunker as modest and retiring in character, but who was obviously perceptive and sensible in difficult situations. A side light is given by Davidson in his "Partisan Picture"; he and a few other SOE agents had ended up at Herceg Novi when Campbell stepped in and enrolled them as press attachés on his staff and maintained this story when he was pressed to surrender any non-diplomats. Shortly afterwards, Italian forces arrived with an advance guard on motorcycles. There was general relief that it was an Italian troop rather than German since there was a much better chance that the British group would be treated according to diplomatic protocols, as turned out to be the case.

Initially, the British were allowed to move around the town to find food but were then confined to their hotels. On 22 April, a British submarine, the HMS *Regent*, entered Kotor Bay at Zelenik but, while her second-in-command, Lieutenant Lambert, came ashore to negotiate the evacuation of the British diplomatic staff with the Italian authorities, it was bombed by German aircraft. The submarine had to make its own escape, still under attack as it dived to deeper waters, taking with it two Italian officers who had gone aboard in exchange for Lambert, who was left onshore. The German bombardment came, to the annoyance of the Italian admiral in charge of the port, who had already assured the British that the submarine would not be attacked while negotiations were in progress. (The commander of the *Regent*, Lieutenant Commander Browne, was awarded the Distinguished Service Order for his handling of the situation.) On 24 April, the Italians arranged a convoy of lorries and coaches to take the British to the Albanian port of Durazzo. Kingscote was taken with the other women and children in the first bus – driven by a "cocky" Italian soldier who managed not only to take the road to Ulcinj rather than the border but to overturn the bus into a ditch, luckily without causing serious injuries. After a night in Scutari, the convoy proceeded to Durazzo, where the diplomatic staff was lodged in the Albergo dei Dogi while the Trepča staff and others were housed in wooden army huts near the airport, but all ate together at the Albergo. They were closely supervised and allowed only brief walks on the street. Having worn only what they stood up in for more than a fortnight, there was an opportunity to buy some spare clothing, albeit at high prices. (Before leaving Trepča, Wharton-Tigar had taken 500,000 dinars, then worth about £2,500, from the company safe to finance his group's journey.) Hot baths and more plentiful food and drink were also very welcome. The roof of the hotel allowed some opportunity for open air and exercise and, amusingly, since this story is about the lives of ballet dancers, Kingscote describes the antics of a male dancer who used a chimney pot as a *barre* and jumped and pirouetted around. Rather sharply, she adds that, once in England, he successfully appealed his call-up saying his work was of national importance.

On 1 May, the entire party was taken in small groups to the airport at Tirana, where, finally, they were flown out in Italian Savoia bombers, seven at a time, to the military airfield at Foggia north of Bari in southern Italy. This was not without some trepidation since the bomb hatches were in the centre of the fuselage and could have been used for the convenient release of unwanted passengers, as well as the fact that the Savoias could be attacked by Allied aircraft. Kingscote was among the last to leave, on 6 May, in a civilian plane rather than a bomber. However, all were landed safely and taken under American protection by train to Rome and then to the northern Italian spa town of Bagni di Chianciano near Perugia. Kingscote describes how, on the way to Rome, they travelled through groves of oranges and lemons, and then forests of cork oak. The six weeks at Chianciano were much more comfortable, albeit still under American guard. The diplomats were housed in the Hotel Principe and others in the Imperiale and the Patria. The local population was amused by the games of baseball and cricket which were played between diplomats and miners. A newspaper, *Imperial Affairs,* was typed up daily. Wharton-Tigar also notes the friendliness of the Italians who had already had enough of hostilities and dreaded the prospect of German control.

To the surprise of everyone, on 11 June, the entire British party was transported by road to Chiusi and then by train to unoccupied southern France, along the Riviera to Barcelona and on to Madrid. Their release had been arranged in return for the freeing of an Italian group which had been captured in East Africa. Among that group of Italians was the Duke of Aosta – Campbell had suggested to the Foreign Office that a fair exchange should include the entire British party, including the ad hoc press attachés and the Trepča staff. Once in Barcelona, the group was placed in the care of the British Embassy in Madrid. The diplomats were treated with every consideration, travelled on to Lisbon and were flown home later in June. Campbell was knighted in the same month. Everyone else, on the other hand, was lodged in small, ill-kept hotels and required to use their own credit to obtain limited amounts of Spanish currency. In the end, those who were not part of the diplomatic group (about sixty people) went by train to Gibraltar, where, eventually, they and over one thousand refugees from all over Europe were taken on board the Cunard liner, the RMS *Scythia*, which was being used as a troop and supply ship. According to Wharton-Tigar, the *Scythia* sailed on 15 July. She travelled within a convoy of an aircraft carrier, cruisers and destroyers since part of the Mediterranean fleet was en route for Britain, and Kingscote notes that they were attacked on at least one occasion. She was surprised to see the shipyards of the River Clyde deserted because it was a Saturday, possibly 26 July.

❧

By July 1941, William Morgan had reached London. He was posted to the Russian section of SOE with the rank of captain and completed a training course in industrial sabotage at Lerwick in the Shetland Islands and the "finishing course" at the Rings, one of the country houses near Beaulieu. The finishing course prepared agents for work in occupied territory and included instruction in security, surveillance, wireless operation, codes, burglary, the use of carrier pigeons, recognition of enemy uniforms and so on. In October 1941, he sailed for Cairo via Accra, a voyage round the Cape of Good Hope to Port Said, and was destined for Teheran. However, after a temporary assignment in Cairo, where his wife was already working for the British government, he was posted to Turkey, where he worked on Hungarian and Balkan affairs, rather than Russian concerns. But he was able to join her in Cairo for Christmas 1942. A year later, he was posted to the SOE advance office for Yugoslav operations in Bari and was promoted to the rank of major. That posting, however, effectively ended his active SOE career. In December 1943, having worked non-stop for five days and nights in occupied territory, he was involved in a vehicle accident on the road between Brindisi and Bari in which both his legs were broken. He was in hospital in Italy for the next three months and was then transferred to the RAF hospital in Church Village, Glamorgan. By the end of the year, or very early in 1945, he was fit enough for a short overseas mission but signed off from service with SOE at the end of January. His final posting was to work with the internment camps in the Isle of Man.

Morgan's wife's journey to Cairo in 1941 is likely to have been at least as arduous as any others', with food difficult to come by and transportation crowded with refugees of all nationalities. Amid the squalor of Egypt, the hot spring *khamseen* wind brought choking sand and dust. While the nature of her work is not known, almost certainly it took advantage of her languages. She may have been able to buy fabric for dresses and would have socialised in the various clubs and restaurants that are described by Artemis Cooper in "Cairo in the War, 1939–1945". She and Helen and Donne Parsons used to go to the Gezira Sporting Club, where they could relax among its shady trees. Bickham and Louisa Sweet-Escott were among the people she would have known already and, even if she was not directly involved in their work, she would have heard about the intrigues and back-biting within SOE, and the burning of files in 1942 and a fire which destroyed SOE records in 1945. While it was possible to send letters, correspondence with family was infrequent and Katherine's grandmother, by then in London, bemoans the lack of news in one of her own.

Bill Hudson was a close friend of Mary and Germano and saw them often on his regular trips from South Africa to England after the war. He also knew Ana Roje and Oskar Harmoš well but, unless he was able to meet one or other of them on those visits, they would have seen little of each other except, possibly, when he was finally able to go back to Yugoslavia in the winter of 1983–1984 for the filming of a BBC documentary on SOE in Yugoslavia, "The Sword and the Shield". In 1936, Hudson was married briefly to a Russian ballet dancer, Ada, or Ariadna Proskurnikova. As dancers, Ada and Mary may well have known each other in Belgrade, and possibly it was through her that Mary came to know Hudson, although it is more likely that the contact came through the social group which centred on the legation. His wartime activities do not directly touch what was happening to Mary and Germano in those years but his story is worth telling briefly because no biography has been written to make his work more widely known, and he did not publish a memoir of his own. In 1946, Jasper Rootham wrote at the beginning of his book, "Miss Fire: The Chronicle of a British Mission to Mihailovich, 1943–1944", that he hoped Hudson's story would eventually be "properly and fully told" and a similar wish was expressed by Davidson in "Partisan Picture". That his obituary in the *Independent* (and, almost certainly, *The Times* as well) was written by M.R.D. Foot, the military historian and historian of SOE, who was himself a former SOE officer, is a measure of the regard in which Hudson was held. As for research on Mary's background, I have looked to first-hand accounts and memoirs of people who knew Hudson and worked with him for information on his early life; his mission to Yugoslavia in 1941–1943; his mission to Poland in the harsh winter months just before the Yalta conference of February, 1945, and which entailed dropping by parachute to a rural area north of Kraków; and his work with a British military mission in Romania after the war. "The Sword and the Shield" centres on him and took him, and some of his SOE colleagues back to Yugoslavia to revisit the scenes of their wartime exploits. Hudson received many medals and honours: the Distinguished Service Order in 1942 and the military Order of the British Empire in 1945, as well as the War Medal, the 1939–1945 Star, the Africa Star, the Italy Star, and the Defence Medal, and he was presented with a Lindberg watch made by Longines for his services to SOE. The medals and the watch are held at the Imperial War Museum, where there is also an archive of paper records and photographs.

Hudson was the first British liaison officer sent to Draža Mihailović, leader of the Royalist Četnik resistance group. His mission, codenamed Operation Bullseye, was landed from the submarine HMS *Triumph* on the coast of Montenegro in September 1941. While the British government recognised and gave a home to King Peter and his government in exile, in the early years of the war it had almost no knowledge of Tito and the partisans, and only a little more about Mihailović and the Četniks and, as a result, had only limited understanding of the conflicting attitudes of the two groups. People who had personal knowledge of Hudson's work with SOE describe his courage and his sense of justice and right, and his physical strength and endurance. These qualities were tested to the limit and allowed him to survive during the two and a half years he was in Yugoslavia, particularly in the winter of 1941–1942. Filming of "The Sword and the Shield" in the winter of 1983–1984 allowed Hudson to hold a service in memory of all who had lost their lives in the war. The film gives some idea of the landscape under thick snow, although factual accounts and memoirs rarely describe in any detail the landscape and scenery of Serbia which Hudson and, of course, Morgan, Glanville and Parsons knew so well. But Captain Charles Hargreaves, a later liaison officer with the Četniks, recalls the great contrast of the Serbian countryside in springtime with the heat, dust and flies of Egypt. He also describes the peasants' cottages with dirt floors covered with rushes or bracken and only the most simple, rudimentary furniture. Their way of life was not only medieval but even "biblical" since, when he and a companion returned to their lodging after a long journey on foot, two daughters of their host not only removed their boots and washed their feet but dried their feet with their hair (see Bailey's "Secret Voices of the Forgotten War"). In his adventure story for young people, "White Eagles over Serbia", Lawrence Durrell captures the sounds, smells and vistas of summer in the mountains around Janko Stone (Jankov kamen) south of Belgrade in what is now the Golija Nature Park. It draws on his own experience as a press attaché to the embassy in Belgrade between 1949 and 1952. Knowing something of Hudson's life in Yugoslavia, Durrell's descriptions allow him to be pictured in those hills and valleys.

Having left Yugoslavia with the legation group, in November 1941, Trevor Glanville resigned his army commission and took a civilian job in the British embassy in Lisbon while also working for MI6 and SOE. In April 1943 he joined 30 Assault Unit as a sub-lieutenant in the Royal Naval Volunteer Reserve and went to Sicily in the Technical Wing. He returned to Yugoslavia with 30 Assault Unit on a mission to link up with Brigadier Fitzroy Maclean, Churchill's liaison officer, and then to meet Tito. However, Tito was suspicious of Glanville's political sympathies and 30 Assault Unit was barred from working in Yugoslavia. He went on to command a unit in Indo-China in 1945 and, after the war, to edit the history of the 30 Assault Unit for Naval Intelligence. He was awarded the Distinguished Service Cross in 1945 when he was acting lieutenant commander, Royal Navy.

For the remainder of the war, Ernest Bunker worked for the United Kingdom Commercial Corporation, which was set up by the Ministry of Economic Warfare in 1940 to make preemptive purchases of critical materials from neutral countries such as Turkey, Spain and Portugal to prevent them going to enemy hands. He was based in Lisbon with a number of other colleagues from Selection Trust, from where he was particularly engaged in buying tungsten ores and concentrates used in hardening steel for armaments. Bunker went back to Trepča in 1946 with a group from Selection Trust to evaluate the cost of bringing the operations back into production, although, in the event, the company was compensated for the facilities being transferred to Yugoslav hands. The Bunker family and Wharton-Tigar remained friends and after the war they were colleagues again in Selection Trust. Wharton-Tigar was godfather to Bunker's daughter, Frances.

Wharton-Tigar does not reappear in Mary's story. He was recruited into SOE in Gibraltar through one of the members of the Belgrade legation and went on to Tangier in Morocco. He did not return to Yugoslavia and the account of his work with SOE in North Africa and China is described in "Burning Bright". He says that his former colleague at Trepča, Bill Bailey, who took over from Julius Hanau, recommended to SOE that he should be transferred back to Yugoslavia at the end of 1942 but, in view of the planned landings in North Africa, he was kept in Tangier. He was also considered as a member of Fitzroy Maclean's team in to go into Yugoslavia in 1943 but ended up in Madrid facilitating the movements of agents in and out of occupied Europe. (He notes that, because he was too late to get a seat, he was not on the KLM flight to London, which was shot down on 1 June 1943, with the loss of everyone on board, including the actor Leslie Howard, whose roles included Ashley Wilkes in "Gone with the Wind" and the title role in "The Scarlet Pimpernel".)

⁊

Hugh Pearse, who was so important to the careers of both Mary and Ana, seems to have returned to England several years before the outbreak of war. The 16 May 1939 issue of the *London Gazette* carried a notice in the Special List that Captain Hugh Armine Wodehouse Pearse, then retired from his regiment, was given the rank of captain in the Special Reserve. He was nearly fifty and not required to join up but would have served in the reserve if needed. He may have made his home near his mother and sister in Dorchester. After his death, a notice in the *London Gazette* under the Trustee Act lists him as a retired schoolmaster, rather than a retired barrister or solicitor,which would have been the case if he had gone into law as suggested by the entry in the Wellington College Yearbook, and that he was a member of the Wellington Club (the sports club associated with the College) and the Dorset Yacht Club (possibly, the Royal Dorset Yacht Club) in Weymouth. Since his time as a master at Wellington was so short, it seems likely that, having left Belgrade, he may have taught at another school and may have retired not long before he died at the age of sixty-six. His sister, Dulcibella, may well have lived with her mother in Dorchester, in the house named Heddington where they moved to from Somerleigh Court, and she certainly lived in the house from the mid-1950s. Hugh, himself, died at Heddington, "after a long illness, bravely borne", only ten years after his mother, in 1958. The brass plate on a wooden bench at Holy Trinity Catholic Church in Dorchester states that the churchyard was restored in memory of Hugh and his mother; the restoration of the churchyard and installation of the bench are thought to date from around 1968 and were almost certainly undertaken by Dulcibella. (The bench is no longer in the churchyard and is kept in a storage area.) Mary regularly visited her in Dorchester until Dulcibella's death in 1984.

CHAPTER 16
A NEW LIFE IN ENGLAND

Alternating pink and white horse chestnuts lined Copers
Cope Road and when the flowers fell, it was as if there was a
striped carpet all the way down the street.

Tamara Jakasha.

Mary and Germano may not have planned to leave Split immediately after the war – it would have been difficult to arrange exit papers for Germano, although Mary would have been able to travel freely on her British passport. But, sometime towards the end of 1945, a telegram came from Mary's brother-in-law, Robert, in London saying that her sister Tatiana was seriously ill and that Mary should come at once. Mary hurried across Europe with her young daughter Tamara only to find that there was absolutely no reason for her journey and, moreover, that Robert apparently knew nothing about the telegram. It is believed that someone in their circle had decided that she and Germano should not make their lives in post-war Yugoslavia and devised a plan to bring them to England. To this day, the family does not know who sent the telegram summoning Mary to London, nor who arranged forged Italian papers for Germano, and for him to be brought from Split to Trieste. Being carefully orchestrated, it would also have cost a certain amount of money for the papers and for an escort, and potentially for bribes along the way. It is tempting to speculate that Hudson or Lethbridge, or the two of them together, were the instigators, or even Charles Parsons or Robert. But Mary and Germano did have a number of other friends who may have had both the contacts and financial resources to see the plan through, although Mary certainly paid for the guide, or guides, for the last part of the journey over the rugged limestone hills of the Karst plateau (Krš in Croatian) to Trieste itself.

While she would have liked to return to Yugoslavia, the plan had been devised, however, and Mary travelled back from London to Trieste with Tamara to meet Germano who had been smuggled out of the country on the forged Italian papers. Germano, himself, had been enjoying an evening drink in Split with some friends when he was told to accompany his escort without changing out of his light clothes, or even being able to say goodbye to his parents – it was the last time he saw his mother. Germano spoke Italian as well as Serbo-Croat and the plan rested on him being able to pass himself off as an Italian returning home as they travelled north. The final part of his journey involved walking over the plateau and into Trieste, which he would have known as Trst. As he and his guides neared the city, his cover story would have been viewed with even more suspicion since at that point he was essentially defecting from Tito's Yugoslavia. Villagers would have been wary of strangers passing through their isolated hamlets, especially in the harsh winter, and the rough stone buildings would have shown the recent scars of flying bullets. Germano's guides were critical to his safe crossing of the plateau ,which is riddled with sinkholes (*polje*) and steep valleys (*uvala*). The mix of pine trees and shrubby vegetation would have provided some cover, but hardly enough in the deep snow, and it would have been difficult to keep to local paths. As they came down the steep, western edge of the Karst, Trieste and the Adriatic would have come into view and they may have used the citadel on its hilltop as a landmark before dropping down into the city itself. When they were stopped by the Italian border guard, Germano thought, "This is it!" But the guard, asking only if Germano was Italian, was satisfied by Germano's cautious "*Sì... Sì*".

By then, Trieste itself was administered by the British-American Allied Military Government but its future had not been determined. The Yugoslav army had entered the city on 1 May 1945, followed the next day by a New Zealand division to which the remaining German troops surrendered. (As a young soldier, the writer Jan Morris, then James Morris, was stationed in Trieste as the war ended. Her "Trieste and the Meaning of Nowhere" evokes memories of those days when she describes the battered tanks of the New Zealand divisions rolling past the railway station.) Although the shipyards had been subject to Allied bombing, the city itself was largely unscathed, but uneasy even under Allied administration. The memory of violence meted out on opponents of Communism during the forty days when the partisans controlled the city would have been raw. Despite their situation, Mary and Germano may have felt it easier to live in Trieste than in Split under Tito's new rule and the imposing Austro-Hungarian architecture would have reminded Germano of his university days in Vienna. The *bora* wind blew in Split too, but in the grey of winter in Trieste it would have been even stronger and colder when it rushed down from the mountains in the north-east, driving everyone off the streets.

For the second time in her life, Mary had left her home, and a country, with minimal possessions. When she received the telegram summoning her to England, she would have expected to visit Tatiana and Robert but not to move there, and Germano had left Split with very little. His parents took care of their belongings, to be retrieved by Mary on later visits. When she comments in the interview that having a British passport meant more to her then than it did before her marriage to Hugh Pearse, she would have been thinking back to how she was able to arrange Germano's papers for immigration to England. They stayed in Trieste for a few months and some of Tamara's earliest memories are of when they lived with an Englishman in a villa with a beautiful spring garden. By the time they were ready to travel to London, Mary was familiar with trains in Europe, but the journey back through Venice and northern Italy would have been slow and the connections not smooth in those post-war months. Even with his official documents, Germano would have been apprehensive as they crossed from Italy into Switzerland and then France. They would have been thankful to reach the safety of London and a flat in Shepherd Market, not far from Robert and Tatiana.

Between 3 March and 20 May 1946, Mary and Germano lived in flat number 11 in Shepherd's House while Robert and Tatiana lived around the corner at 33 Curzon Street. In those days, Shepherd Market was the same warren of old narrow streets and lanes between Curzon Street and Piccadilly as it is now, with Market Street running east–west between White Horse Street and Stanhope Row. The buildings, many of them Georgian, would still have been blackened from years of smoke and soot, and damage from air raids would still have been unrepaired (buildings opposite Shepherd's House were particularly badly hit), but, after Belgrade and Split, such damage would not have been unexpected. Shepherd's House is an art deco-style block of flats located on the south side of Shepherd Street surrounded by a mix of Georgian and Victorian buildings. Rationing was still in effect but there were shops for everyday needs – tobacconist, newsagent, greengrocers and butchers, and several restaurants and pubs, including the conspicuous Ye Grapes, and at least one cobbler, both of which still exist. (Robert Henry describes Shepherd Market in the early years of the war in "A Village in Piccadilly".)

Then, for the next two years until June 1948, they lived at 17 Copers Cope Road in Beckenham, Kent, before moving into number 7. Mary is listed as Mary Pearse living at number 17 in the electoral register for 1947 but when her divorce from Hugh was made absolute on 6 June 1947 she was able to marry Germano in an English civil ceremony at Caxton Hall in London on 14 February 1948. She is listed as Maria Jakasha at number 7 in the electoral register for the same year. Copers Cope Road was lined with alternating pink and white horse chestnut trees, which may still have been in bloom when she and Germano moved there from Shepherd Market. Until the early 1960s, Copers Cope Road, and the other residential roads of what was known as the Cator Estate in Beckenham, remained gravelled and lined with mature trees. It was typical of the roads and avenues of large, detached houses and gardens developed originally by John Cator in the late 1700s. Because of bombing, number 7 was the first Victorian house remaining on the southern side of the road which backed on to the railway line between Beckenham Junction station and Victoria station in London. Newer houses were being built to replace those destroyed by bombing, but even in the late 1950s there were areas near the station where extensive damage had not been cleared.

Mary and Germano on their wedding day in London, collection of Tamara Jakasha.

Mary owned number 7 through a long lease, while number 17 became the home of the Morgans and the Parsons. It was jointly owned by William Morgan and Charles Parsons, and Katherine's grandmother lived with them, as did her aunt Joyce Parsons when she was not working abroad. The two houses quickly became gathering places for family and friends, for meals and to share stories – Katherine remembers being sent to bed just as she thought the conversation was getting interesting. There was a small Russian community, including some school friends of Katherine's mother and her aunt Helen from the days in Kikinda in Serbia, and an older gentleman who, even in the 1960s, continued to click his heels and kiss the hands of ladies as he greeted them. There was no Russian church in Beckenham and at first they all went to St Philip's Church in Buckingham Palace Road (where the funerals of both Nicolai Legat and Anna Pavlova were held). But, later, Mary and Helen celebrated Easter and the major feast days at the Orthodox cathedral in Ennismore Gardens which had moved there from St Philip's in in 1956, while Katherine's mother took her children each week to the Russian Church in Exile in Gloucester Road.

From as early as 1945, Katherine's mother worked in the information department of the Royal Yugoslav Government in London and, a few years later, joined Helen as a translator at the Government Communications Headquarters. Her father worked as an accountant for British Rail until his retirement. Charles Parsons travelled extensively for the Consolidated Pneumatic Tool Company and Helen often accompanied him. He was older than the others and, sadly, he was the first of the group to pass away, dying suddenly in Beirut in 1957 while on a business trip. He is buried in the Anglo-American Cemetery there.

As a foreign national, Germano's identity document was his certificate of registration, which sets out his employment and addresses until he was granted British citizenship by naturalisation in May 1957. His first employer, in February 1948 was Clavell Engineering Ltd, located at 7 Copers Cope Road, suggesting that he may have set up the company and was working from home. Of course, Mary had her father's example to follow in setting up a company for personal business activities. By March, he worked for Buildings Plant Hire (On Site) Ltd, in St Mary Cray, as a mouldings and bushings engineer and, in some capacity, he went to Iraq in May 1950. At the end of that year, he was given permission to take up employment with the Aerograph Co Ltd in Lower Sydenham, which was a leader in aircraft spray painting equipment. He then worked as a quality control engineer at the Muirhead and Co electrical and mechanical engineering factory in Elmers End, but later moved to a similar job closer to home in Lower Sydenham. Germano was tall and square-set, and Mediterranean in his outlook – he loved to while away the hours with his friends, visiting William Morgan at number 17 to reminisce and talk Serbo-Croat on Saturday mornings over an aperitif while Mary was teaching.

Bill Hudson visited Mary and Germano, and the Morgans and the Parsons, whenever he was in England. In London, and probably in South Africa as well, he led an intensely social life, enjoying parties and dances which Donne Parsons remembered, being a little older than Tamara Jakasha. Hudson maintained a *pied-à-terre* in London, at first near the Russian church in Ennismore Gardens, but later, and probably on the strength of the sale of his tungsten mining property in South Africa, above Prunier's famous French restaurant at 72 St James's Street on the corner of St James's Street and Little St James's Street. The building is French in style, with wrought-iron balconies and a mansard roof – although these days the white limestone is clean and crisp. Between Piccadilly and Pall Mall, St James's Street is still home to long-established businesses like Lobb the bootmaker, Lock's the hatter and wine merchants, Berry Bros. and Rudd, all of which Hudson may have got to know well on his visits.

Tatiana and her husband Robert make only brief appearances in this story but Robert played an important role if he was instrumental in finding Hugh as a prospective British husband for Mary, and he must have helped to find the flat in Shepherd Market when Mary and Germano first arrived in England. He travelled for business throughout Europe. His passport from the 1920s was valid for travel in Eastern Europe and Constantinople as well as Western Europe, including Germany and German-occupied territories, under the auspices of Messrs. Drysdale, Smith & Co. He was authorised to deal in silver bullion on behalf of the precious metal merchants Johnson Matthey & Co. and to deal with the Yugo-Slavian ExportTimber Company of Belgrade. By the late 1930s, his passport permitted travel to the countries of the Soviet Union and Turkey. Tatiana and Robert did not have children and she may well have accompanied him on some of his business trips, especially if they took her to see Mary and Kitty in Yugoslavia. They seemed to have lived in and around Piccadilly and, as war loomed, they made their home at 33 Curzon Street and then in Kensington. In the early 1960s, they moved to the Ladywell Lodge retirement home in Lewisham, where Robert died at the age of eighty-five in 1965. Tatiana came to live with Mary and Germano and went with them on some of their visits to Italy and Yugoslavia. In time, she needed more care and moved to a retirement home in Shortlands, not far from Beckenham and where, in 1976, she remarried an old friend, a widower called Robert Beggs. He died in 1984. The eldest of the Zybin children, Tatiana, survived all her siblings, dying just before her ninetieth birthday in 1992.

࿇

Mary opened her ballet school in 1950, when Tamara would have been settled in primary school, although she was already teaching at other studios in London, which was easily reached by train from Beckenham Junction and New Beckenham stations. As she says in the interview with Patricia Deane-Gray, she needed to support herself and, with dedication and hard work, she built a successful school and her reputation as a teacher of both classical ballet and character. By then, she had her own experience in Split and would have had the example of Eduardova, Poliakova and Preobrazhenskaya, and many others, to see that in the dance world women were well able to make their own mark running studios and companies. And she would also have seen the advantages of having her school within her home, while teaching in London at the same time.

Number 7 was big enough for the two main reception rooms to be used for the studio and changing room, as well for several flats for tenants on the upper floors. Until the studio was renovated in the early 1960s, the overwhelming impression was of an imposing and rather dark house, since the hall and changing rooms were poorly lit, as they often were in those big Victorian homes, and the floorboards were stained black or dark brown. The houses were almost impossible to heat adequately and even in summer the hall felt cool. In winter, the focal point of the old changing room was the round, black paraffin heater with its perforated top, which sent dancing patterns of light to the ceiling. The hall led into a dark passage where a black, pay telephone was installed (just like those in public telephone boxes with their chrome Button A and Button B), and a few steps down the passage led to Mary's sitting room and a dining room, and then the kitchen. It was a great treat to be invited into Mary's own part of the house and to be given such unheard-of delicacies as dried apricots and, later, Turkish coffee, which, of course, she knew well from the Ottoman influences in Yugoslavia. For some of us, the idea of a bar from which to serve drinks at home was quite unfamiliar – but it would have been something that Germano particularly enjoyed when entertaining his friends.

The studio walls were lined with photographs, two large mirrors leant against a wall and the *barres*, like the mirrors, were mismatched. The *barre* in front of the window had a particularly comfortable diameter and height. The window looked out onto Copers Cope Road and had a net curtain. The piano was a polished upright. The floor was refinished, since it was

Studio portrait of Nicolai Legat in the 1930s, courtesy of the Legat Foundation.

not splintered and full of nails (as was the case of the Max Rivers Studios in London), and it had a good spring. Mary allowed the use of rosin so, unlike Legat in St Petersburg and at his studio in Colet Gardens, she did not have a ritual of sprinkling the boards with a watering can before class. Since she told a few anecdotes about Legat, his photograph, a studio portrait, was particularly memorable with his long face and bald head. Among the other photographs there was at least one of John Gregory and another of him and his wife Barbara Vernon in a *pas de deux*. As part of the renovation in 1964, Mary opened up the cellar underneath the studio to make a comfortable changing room. There was good height in those Victorian cellars and the walls were whitewashed and rush matting covered the concrete floor. The renovation also made the studio much lighter with the addition of a large rear window and allowed the floor area to be extended. The mirrors remained in place, although for some reason the photographs did not. At the same time, a separate entrance to the school was installed at the side of the house.

Mary had a good head for business and, given her father's investments in property in Berlin, she may well have learned about the benefits of being a landlord from him. A friend of Mary's from Berlin, Erica Esslinger, was secretary for the school. They had known each other from Eduardova's classes but had lost touch for many years until they met by chance in London after the Second World War. Until the late 1970s, Erica lived in a small flat on the landing halfway up the stairs in rooms originally intended as servants' quarters since there was not a separate staircase. It was in the early 1950s that Mrs Courtney and her daughter Claire came to live in a flat above the studio. Mrs Courtney, ample and good humoured, took attendance for classes and supervised behaviour in the changing room. Claire was completing her ballet training in London at Mona Inglesby's International School of Ballet and tried to look after the rather neglected garden before she went to Yugoslavia to work with Ana Roje. On her return, she studied for her teacher's certificate, taught some classes for Mary, and helped with school performances, all at the same time that she was performing at the London Palladium. (Mr Courtney moved to number 7 when he retired from his work in Ireland, and he died there in 1961.)

Through her connections with other students of Legat's London studio, Mary became an examiner for the Association of Russian Ballet, the Federation of Russian Classical Ballet and, later, the Society of Russian Style Ballet Schools, and she maintained a busy teaching schedule. She joined the faculty of Barbara Vernon and John Gregory's recently established School of Russian Ballet early in 1950 to teach ballet and character, and continued to teach character there, if not ballet as well, at least until 1958. (The *Dancing Times* of October 1950 reports that Mary's former colleague in Belgrade, Anatoli Zhukovski, had given a series of classes in Balkan dances at the school.) In the early 1950s, she taught in summer courses at the Legat School, by then located in Tunbridge Wells. For some years, Mary also taught at the Judith Espinosa School and she choreographed ballet scenes for Judith Espinosa's troupe in the Christmas pantomime, "Dick Whittington", in Folkestone in 1952. She became the representative in England for Ana and Oskar's school at Kaštel Kambelovac in 1953 and taught there in the summers. From 1954, advertisements in the *Dancing Times* for the Roje-Harmoš International Ballet School referred readers to the Maria Zybina School of Russian Ballet, although earlier only her name, address and telephone number had been given.

Mary probably first met Anton Dolin at Legat's studio in the 1930s and later they were both examiners for the Association of Russian Ballet. But, while Dolin's links with Ana and with Nadine Nicolaeva were close, he and Mary did not work together. (I was entranced to see Dolin with Alicia Markova in the pantomime "Where the Rainbow Ends" as a family Christmas treat in 1958. It was probably my first experience of ballet performed on stage. Dolin was St George and Markova the Spirit of the Lake.)

Mary taught at the school that Mona Inglesby founded to support her International Ballet Company, whose studios were at 17 Queensberry Mews West in Kensington. According to advertisements in the *Dancing Times*, Mary taught classical ballet and then, in the last couple of years of the school's existence, she taught character. While she may well have taught at Kathleen Crofton's studio in the early 1950s, her name does not appear on those advertisements until around 1956, when she took over the character class from Lydia Sokolova. Crofton's classes were held at the Max Rivers Studios in Leicester House, 10/11 Great Newport Street. A little later, Mary taught professional level ballet for her on Monday, Tuesday, Thursday and Friday mornings, and character on Wednesday afternoons. They worked together quite closely in those days; in an advertisement from 1958, Mary's school in Beckenham is referred to as a branch studio for students and children. The Max Rivers Studios, surrounded by theatres and with Covent Garden nearby, were well used for rehearsals by opera singers and show people, as well as for ballet and character classes. The changing rooms were small, the walls and doors of the toilets, which were on half-landings in the stairwell, were covered with scurrilous graffiti, and the floors of the studios often needed sharp strokes of a hammer to deal with nails that had popped up. (Max Rivers, himself, was a performer and dance director who worked in film and on stage at least from the 1920s.) In Beckenham, Mary taught children's classes through the mornings on Saturdays and a limited number of classes in the evenings for older pupils. But by around 1961, she expanded the evening classes at the request of Katherine Morgan and another student who had attended the Association of Ballet Clubs summer school in Oxford and wished to have classes two or three times a week. Mary's own regular advertisement was a "professional card" that appeared each month in the "Where to Learn" pages of the *Dancing Times*.

Neither Mona Inglesby nor Kathleen Crofton was part of the Federation of Russian Classical Ballet but both had attended Legat's classes. Crofton was a few years older than Mary and Inglesby was a few years younger and they would all have known each other then. Crofton was born in December 1902 at Fyazabad in India, where her father was a soldier, and her mother had also been born in India. Her early training was with Legat's friend Laurent Novikoff in London, after which she toured with Pavlova's company for four and a half years and was a soloist in Pavlova's last season at Covent Garden in 1928. The writer Wendy Roxin Wicks includes biographical material on Crofton in her book, "Tim Draper: From Eastman Theatre's Muses to the Founding of Rochester City Ballet", calling her Pavlova's "baby ballerina". Crofton also toured in the United States and worked again with Novikoff in 1929 at the Chicago Opera Ballet. On her return to London in the early 1930s, Crofton studied with Legat but, when the plan to run a branch studio in St John's Wood failed to materialise, she went to Paris to study with Preobrazhenskaya and then danced with Nijinska's Théâtre de Danse, the Ballet Russe de Monte Carlo and Victor Dandré's Russian Ballet. Crofton's final professional engagements were with the Markova-Dolin Company, after which she returned to Paris to study again with Preobrazhenskaya and did not return to London until the outbreak of war. From 1939 to 1951 she was not involved at all with ballet; both Wicks and E.C. Mason (writing in *Dance and Dancers*, November 1956) say that she was completely occupied with "war work". (E.C. Mason was a regular contributor to the magazine and wrote a series of articles on dance teachers that includes Lydia Kyasht, Anna Lendrum and Patricia Spalding, as well as Mary.) What Crofton did during the war is not elaborated upon in either source. Of course, she might have gone into nursing or any number of other fields, but in writing this I remembered, even at the age of sixteen, being impressed by Crofton's sharp intellect and wondered if she might have worked in intelligence. A little research yielded the fact that she did, indeed, work in some capacity for the Inter-Service Liaison Department, or ISLD, which was the name under which MI6 operated in Asia, since she returned to England by sea from Colombo, Ceylon (Sri Lanka), in August 1945. Her name on the passenger list is under "ISLD", her occupation given as "War Off. Civ" and her permanent residence (residence for more than one year) as Ceylon. ISLD was based in New Delhi between 1941 and 1944, and then in Kandy, Ceylon, until 1946. This suggests that Crofton may have spent enough time in India as a child, and even through touring in Asia with Pavlova and others, to have the understanding of Asian customs and language that MI6 looked for in its civilian staff. That neither Mason nor Wicks give any details suggests not only that she was reticent about those details, but that she was, almost certainly, bound by the Official Secrets Act. (She and Mary may have discovered that they both worked for the British government during the war, but would not have attempted to learn any of the details.) The fact that Crofton did not return to ballet until 1951 suggests, too, that she was not simply demobilised after the war but held a position of some importance.

Crofton was a masterful proponent of the Russian classical tradition, although relatively little has been written about her. She did not wear any sort of practice costume for her classes and taught in elegant low-heeled street shoes. Her hair was parted and draped over the ears, and then drawn into a bun at the nape of the neck. She was particularly memorable for the fact that, rather than giving the names of the steps she wished to demonstrate, or even counting out the timing, she simply marked the movements with her hands and feet and accompanied herself by whistling, which was a challenge to both her students and her pianists. Crofton ran her studio in

Great Newport Street for about fifteen years until the beginning of 1966, when she moved to the newly established Dance Centre at 12 Floral Street behind the Royal Opera House in Covent Garden. Later that year, however, she accepted Markova's invitation to work with her at the Metropolitan Opera in New York and entrusted her students in London to Roger Tully, a student of Marie Rambert who went on to dance with International Ballet and Les Grands Ballets Canadiens, among other companies, before taking over Crofton's classes. Shortly after arriving in New York, Crofton moved to Buffalo to establish the Niagara Frontier Ballet and worked with other regional companies. After a disastrous fire in 1973, the studio and associated ballet company, Festival Ballet of New York, were disbanded and she became the artistic director of the Maryland Ballet Company until 1978. Having been appointed artistic director at the newly created Ballet Concordia in Rochester, New York, Crofton died suddenly at her desk on 30 November 1979. Her obituary appeared in the *Dancing Times* in January, 1980. She has not left a memoir and did not write extensively for the dance magazines. In a short piece in the *Dancing Times* in January 1951 she describes Preobrazhenskaya's approach to teaching and, in July 1954, she contrasts film images of Pavlova with the great variety of her roles and the breadth of her technical abilities.

Much younger than Crofton, Mona Inglesby was born in London as Mona Vredenberg in May 1918, just before the end of the First World War. Her memoir, "Ballet in the Blitz", deals more with the company than with the school so it is not surprising that Mary is not mentioned. Inglesby was something of a prodigy since she played the piano in concerts at London's Wigmore Hall from the age of nine, and won prizes in riding shows, as well as studying ballet. Between the ages of twelve and seventeen, she was a student of Marie Rambert and joined Ballet Club at the age of only fourteen. But she became increasingly dissatisfied with the Cecchetti method followed by Rambert and was encouraged by the dancer Diana Gould to go to Paris to work with Mathilde Kschessinskaya. Kschessinskaya's classes, and performances at the Paris Opera, were a revelation. Inglesby learned about Legat at this time too and worked with him at the Colet Gardens studio whenever his classes could be fitted into the Ballet Club schedule. She went to Paris as often as possible and studied with Lubov Egorova and Preobrazhenskaya, as well as Kschessinskaya. Working with these teachers of the Russian system provided the "release" from Cecchetti's method that she had been looking for and resulted in a rapid improvement in her technique.

However, her embrace of the Russian approach was seen by Rambert as a betrayal and life became increasingly uncomfortable at Ballet Club. Egorova was instrumental in introducing her to Victor Dandré, who, as manager of the company, took her on for a short season with the Covent Garden Russian Ballet in 1939. She may well have taken the company classes with Ana Roje that summer.

Although Inglesby was invited to join de Basil's company for the Australian tour she declined as war was looming. She volunteered as an ambulance driver but managed to persuade her father to support the formation of International Ballet, for which she would both choreograph and dance using her mother's maiden name. Her objective was to keep a group of dancers together since so many had become dispersed because of the war, and to present ballet to audiences outside London. Central to the company's success was its association with Nicolai Sergeyev, who, unhappy in his position as ballet master with Ninette de Valois's Vic-Wells company, was ready to support the new venture. He still possessed his copies of some of the notations made by Vladimir Stepanov of the Mariinsky ballets that he had brought with him when he fled Russia in 1919. As a result, International Ballet became the western custodian of these Mariinsky works and staged "Giselle", "Aurora's Wedding/The Sleeping Beauty/Grand pas d'action", "Coppélia", and "The Polovtsian Dances" from "Prince Igor" and "Swan Lake". (On Stepanov's death in 1896, Alexander Gorsky worked further on the notation system and, when Gorsky left St Petersburg for Moscow, Sergeyev took over the task, assisted by Alexander Chekrygin, Victor Rakhmanov and Nikolai Kremnev.) Sergeyev's copies found their final home at the Harvard Theatre Collection in 1969. Both the Royal Ballet and the Kirov companies had turned down Inglesby's offer of the papers but both have drawn on the Harvard collection for the original choreography. Sergeyev was instrumental in establishing the International School of Ballet in 1943 so that he would have young dancers coming into the company, despite the difficulties of running a ballet school in London during the war. In her memoir, Inglesby makes only passing reference to Sergeyev's days when he was *régisseur* at the Mariinsky and sided with the management of the theatre during the strike of 1905. On a visit to Paris, she observed that Kschessinskaya seemed to dislike him, while Egorova, on the other hand, was enthusiastic that he was working with Inglesby, perhaps recognising the opportunity it gave her company to present the Mariinsky choreography. Nevertheless, Sergeyev was integral to the success of International Ballet and his death in June 1951 was a personal loss to Inglesby and the loss of a mainstay of the company.

A mark of International Ballet's accomplishments was the invitation to appear in the inaugural performance at the Royal Festival Hall on 3 May 1951, attended by King George VI and Queen Elizabeth, followed by an engagement at the Coliseum and return to the Royal Festival Hall in July and August. For that season, the stage was extended over the orchestra pit to provide space for the Mariinsky classics as well as "Capriccio Español", "Gâité Parisienne", "Carnaval" and "Les Sylphides". Claire Faraci (Courtney) remembers that the stage was well-sprung, but the open area underneath meant that *pointe* shoes had to be quite soft so as to make less noise. However, only two years after the successful season at the Royal Festival Hall, Inglesby was forced to disband her company when the Arts Council turned down a modest request for support. The school continued in operation until the mid-1950s. It is only recently that Inglesby's contribution to the development of ballet in Britain during the war and in the following years has been recognised. (See Brown's "The Black-Out Ballet: The Invisible Woman of British Ballet" and Eliot's "Albion's Dance".) Unlike de Valois, she was not trying to foster "British ballet"; she was simply determined to maintain Russian traditions and the Russian classics in her company's *répertoire*. She was much younger than both de Valois and Rambert and was very young when she founded International Ballet. Even though she had Sergeyev to lend his weight and experience, and Stanislas Idzikowski as ballet master in the early 1940s, the company had a relatively short life and Inglesby was never accepted as part of the British establishment. And, unlike both de Valois and Rambert, she was never honoured.

Mary would have gone to the performances of International Ballet because other students from Inglesby's school were dancing, as well as Claire Courtney, and she must also have gone to see the Yugoslav National Opera and Ballet Company in their three-week season at the Stoll Theatre in January 1955. By then, Ana Roje and Oskar Harmoš were no longer directors of the ballet company in Zagreb, but Mary knew Nenad Lhotka and his English wife Jill from her teaching in Yugoslavia and, because of the close links between Split and Zagreb, she would have known a number of the other dancers, as well as Margarita Froman, who accompanied the tour. She would have been interested to see performances of "The Devil in the Village", "Ero the Joker", "The Gingerbread Heart", "Romeo and Juliet" and "Prince Igor"; "Ero the Joker" was conducted by Gotovac himself. A special train was arranged for the two hundred and fifty-strong orchestra, ballet and opera companies. The presentation of works, such as "The Devil in the Village", combining both classical ballet and folk-dance elements, was unfamiliar to the audiences, and at the time, so was the idea of a ballet version of a Shakespeare play in "Romeo and Juliet" danced to Sergei Prokofiev's music (despite Nijinska's ballet for Diaghilev in 1926). Generally, "Romeo and Juliet" seems to have been the least well received. The critic A.V. Coton wrote in the *Spectator* (11 February 1955) that the performances were well danced, although he felt that the choreography for "Romeo and Juliet" was "over-simple" and used "too much 'literal' mime". In the *Dancing Times* (March 1955), the dance teacher and writer Joan Lawson enjoyed "The Devil in the Village" and praised the dancing and acting of Nenad Lhotka and Sonia Kastl but was less excited about Margarita Froman's choreography for "Romeo and Juliet" and "The Gingerbread Heart".

From the earliest days, Mary worked very hard to build up her school in Beckenham and to find as many opportunities as possible for her students to perform. On a small and local scale, for several years her students were a fixture at the annual summer fête of the League of Pity and at the autumn fair in the Beckenham Public Hall. Mary choreographed and staged the dance numbers for three pantomimes produced by the Beckenham Amateur Dramatic Society and she mounted a school performance at least once a year. In the mid-1950s, she took over the Lewisham Ballet Theatre Club from Maria Balinska, who was a fellow member of the Federation of Russian Classical Ballet and who Mary would have known from Legat's studio as well. Mary's pupils could be coopted into the Club's performances, and vice versa when she needed adult dancers for school performances. This busy schedule took a tremendous amount of organisation and preparation which, in the eyes of her students at least, Mary seemed to undertake almost effortlessly. The Lewisham Club was certainly active by 1950 and probably had been for a few years before that. Referred to simply as "Lewisham" in most conversations, the Club met, took class and rehearsed in secondary schools as part of the borough evening adult education system. In the first half of the 1950s, classes were held at Brownhill Road School in Catford (Catford Boys' School) and may have continued there when Mary took over from Balinska, teaching classes in ballet and character at least once a week.

With her school in Beckenham well established, in the 1960s Mary's classes in London became more focused on character rather than ballet. The field was less crowded and she was becoming a recognised expert in European character dances. She did not teach at the Dance Centre in Floral Street as soon as it was opened by Gary Cockrell and Valerie Hyman in 1964, because their primary aim was to provide modern and jazz classes in London. But by early 1966 she was listed among the instructors, giving classes in "Central European National" in an advertisement in the *Dancing Times*, while Crofton and Eileen Ward (who had danced with Ballet Rambert and also taught at the Royal Ballet School) were among the teachers of classical ballet. Mary took out her own advertisement in the May issue of the magazine to announce open classes for students and teachers on Tuesday evenings and Saturday afternoons, as well as to give information on the studio in Beckenham. Probably because of being well known at the Dance Centre, Mary was asked to coach the pop singer Dave Dee in Russian character steps for the television show, "Top of the Pops". Dee was the lead for the group Dave Dee, Dozy, Beaky, Mick & Tich and he wanted a Cossack dance for the launch of their Russian-influenced record "Okay!" The note and photograph in the *Dancing Times* of July 1967, show Mary wearing Russian character boots and Dee in Russian costume – evidently, he was a capable pupil. From mid-1967, Mary taught character on Mondays at 1.45pm at 26 West Street, Cambridge Circus (classes were offered at six shillings and sixpence). At that time, the studio in West Street was run by Anna Northcote who had started teaching there in 1941, sharing space with Vera Volkova. Northcote was another student of Legat at Colet House and she went on to dance with de Basil's Ballets Russes and the Dandré-Levitoff Russian Ballet using the name Anna Severskaya. (The *Dancing Times* of January 1969 carried a note on her closing the historic location after a ten-year tenancy, presumably when she was responsible for the lease. The premises had been used for ballet since the 1920s and in the 1930s Margaret Craske had her studio there, the Craske-Ryan School with Mabel Ryan.)

Mary and Vera Volkova must have known of one another, possibly from Legat's studio. Although she hardly comes into Mary's story, like Cleo Nordi, Volkova is an important link between Legat's years in London and when he taught in Russia. She trained at Akim Volynsky's School of Russian Ballet in Petrograd where Legat taught before leaving Russia, and she also attended the studio in Colet Gardens for a brief period before his death. She was born in May 1905 in Tomsk, where her father was stationed, though the family home was St Petersburg. Alexander Meinertz's "Vera Volkova, A Biography" provides detail on Volkova's early life and her training at Volynsky's school, where Legat's student Agrippina Vaganova was her principal teacher. She graduated in 1925 but found it difficult to establish a career as a dancer. She left Russia in 1929, travelling to the Pacific coast, where she danced in Shanghai. She did not arrive in England until 1936, having met the man who secured her passage and who she later married. Ninette de Valois engaged her to take over from Sergeyev at the Sadler's Wells School but she did not remain in de Valois's favour and from 1942 she taught in London only from the studio in West Street.

∽

Unlike Mary, Germano did not go back to Yugoslavia for many years. Given the circumstances of when he left in 1946 it was not until he had a British passport that he felt confident of being able to travel freely. Tamara recalls that his passport application was signed by an influential person in the British government. That could not have been Bill Hudson but could have been another friend from the war years, possibly even the same person whose telegram brought Mary to London with the fabricated news of Tatiana's illness. Before Germano had his own passport, he and Mary would drive with Tamara across Europe to Venice, where he would stay at the then relatively undeveloped beach resort of Lido di Jesolo while Mary and Tamara went on into Yugoslavia. Mary and Germano shared the driving, although she may have been more comfortable undertaking these journeys for the first few years at least. Certainly, it was not unusual that Mary drove – it was essential in order for her to get to the adult classes she taught at the Lewisham Club – but she was a good and confident driver. Hugh, or one of the legation staff, had taught her in Belgrade and she would have honed her skills in the days when she had her father's car and drove across Europe between England and Yugoslavia, and maybe to other countries as well.

Germano first returned to Yugoslavia in the early 1960s, shaking with apprehension as he approached the border with Italy and fearful that he would not be able to leave again. By then his mother had died. There were letters, of course, but she had had to live without ever seeing her son after he left Split. Germano's father still lived in Split on the upper floor of his large square house at Francopanska ulica 27. On a family holiday in 1965, my family met up with Mary and Germano, and Tamara and her husband,

Claudio, and visited Germano's father one evening at his flat. My memory is hazy, but we all sat around the table in the big kitchen and I am sure there was *šljivovica* for the adults and delicious snacks for everyone. Germano and his father looked very much alike – his father was simply an older version of Germano himself.

As travel from Yugoslavia became easier in the 1960s, Mary's sister Kitty and her husband Viktor Starčić came to England for a visit in the spring or summer of 1964. By then, he was a well-known theatre and film actor, and had worked with a number of British stars. His arrival prompted an article in the local paper. (It also refers to the renovated studio and a planned trip to Russia.) Many years later, I met an actor and director who had studied with Starčić at the Theatre Academy in Belgrade and immigrated to Toronto with his wife after the breakup of Yugoslavia. He remembered Starčić fondly and with a degree of reverence, both for his work and for his personality. Viktor himself estimated that he had played some five hundred roles in theatre and film. He appeared in over one hundred films, starting in 1927 in the role of the thief Lajoša in the silent film "Gresnica bez greha" ("The Sinner without Sin"), directed by Kosta Novaković, and ending with an episode in the television drama series "Sedam sekretara SKOJ-a" ("Seven Secretaries of SKOJ"), which aired after his death in 1981. (SKOJ was the League of Communist Youth.) He received numerous awards and honours, including a set of crystal water glasses and jug presented to him by Tito, and a lifetime achievement award in 1964. As well as appearing in Yugoslav productions, Viktor worked with internationally known actors including Anthony Quinn, Michael Redgrave and John Le Mesurier in the satirical drama "La Vingt-cinquième heure" ("The 25th Hour"), and Broderick Crawford in "Square of Violence". He continued to work through his seventies and died in 1980, some years after Kitty. In recognition of his life's work, he is buried in the Aisle of the Deserving Citizens in the New Cemetery in Belgrade.

Mary returned to Russia only once after her family left in 1918 when she went on a trip for ballet teachers led by Joan Lawson. The visit was organised by the Society for Cultural Relations with the USSR (now the Society for Cooperation in Russian and Soviet Studies) and included some members of the London Ballet Circle and the Children's Theatre Group.

The Annual Report for 1964 has a brief note on the tour. It acknowledges the assistance of individuals in the USSR–Great Britain Society in Moscow and the Leningrad Society, as well as the well-regarded teachers, Asaf Messerer and Mme Golovkina of the Bolshoi school and company, Mme Dudinskya of the Kirov company, Mme Balabina of the Vaganova School and Igor Moiseyev, founder of the Moiseyev Folk Dance Ensemble, who assisted in arranging attendance at performances, classes and rehearsals. There were eight people in the ballet teachers' group (including John Gregory and Barbara Vernon) and ten others representing the Children's Theatre Group. One of the participants, Jean Currie, wrote a two-part article for the *Dancing Times* (March and April 1965) describing the visit. The party left Liverpool Street Station in London on 28 December 1964 and travelled to Moscow via the Hook of Holland, East Berlin, Warsaw, Brest Litovsk, Minsk and Smolensk. They arrived at the Belorussky Station in the already darkening afternoon two and a half days later, on 30 December. They stayed at the Berlin Hotel, which appeared to be largely unchanged from 1917, although it was built as the Savoy Hotel in 1913 and renamed the Berlin in 1959 (the original name was reinstated in 1989). Located on a side street off Teatralny prospekt, it was within easy reach of the Bolshoi Theatre, which is where the party was taken, almost as soon as they arrived, to see "Giselle" with Natalia Bessmertnova and Maris Liepa. On the next evening, New Year's Eve, they saw Maya Plisetskaya and Nikolai Fadeychev in "Romeo and Juliet", followed by "Swan Lake" with Nina Timofeyeva and "Tixomov" (possibly Vladimir Tikhonov). On the last evening of their four or five days in Moscow, the group saw the first performance of "Leili and Medjnun" with Raisa Struchkova and Vladimir Vasiliev. In Leningrad, they stayed at the Astoria Hotel, which had opened just before the Berlin and which overlooks St Isaac's Square and Cathedral. A second performance of "Swan Lake" was seen at the Kirov Theatre with Margarita Alfimova and Vadim Budarin, and "The Little Humpbacked Horse" followed at the Maly Theatre.

In articles for the *Dancing Times* (March and May 1965), Gregory describes visits to the Kirov and Bolshoi schools, which must have been attended by all the ballet teachers. In addition to the ballet performances and visits to the Bolshoi and Kirov schools, Mary would have been particularly interested in attending a specially arranged rehearsal of the Moiseyev Ensemble and performances of the Red Army and Moiseyev ensembles, as well as a Ukrainian group which may have been the P. Virsky Ukrainian

National Folk Dance Ensemble. Mary would have known Joan Lawson, who by then was teaching character and mime at the Royal Ballet School, and in Russia they must have compared notes on their shared interest in character dance. Indeed, the two of them may have made sure that rehearsals as well as performances of the Moiseyev, Red Army and Ukrainian groups were on the itinerary. Mary must have known also of Legat's granddaughter Tatiana (from his marriage to Antonina), then a soloist with the Kirov company and married to principal dancer Yuri Soloviev, but it is impossible to say if they ever met, either when Mary was in Leningrad or when the company toured to London. After their full programme, the group left Leningrad on 8 January 1965. The cost per person was just under £100. At approximately £2,000 in today's terms, it was very good value and may well have been subsidised.

While in Moscow, Mary took the opportunity to look at the outside of her former family home in Pokrovsky Boulevard, discovering that it was occupied by the Embassy of Persia. Like Farhad Sepahbody (whose recollections are mentioned in Chapter 3), she must have found it drab and grey compared to her memories. Parts of the train journey to and from Russia would have been familiar from Mary's earlier travels. But it must have been tantalising to go through Berlin in both directions, perhaps stopping at the Friedrichstrasse station in East Berlin at the border, since she would have had little time or opportunity to search for familiar streets and buildings. (However, a few years later, Mary was able to join a group on a short visit to East Berlin and saw the buildings that had been owned by her father.)

Mary would have met Anatoly Borzov, choreographer and instructor with the Moiseyev Ensemble, on this trip, if not earlier on his own visits to London. Later in 1965, Borzov came to England for three weeks to give classes in Russian character dance to teachers and students at the invitation of the Society for Cultural Relations with the USSR, and wrote an account of his visit, "The Russian Rope that Tied Them in Knots" in the *Dancing Times*, January 1966. In an accompanying note to Borzov's article, Kathleen Crofton credits Joan Lawson for the idea and organisation of Borzov's visit. In his article, Borzov says he found it particularly difficult to get across to his English students what he called the "dancing image" of the Russian character, an idea quite similar to the fire or spirit that Legat describes in his own article, "What is 'Élan' in Dancing?" Borzov lists some of the basic steps, the rope (or chain) step (*vereovshka*), double rope step, rope step with a stamp, *pripadanye, koveryalochka* and the accordion step, steps which Mary's students already knew, but not then by name. She invited him to give a class to students of her school and at former student, Linda Neech's Russian Dance Theatre Club at the Churchdown Evening Institute in Bromley on 24 November. This was followed on the next Wednesday by a class at the Malory Comprehensive School at Downham. Perhaps Mary's students, already well experienced in character, and with the benefit of her teaching, especially following her trip to Russia, were better able than most to show the "dancing image" which Borzov was looking for.

∾

In 1967, Mary and Germano celebrated the silver anniversary of their marriage in Split with a party in the studio. But, while Tamara's wedding to Claudio Campanati and their silver wedding anniversary were important family occasions, perhaps even more significant was finally gaining ownership of a house at Milna on the Adriatic island of Brač. This had been arranged through the government in Yugoslavia in exchange for Germano's father's house in Split when the land was needed for redevelopment for the modern buildings which now line Francopanska ulica. (In the event, the house was not pulled down and still stands.) There were no direct family links with Brač and Milna, but friends already had homes there. I remember Mary's joy when, at last, all the paperwork was completed. Later, politics intervened once again; after the breakup of Yugoslavia, Tamara had to prove ownership of the house but was able to secure it in 2003. As well, Mary had started the task of establishing the rights to her father's property in Berlin, even as early as the early 1950s, and expressed hope that Tamara would be able to achieve what she had not. After the fall of the Berlin Wall, Tamara was able to demonstrate prior ownership of the buildings and was granted possession of a large flat, close to, but not in, one of the buildings owned by Nicolas Zybin. She also looked into claiming ownership of the house in Moscow as the Soviet Union crumbled but, whether or not the claim was well founded, the bureaucratic barriers were impossible to penetrate. Knowing so well the value of property, Mary had repeatedly tried to purchase the freehold of number 7 Copers Cope Road without success. Tamara continued those efforts but, by the 1960s, the Victorian houses with their big gardens were being replaced by flats and townhouses and, with competitive interest from developers, it was out of reach. The house was eventually sold after Mary's death and a three-storey block of flats, known as Sycamore Court, stands in its place. Now, just one Victorian house, number 11, remains between the lots for numbers 7 and 17, and number 17 has been replaced by another low-rise development, Nettlestead Close.

CHAPTER 17
ANA ROJE AND OSKAR HARMOŠ AND THEIR INTERNATIONAL SCHOOL OF BALLET AT KAŠTEL KAMBELOVAC

She [Ana] was already his [Legat's] assistant. He was very interested in her and thought her very talented.

Maria Zybina, interview with Patricia Deane-Gray.

Meanwhile, Ana and Oskar pursued their own careers in Yugoslavia. Having been reinstated as directors of the Zagreb National Ballet after the Second World War, they held those positions until 1950. Early in their tenure they staged "Schéhérazade", "Carnaval" and "Rhapsody", as well as "The Devil in the Village". In 1947, they mounted "Petrushka" and "Bolero", "Simfonijsko kolo" ("Symphonic Kolo") to Gotovac's music and "The Fountain of Bakhchisarai". Margarita Froman's "Romeo and Juliet" was staged in June 1948, with Ana as Juliet, Oskar as Tybalt and Nenad Lhotka as Romeo. Ana's moving and dramatic performance was rewarded with a Federal prize the following year. Oskar then produced Hristić's "The Legend of Ochrid", which must have been based on Froman's choreography, although a poster for the performance on 24 April 1949 credits him with direction and choreography and lists Nenad Lhotka as assistant choreographer. "The Sleeping Beauty" was staged in November 1950 with Ana as Princess Aurora and Franje Jelinčić as the Prince. This was Ana and Oskar's last performance as directors and the running of the company was taken over by Đurda Đurdan, one of the soloists. They were then invited to Split by Silvije Bombardelli, director of the National Theatre there, since he wished to have more full evening programmes of ballet. Initially they staged the dance pieces for the operas "Carmen" and "Faust", and then longer works including "Chopiniana", "Pictures at an Exhibition" to Modest Mussorgsky's music, and the second act of "Swan Lake". The first performance of "Pictures at an Exhibition" was in January 1954.

Although Yugoslavia was somewhat more open than countries behind the Iron Curtain in the 1950s, international travel to the West was possible only for those who could justify scientific or cultural purposes and Ana's and Oskar's trips in the early years of the decade may have been facilitated by the political connections of Ana's brothers. After their years directing the company in Zagreb, it was recognised that, as they moved away from performing into teaching, they needed to see what was being done outside Yugoslavia, as well as the fact that Ana had recently been appointed technical adviser to the Federation of Russian Classical Ballet. Over the three summers of 1950 to 1952, they travelled to England where they taught for Nicolaeva at the Legat School and lived in the lodge near the entrance gate at Warberry House. Ana appeared in her costume for the role of Biljana in the "Legend of Ochrid" on the front cover of the March 1951 issue of the *Dancing Times*. On that visit, they contributed *pas de deux* from the second act of "Swan Lake" and "Les Sylphides" to the programme for the second of twelve lectures on the Legat system given by Nicolaeva at the London studio of her school in Drury Lane. Later in the year, a Yugoslav group presented "The Legend of Ochrid", "A Ballad of Medieval Love" and "The Gingerbread Heart" at the Edinburgh Festival on 3 and 8 September in the Empire Theatre. Many of the dancers were from the Belgrade Theatre but Nenad Lhotka danced the role of the Prince in "A Ballad of Medieval Love" and Veseljko Sulić, another student of Ana and Oskar, was in the *corps de ballet* for all performances.

Franje Jelinčić and Veseljko Sulić were among the principal dancers in Ballet Legat, which was founded by Nicolaeva to provide her students with formal stage experience. The first performances took place in November 1951, first in Hull and then at the King's Theatre, Hammersmith, followed by a tour in England and then an engagement in Amsterdam. A challenging undertaking at the best of times, even a short tour would have been demanding in the post-war years. Jill Lhotka's description in "Dance to the Challenge" captures the trials of such a life – dismal lodgings, poor food and uncertain pay. The tour ran out of money and she goes on to recount how her stepfather helped to bring home the dancers who were stranded in Amsterdam.

∽

Ana and Oskar founded the Roje-Harmoš International Ballet School in 1953 at Kaštel Kambelovac, a small town on the Dalmatian coast about fifteen kilometres north of Split. A villa on the water's edge was made available by the municipal authorities in Split and, despite its seaside setting, a strict schedule of lectures and classes was maintained. A note in the *Dancing Times* of July 1954 reports that a maximum of twelve carefully selected students between the ages of fifteen and eighteen would be subject to a six-month trial period. The curriculum extended to character and national dances, *pas de deux*, teacher training, music, history of ballet and study of the Croatian language. All those who have described the relationship between Ana and Oskar observe that Ana devoted herself to her dancing and teaching, while Oskar took responsibility for the organisation of the school and practical issues such as buying and preparing food, although of course he maintained his own performing and teaching activities. Ana's connections with the Ballets Russes companies resulted in her first visit to New York in 1954, when she taught for five months at the Ballet Russe de Monte Carlo School of Ballet and she also taught regularly for Serge Denham at the Ballet Russe de Monte Carlo in the United States through the 1950s.

It was possible, although in those days rather unusual, for young students to travel from England to Yugoslavia but, in the early 1950s, a number went from the Legat School to study with Ana and Oskar, first in Zagreb and then in Kaštel Kambelovac. They made sure that their students had opportunities to perform regularly at the theatre in Split. This also allowed some of the larger works to be staged there and gave many of the dancers their first semi-professional experience. Ana's brothers' connections with Tito allowed a jeep to be imported from England and, for a while, it was the only motor vehicle in the area. Oskar would drive the overcrowded jeep between Split and Kaštel Kambelovac on roads that were full of cows, chickens and people, but few other cars. In August 1954, an evening of ballet was put on by the school with a programme of excerpts from "Les Sylphides", two of the pictures from Oskar's "Pictures at an Exhibition" ("Gnome" and "The Old Castle") and "The Dying Swan", performed by Ana to the accompaniment of pianist Krešimir Šipuš. (In Ana's biography, Legat is credited with the choreography, and Nicolaeva notes that he did create a version for her. However, Jill Lhotka recalls in "Dance to the Challenge" that Victor Dandré taught the solo to Ana since it was planned that she would dance it in a film to be made about Pavlova – a project that was not completed because of the outbreak of the Second World War.) Oskar's ballet "Stranac" ("Stranger"), to music by Bombardelli, was first staged in January 1956 and was taken to Belgrade and Zagreb the following year. The links between Ana and Oskar and dancers in England from their years at Legat's studio included Anton Dolin, who mounted "Giselle" on the company in Split in January 1957. Later in the year, the production was also taken to Zagreb.

Then Jill Morse, Jill Lhotka was one of the first students from the Legat School to study with Ana and Oskar. She had been ill while at the school and had been advised by her doctor that she should recover away from the cold and damp of England. That advice would have been impossible to act upon had Ana and Oskar not been on one of their visits to the school and they suggested that she should study with them in Zagreb for a few months. Jill's adventures on the journey from Paris, not on the Simplon–Orient Express as planned but on a series of trains and with various people who helped her on her way, are recounted in her memoir. Deirdre Hodgens and Jürgen Pagels, also students at the Legat School, went there at the same time. (Deirdre Hodgens later took the stage name of Deirdre O'Conaire.) Classes were taken in a studio in Ana and Oskar's flat at number 20 Bulatova ulica and a photograph in Ana's biography shows a picture of Legat on the studio wall. For Jill, the food, the climate, and the wine, as well as the ballet classes, were the tonic she needed. Food was more plentiful and more varied than in post-war England, although household items and clothes were scarce. Not only was Oskar a good cook himself (delighting Legat years earlier with artichokes and *hollandaise* sauce in their lodgings in London), but their Austro-Hungarian cook Tante Lise prepared wonderful central European dishes.

Over the years, other students from the Legat School who went to train with Ana and Oskar included Patricia Sherwood from Bermuda, Myles Marsden from the United States, Shirley de Burgh from Brazil and Annie Vertabedian from Armenia. Claire Courtney went from Inglesby's school in London and Jelko Yuresha, Herci Muntić and Marijan (Marjan) Jagušt were among the students from Croatia. Mary's daughter, Tamara, joined them in the summer. (Rather later, in 1957, Kathleen Crofton's pupils Donald Barclay and Joselyn Matisse were engaged with the company in Split, but would have continued their training with Ana and Oskar.) Oskar also wanted to show the young dancers more of his country and arranged at least one tour for Ana and himself, with Jill, Deirdre and Jürgen, and with Šipuš as accompanist. They travelled by train to a number of cities including Dubrovnik and also performed at an army camp at Slavonska Požega. The training of these students at a pre-professional and professional level stood them in good stead and most, if not all, went on to join major ballet companies, to perform in musicals and films, and to found their own schools.

Ana had special qualities, both as a dancer and as a teacher. Anna Lendrum notes that she was a true ballerina with brilliant technique and tireless energy as a teacher, and Ana herself says that she followed Legat in seeing every student as an individual, helping them with honesty, to find their own path in ballet. In an article first published in December 1954 in *Dance Magazine* and reproduced in her biography, she writes that a teacher must work with the psychological as well as the physical characteristics of a pupil and to develop a real friendship between them. Fernau Hall visited the school at Kaštel Kambelovac in 1958 and wrote an article for *Ballet Today* in which he compared the atmosphere of Ana's classes to those of Legat's studio in London two decades earlier. Ana's regard for technique is reflected in a short note which appeared in the *Dancing Times* (May 1958). She had been asked to write a review of the visit of the Kirov company to Zagreb in 1958 for the paper *Vesnik* and had great praise for the *corps de ballet* in their precision, elegance and épaulement, and for the freedom of their soaring jumps. However, she also observed that Vaganova had not maintained Legat's approach to "the laws of balance", that balance *en pointe* was no longer than a few seconds and the number of turns in *pirouettes* was also limited. Ana had particularly good balance *en pointe*, and Legat wrote about the ability of his brother Sergei to turn multiple *pirouettes*, so she must have made sure that her pupils understood how to master these technical feats but, in accordance with Legat's approach, without strain or showiness.

♺

After Ballet Legat folded, Jill Lhotka (who used the stage name Alis) joined the cast of "Three Cheers", a revue at the London Casino to celebrate the coronation of Queen Elizabeth II. Ana arranged for her to lodge with the Vladimiroffs at number 1 Colet Gardens and with whom Ana had stayed when she was studying with Legat. (As we have seen, the house was occupied by Mrs Viatkin in those days. Widowed, she had recently married Alexander Vladimiroff.) In "Dance to the Challenge", Jill says that the Vladimiroffs worked for the British government deciphering codes and were part of a group that had been involved in intelligence during the war as, of course, had Mary during her time as a translator in Split. (If there is little information on the work that Mary did, there is even less on Ana and Oskar's activities. But, as the photograph in Ana's biography shows, former British prime minister Clement Attlee visited the school at Kaštel Kambelovac in August, 1953 when he was invited to Yugoslavia by Tito. Attlee, himself, says only that he holidayed as a guest of the government.) Mary and Germano introduced Jill to their friend Bill Hudson, who then often came to watch "Three Cheers" and took her to nightclubs after the performance, and to the Hurlingham Club in the afternoons where he played tennis. Hurlingham House was built in 1760 as a gentleman's residence and afternoons at the club and in its extensive grounds must have seemed for Jill a world of comfort and luxury far removed from the theatre. At Hudson's suggestion, they also visited her parents at their home in Swindon. But, inexplicably, after "Three Cheers" closed in June 1953, he vanished from Jill's life. Many years later, she learned from Oskar that, despite his feelings for her, Hudson believed that the twenty-year difference in their ages was too great and that he should simply disappear. She never heard from him again.

Ana and Oskar invited Jill back to Yugoslavia to dance with the company in Split. A romance blossomed between Jill and Nenad Lhotka, who was with the ballet company in Zagreb and came to Split to dance in a production of "The Devil in the Village" in June, 1954. It was encouraged by Oskar, who, even then, may well have known why Hudson decided to disappear. At Nenad's urging, Jill applied to and was successful in joining the company in Zagreb, and they were married later that year. She was given away by Oskar and, since they both had to be back at work in the theatre on the following Monday, Oskar drove them from the wedding reception to Nenad's brother's flat – in the jeep, of course. By the autumn of 1955, Jill and Nenad were preparing to move to Canada, where he had been invited to join the Royal Winnipeg Ballet as ballet master and she was engaged as a soloist. One of his first ballets for the company was a staging of "The Devil in the Village". However, their time was cut short by a clash of temperaments with the newly appointed principal dancer Ruthanna Boris and her husband Frank Hobi. Nenad resigned in September 1956, taking Jill with him, and opened the Nenad Lhotka Academy of Dance in Winnipeg. In her memoir, Jill notes that Nenad had been brought to the Royal Winnipeg Ballet at least in part because of his European classical background. In practice, however, their experience and training in Legat's Russian system did not fit easily with the company's approach.

Claire Courtney first met Ana in 1952 through Mary, who arranged for her to have private lessons at the studio in Beckenham in order to get over an injury. Mary believed that Ana was particularly able to work with and rehabilitate injury and Claire made a full recovery. She remembers that Ana's understanding of how the body works allowed her to look at a pupil's physique and see what needed correction or strengthening – the same approach as taken by Legat – and showed Claire how to take full advantage of her jumps. Wishing to continue her training with Ana, she turned down an offer to join the Sadler's Wells Theatre Ballet and travelled back to Kaštel Kambelovac with Ana and Oskar in a convoy consisting of a truck and the famous jeep. She spent a year there, at the same time as Patricia Sherwood, Deirdre Hodgens, Myles Marsden, Shirley de Burgh and Annie Vertabedian. A particular memory is of Oskar taking her to find ingredients for her birthday cake, as specified by Tante Lise. Since the required quantities of luxuries like eggs and chocolate had to be obtained on the black market and Oskar told Claire to look pitiful as he negotiated the purchases. But she also remembers Oskar as a wonderful partner, as does Jill, and able to do spectacular lifts. Both the partnering and the lifts would have been due to Legat's teaching. Photographs show Legat instructing Serge Renoff how to lift Nicolaeva above his head on one outstretched arm and similarly spectacular lifts are shown in photographs of Ana and Oskar in Ana's biography. When the time came for her to go back to England, Claire travelled with Shirley on the Simplon–Orient Express; the thought of two young girls travelling alone across Europe might have caused almost as much anxiety for their parents as the outward journey by road would have done. On her return to England, Claire auditioned successfully for the popular television variety show "Sunday Night at the London Palladium", hosted by comedian Tommy Trinder and entertainer Bruce Forsyth. That would have been another surprise decision since she was expected to audition instead for the London Festival Ballet, which was founded in 1950 by Alicia Markova and Anton Dolin. Claire continued to live at number 7 Copers Cope Road and taught some classes for Mary. Her colleagues from the Palladium came to celebrate her twenty-first birthday at a party in the studio in 1958. Claire then went to Paris to rehearse "La Parisienne" in preparation for the show opening in Las Vegas and, after Las Vegas, she took a short engagement in San Francisco. Although Claire and Donne

Parsons went out together for a while, and the families at number 7 and number 17 expected them to marry, she had already met Jimmy Faraci at the Palladium. Also known as Jimmy Vincent, he was a noted jazz drummer from the United States, where they met up again. They married and settled near Las Vegas.

Among Ana and Oskar's other students, Deirdre Hodgens (O'Conaire) joined the London Festival Ballet around 1958 and then the Royal Ballet where she was a soloist until she retired in the early 1970s. Shirley de Burgh became a dancer on Broadway, appearing in "Oh, Captain!", "Redhead" (for which Bob Fosse was the choreographer), "13 Daughters" and "Coco", and in the film "Pepe". She went on to act in the popular television series "Out on a Limb", "Fantasy Island" and "Days of Our Lives". Annie Vertabedian taught and founded her own dance company in Lebanon. Veseljko Sulić appeared with the Milorad Mišković company at Sadler's Wells in the summer of 1958 and then moved to the United States, where he joined the Folies Bergere dance troupe at the Tropicana Hotel and Casino in Las Vegas. In 1972, he brought together dancers in Las Vegas to perform at the University of Las Vegas Performing Arts Center and, two years later, founded the Nevada Dance Theatre with Nancy Houssel. He remained as artistic director and choreographer for the next twenty-five years. Claire and Sulić did not know each other well but shared memories of their time as students with Ana and Oskar. Marijan Jagušt went from the company in Zagreb to the Wuppertal Ballet in Germany and was ballet master at the Staatstheater am Gärtnerplatz. (I first learned about him from my Croatian geologist friend, who went to school with him in Zagreb.) Jürgen Pagels was a soloist and principal dancer with companies in Germany in the 1940s, and then with Ballet Legat, the Yugoslav National Ballet and the Paris Opera. He moved to the United States and founded the Pagels Legat School of Ballet in Dallas before becoming a professor in the dance department at Indiana University. He received his senior teacher's certificate from the Association of Russian Ballet in 1969.

Myles Marsden had persuaded his parents to let him go from the Legat School to Kaštel Kambelovac at the young age of sixteen and Ana and Oskar became his legal guardians. In 1955, he became a soloist in the company in Split and partnered Ana in several productions, including "Giselle", in which he was coached by Dolin. He and Herci Muntić were married in 1957 and named their first child after Ana, her godmother. (Dolin was her godfather.) They opened the Brae Crest School of Ballet in 1958 at Lincoln,

Rhode Island, and founded the State Ballet of Rhode Island in 1960. Links were also maintained with Dolin, who was guest choreographer and artistic adviser and appeared in "Hamlet" and "Giselle" and staged his "Pas de Quatre" for the company in 1976. Nearly a century after its first performance, Dolin's version of 1941 recreated Jules Perrot's original ballet for the four romantic ballerinas, Marie Taglioni, Lucille Grahn, Carlotta Grisi and Fanny Cerrito. He set it on principal dancers of the Ballet Russe de Monte Carlo, Alicia Markova as Taglioni, Natalie Krassovska as Grahn, Mia Slavenska as Grisi and Alexandra Danilova as Cerrito. Oskar staged "Stranger" for the company in 1968 and returned to perform the title role in the 1970s.

Yuresha was inspired to become a dancer when he saw Ana in a wartime performance in Zagreb. After training with Ana and Oskar, he became a soloist with the company in Split in 1953, remaining there until he joined the London Festival Ballet in 1959, and then danced with the Royal Ballet between 1962 and 1965. He partnered Ana in her last performance of "Giselle" in 1960 at the Bermuda Ballet Week. Yuresha remembers Ana's flair and style, both as a performer and as a teacher, but writes in his contribution to her biography that their personal relationship was detached, for reasons which he did not understand and found disappointing. As a young student, she seems to have underestimated his potential, which is surprising given his successful international career. Nevertheless, he acknowledges that she was instrumental in his development as a dancer. Yuresha first performed with Belinda Wright in 1959 at a Royal Command Gala in Manchester before Queen Elizabeth, the Queen Mother, and they were married in 1961. Having danced major roles with both the London Festival Ballet and Royal Ballet companies, including "Giselle", they performed independently and were "Ambassadors of Dance" for ten years under the auspices of the British Council. Dolin had a close relationship with Jelko Yuresha and Belinda Wright, and after his death, the rights to his version of the "Pas de Quatre" were conveyed to them. Davor Schopf and Mladen Mordei Vučković published "Yuresha: Visions and Dreams", a compilation of biographical information, photographs and programmes, in 2011. Mary knew Yuresha well from when she taught for Ana and Oskar. She took the opportunity to introduce me to him and he is remembered fondly by his fellow students from the ballet school at Kaštel Kambelovac.

This successful and influential period in Ana and Oskar's lives ended abruptly in the middle of 1959. While there seems to have been disagreement with the local authorities over the future of the school – there were plans to expand its scope to introduce a four-year advanced ballet course and to include classes for adults – conflict had arisen between Ana and Oskar themselves. This resulted in their divorce at the end of July and closure of the school at Kaštel Kambelovac. (Now, the nearby Hotel Baletna škola, or Hotel Ballet School, acknowledges their importance to ballet in Croatia and the school building itself is used as a performing arts centre.) Oskar went back to the National Theatre in Zagreb as ballet master. He also taught at the school of Nenad and Jill Lhotka in Winnipeg when they were away in Europe and it was in the 1960s that Oskar came periodically to Beckenham to visit Mary and Germano and to teach classes.

Ana went to Bermuda where her former student Patricia Sherwood, by then Patricia Deane-Gray, had founded the Bermuda School of Russian Ballet. Deane-Gray describes how she took over all the practical arrangements of Ana's life in Bermuda while, slowly, Ana learned how to become more self-sufficient. Together they established the Bermuda Ballet Week, which was inaugurated in August 1959 and which in its early years featured dancers from the days in Split and Zagreb, including Deirdre O'Conaire, Myles Marsden and Jelko Yuresha, guests from the London Festival Ballet and Milorad Mišković and his company. (Mišković was nearly twenty years younger than Ana but his early training was with Poliakova in Belgrade.) Ana and Deane-Gray also founded the Bermuda Ballet Association. Ana was its first president and then honorary president for the rest of her life. She started a series of summer schools in Bermuda and these have been held every year in Bermuda or Croatia, most recently under the auspices of the Bermuda Civic Ballet. Deane-Gray was honoured in 1985 as a Member of the Order of the British Empire for her services to ballet in Bermuda.

Although Ana returned briefly to Yugoslavia to dance "Giselle" at the Split Summer Festival in 1960, she did not then go back until 1967 but divided her time between Bermuda and the United States, which she had first visited in 1954. She taught at the Harriet Hoctor School of Dance in Boston and was director of ballet at the Lexington School of Modern Dance but wanted to open her own school. Her biography includes extracts from letters to support her immigration to the United States from Anatole Chujoy, Anton Dolin, André Eglevsky, Margot Fonteyn and Natalie Krassovska, all of whom acknowledged her training with Legat – Fonteyn, in particular, recalled that she worked "in the same class" as Ana, who had been given full responsibility for Legat's junior classes. Finally, Ana was able to open her own school, the Ana Roje School of Ballet, in Boston in 1966, at 667 Boylston Street. It was a member of the Society of Russian Style Ballet Schools and continued to operate under her name until 1994.

A new chapter in Ana and Oskar's lives opened in 1967 when Ana visited one of her brothers at Primošten, a small town on the coast about sixty kilometres north of Split. She decided to re-establish a base there, opening the Ana Roje International Ballet School, which ran courses in the summer. After a separation of ten years, she and Oskar were reconciled and ran the school together. Mary taught for them, as did Patricia Deane-Gray, and both Ana and Oskar continued to teach outside Yugoslavia. Oskar occasionally choreographed for the company in Split, but also taught in Buffalo (presumably for Kathleen Crofton), Los Angeles and San Francisco. As well as staging "Stranger" for the State Ballet of Rhode Island, he produced "The Devil in the Village" in 1972 for the inaugural performance of the Bermuda Civic Ballet.

Ana and Oskar were honoured in Yugoslavia in 1978 when they received the Vladimir Nazor Lifetime Achievement Award. A number of scholarships were established in their names in Croatia, Bermuda and Rhode Island. Material relating to Ana is held in the Jerome Robbins Dance Division of the New York Public Library, including the text from her lecture-demonstrations on the Legat teaching system at the eighth and ninth Conferences on Creative Teaching of Dance to Children in December, 1963 and 1964, respectively.

CHAPTER 18
MARY'S CLASSES

…long into the nights, [Legat] used to sit and talk to us about… even about character dancing and about the life in Russia…

Maria Zybina, interview with Patricia Deane-Gray.

Mary had great elegance, whether she was dressed for teaching or in street clothes. She wore her hair short, as she had since the Legat days, rather than in the somewhat old-fashioned ballerina style adopted by Kathleen Crofton and Cleo Nordi. She discouraged her pupils from advertising themselves as ballet students by walking with their feet turned out, as being affected, and she avoided obviously revealing herself as a ballet teacher. Her personal style was graceful and understated and, characteristically, she rarely raised her voice in class.

While only a handful of Mary's students went on to professional careers – as is the case for most ballet teachers outside the major schools – her great gift was to instil an approach to work and to life that stood us in good stead no matter the course we each took. Legat's pursuit of "precision, discipline and brilliance" noted by Eglevsky was softened somewhat for Mary's young students so that brilliance was replaced by "presentation" and the need to "dance", for even the most routine exercises. We learned the importance of accuracy and precision in the execution of steps, which applies similarly to work outside the dance world; how to concentrate; how to work as a team and be mindful of others – so essential in performance; and we learned the importance of presentation – whether for a clean finish to a *pirouette* or variation, or for a business assignment, and to engage fully – to "dance" – in any serious endeavour. We learned to appreciate the diverse and unconventional characters in the Lewisham Ballet Theatre Club and we learned not to show off. Mary inspired musicality and a love of music from Russia and the Caucasus to Spain, and she did all this without us even realising that we were continually learning from her and putting her lessons into practice.

Like many teachers in the 1950s and 1960s, although unlike Legat, at least in his younger days, Mary did not wear practice clothes for classes. Freedom of movement was given by a fine wool sweater and a pleated skirt. Latterly, she favoured the type in which the pleats were stitched to the hip and were available in reversible soft-coloured plaids – two skirts in one. For class, she wore black ballet shoes that had a full leather sole, a very flat heel and a somewhat pointed toe. But she did not use elastic to keep them on and, certainly, there was no drawstring to be tucked in or tied in a neat bow. They came from Mr Gamba, who knew her well enough to send her away from his shop with a few pairs of *pointe* shoes that had been tried on so many times that they could not be sold but could be used by her students. Mary showed us the correct placement of ribbons for *pointe* shoes – folding the fabric of the heel inwards and marking a diagonal line on the canvas lining. An article in the *Dancing Times* of January 1966 describes how Luigi Gamba immigrated to London from Italy in 1906 and started making patent leather shoes for waiters. He imported ballet shoes but realised that the design could be improved upon and began to make his own. Gamba advertised his range of "Ballerina" flat shoes in the *Dancing Times* of December 1950, forerunner of the ubiquitous "ballerina flats" that became universally popular decades later. His shop at 46 Dean Street in Soho had an almost life-size picture of a ballerina over the front entrance.

Mary had a whippy little bamboo cane to mark time or to draw attention to an inadequately pointed toe or incorrect placement, although she seldom used it. Equally, she seldom spoke sharply but discipline was strict and complete attention was required, and certainly no whispering, talking or giggling was tolerated. On the rare occasions when she needed to halt an exercise or was particularly displeased, Mary would rap her wedding ring on the piano. This was a direct reference to Legat, who, she told us, would do the same. Class proceeded without a break so there was no opportunity for a drink of water, and drinking water immediately afterwards was discouraged as being unhealthy. Sitting on the floor during class was absolutely not allowed, and it was also discouraged immediately afterwards as being bad for the muscles. And it was not permitted to wear watches or jewellery in class, except perhaps discreet ear studs.

Mary's teaching was firmly rooted in the tradition of her own teachers. Like Legat, she never repeated a ballet class and the structure followed those which are set out in Eglevsky and Gregory's "Heritage of a Ballet Master". They differed from a more modern format in that the first exercise was *grands pliés* rather than *battements tendus* facing the *barre*. Interestingly, however, it seems that it was Legat who started this approach. Fedor Lopukhov, quoted in Gennady Albert's biography of the teacher, Alexander Pushkin at the Choreographic Institute in Leningrad, states that Legat started his classes with *battements tendus* because he believed that it was a better preparation than the more strenuous *grands pliés* and Albert goes on to note that many teachers today follow that change in order. Lopukhov was a pupil of Legat through his time at the Theatre School but also observes that Legat had no interest in writing down his classes. It is strange, then, that none of Legat's classes that were recorded subsequently in England, including the ones he gave to André Eglevsky, start with *battements tendus*. For whatever reason, it seems he abandoned this first exercise.

The *grands pliés* which opened Mary's classes almost always started in second position, followed by first and fifth, and usually each *plié* was followed by a *relevé* and short balance. That the exercise started in second position, and *grand plié* was almost never done in fourth position, was in accordance with Legat's approach, which was to minimise stress on the joints, particularly early in the class. Exercises followed the pattern given in "Heritage of a Ballet Master", with *battements tendus, battements tendus jetés, battements fondus*, and *battements frappés*. Unlike virtually all present-day classes, Mary did not do any exercises in which the foot is flexed from a *tendu*, and nor did she use sixth position, with the feet together in parallel, since both of these practices were adopted some years later. Generally, in *battements fondus* the working leg extended to less than ninety degrees, even in the more advanced classes. Preparation for *battements fondus* was the same as for the *battements frappés* which followed, with the working leg taken to *tendu à la seconde*. These were done with the working foot pointed and without the toe striking the floor, as it does when the foot is in the flexed position. *Ronds de jambe par terre* followed *battements fondus* and *battements frappés*, rather than coming before them. The exercise ended with *port de bras* that was repeated on *demi-pointe*. Then came a separate exercise for *ronds de jambe en l'air*. *Petits battements* were given at the end of the *barre*, following *developés* (*adage*) and *grands battements*, rather than being combined with *battements frappés* and, as for *frappés*, the working foot was pointed. Positions *en coup de pied* were with the foot "wrapped" around the ankle. Each exercise was started and completed formally, with the arm in the Russian first position (*bras bas*) and the head turned away from the *barre*. Full use was made of *croisé, effacé* and *écarté*, and correct positions of the head, arms and épaulement were integral to each exercise. Before Mary's trip to Russia in the winter of 1964, preparation of the working arm for each exercise was only to take it through the Russian second position (at waist height in front of the body) and open to the side. Afterwards, she adopted the later Russian custom of a brief opening of the hand in *allongé* from first position before taking it back towards the body through the usual preparation. While the positions of the feet were numbered as in all other schools, simple positions of the arms went from first (both arms down in front of the body, *bras bas*), to second held in front of the torso, to third held above the head and fourth opened to the side; for young students, in fifth position the arms were held in *allongé* behind the back in a "butterfly wings" position.

In the centre, the first exercise was an *adage* which almost invariably included a *grand plié*. Indeed, some of the classes set out in "Heritage of a Ballet Master" include two or three *adage* exercises with *grands pliés*, sometimes in fourth position. (The long tradition of these demanding *grands pliés* is preserved in Bournonville's ballet "Konservatoriet". Created in 1849, it recalls his time in Paris when he studied with Vestris, and he used *grands pliés* in both the opening and the closing scenes. One hundred years later, Harald Lander restaged parts of "Konservatoriet" in his ballet "Études", again using *grands pliés* without the *barre*.) The first *pirouettes* in the centre were introduced in *adage*. Next came *temps liés*, with more *pirouettes*, followed by *battements tendus* and *battements fondus*. *Pirouettes* were done with the working foot in *coup de pied*, rather than in *retiré*, at least early in the centre work and, as well, the preparation for *pirouette en dehors* was with the back leg straight in fourth position, not in *plié*. (This is shown clearly in the illustration to Legat's article on the "The Secret of the Pirouette" in the *Dancing Times*, September 1932.) For *pirouettes en dedans*, the working leg was brought straight into contact with the supporting leg, rather than opening to *à la seconde,* which is sometimes used. Other exercises from the *barre* that were repeated in the centre included *ronds de jambe, battements frappés* and *petits battements*, before moving on to *allegro*. These exercises from the *barre* certainly fostered good placement and balance. I do not recall that Mary started *petit allegro* with simple warm-up jumps and these do not appear in classes set out in "Heritage of a Ballet Master". Following *grand allegro* exercises, Mary's classes often included turns on the diagonal or *en manège* and sometimes *fouettés*. Some of the classes in "Heritage of a Ballet Master" end with *grands battements* or *changements* before the *révérence*, and which Mary also used. In those days, in the Russian school, the position of the arms for certain steps was, or is, different to what was customary elsewhere. For example, in *glissade* starting with the right foot from the back, the left arm, rather than the right, was held in the Russian second position. There are also differences in names for the steps, as described by "Sitter Out" in the *Dancing Times* (November 1936) after watching Nicolaeva give a class at Legat's studio – the familiar *chaînés* were known in England as *déboulés*, the term *manège* seemed unfamiliar to him and *pas failli* was otherwise known as *sissone passé*. (Elvira Roné notes in her biography that Preobrazhenskaya always referred to *sissone* as "*sissol*", which was used in the Imperial Russian system, and "*sisol*" is described also by Volynsky as an alternate to *sissone*. Legat must have used *sissol*, or *sisol*, since that is how I heard it through the time I took Mary's classes, and it is used by John Gregory and Barbara Vernon in an article in *Dance and Dancers*, July 1958.)

While open classes usually end with a round of applause from both students and teachers (with the pianist bowing or nodding in acknowledgement of their contribution), at the school in Beckenham, pupils lined up after the *révérence* to receive a kiss on the cheek or forehead and a final word of encouragement or correction. This must have been a practice which Mary adopted from her classes with Legat (and possibly Eduardova and Poliakova as well) since Gregory and others note the ritual of a curtsey, kiss or handshake as his students left the studio.

Comparison of Zybina's classes with others', particularly those trained in the Vaganova style, suggest that Zybina's offer insight into Legat's own. When she established her school in 1950, it was less than fifteen years since she had studied with him and the intervening years were in an environment that was steeped in the Russian classical tradition. My recollections were confirmed by the classes set out in "Heritage of a Ballet Master" and those published by Nicolaeva after Legat's death. Another link to the structure of classes used in Imperial Russia, if not directly to Legat, was provided when I had a strange and uncanny sensation of *déjà vu* sometime in the 1990s when a new teacher came to take a class. He arrived slightly later than he would have liked, having been delayed by traffic, and then proceeded to teach a class that was very similar to one that Mary might have taught. These classes were special because they seemed to take me back to my ballet roots. The teacher's connections with the Legat tradition came from his training in Winnipeg with David Moroni, and with Chiat Hon Goh and Petre Bodeutz. Moroni considers Vera Volkova his mentor and her teaching a distillation of Vaganova and other Russian teachers. He also trained with Nesta Toumine (Nesta Williams) at the school of the Ottawa Classical Ballet Company and taught there with Toumine. Goh was a pupil of Nicolaeva-Legat at the Legat School in England. Bodeutz was also trained in the Imperial tradition.

Occasionally, Mary's students had the benefit of lessons from visiting teachers. Eeke Thomée's school was a member of the society and, on a visit to England, she taught at least one of Mary's ballet classes. Her bearing was rather strict and severe, and my recollection is that she looked for *épaulement* that was quite open across the upper chest, rather similar to the Vaganova style. One of her pupils, Marijke van Dorp, spent a year in Russia studying at the Bolshoi school (and then spent several months taking class with Mary). Oskar Harmoš came more often and taught both ballet and character on his visits from Yugoslavia in the 1960s. This was in the decade when he and Ana were separated and Ana taught only occasionally for Mary in Beckenham. In class, Oskar was more forceful than Mary, and he had high standards and high expectations of her pupils. But he was also kind and patient. As valuable, however, were his lessons in how to apply stage make-up. For these we sat at the table in Mary's dining room and, at least once, he made himself up as the Devil in "The Devil in the Village". His features were striking even without make-up and, as the Devil, the prominent bridge of his nose, high forehead and cheekbones were dramatically exaggerated with shading. He used blue and green for the eyes, with white liner for the outside corner to extend the appearance of the white of the eye, and maybe a dot of red for the inner corner. With the benefit of Oskar's lessons, we became better able to do our own make-up for performances and to help each other with tricky things like eyeliner. We started to collect our own make-up. Oskar used Leichner greasepaints, thick cylinders wrapped in cellophane and foil, but for foundation we learned about Max Factor "pancake", which was applied with a damp sponge from a round white plastic container. Smaller, thinner coloured greasepaint sticks were used for eyes and for any lines needed for expression or age. We collected our own brushes for applying eyeliner and for brows and lips. Rouge also came from Leichner, along with a large tin of greasy but effective make-up remover. The pancake, greasepaints and remover all had their own particular smells, which added to the special feeling associated with being onstage or backstage. (While it was tempting, as seeming more glamorous, to use ordinary lipstick instead of greasepaint, it was a mistake since it sometimes looked black under stage lights.)

Importantly, too, Mary occasionally took groups of students to professional stage performances. Details are sparse, but the musical "West Side Story" and the State Dancers from Soviet Georgia are just two examples of what she chose to broaden her students' experience.

Mary had a serious interest in character dance that went beyond her belief that, through character, a classical ballet dancer becomes more versatile and less mannered, because character has to be danced with freedom, if not abandon, in order to capture its spirit. Character dance uses syncopation, which does not often appear in classical ballet but is an important aspect of the musicality which Mary strove to foster in her students and, as well, it requires quite different use of the muscles of the feet. So she encouraged all her students to take character classes. Mary's interest originated from her studies with Evgenia Eduardova in Berlin and was particularly reinforced by her time in Yugoslavia, as well as in conversations and classes with Legat in London. E.C. Mason's article on Mary in *Dance and Dancers* (October 1957) notes that she had lived in Finland, Sweden, Holland, Germany, Austria, Greece, Hungary and Italy, and in each country had learned and collected dances. Mary did not actually live in all these countries but she certainly took every opportunity to learn and collect national dances, and to understand their history. She passed on this historical knowledge in class or as she staged a new dance – how the *gopak* or *hopak* of Ukraine had wide and expansive movements because the flat steppe did not confine the dancers (being Russian, Mary pronounced it *gopak*) and how the *kolos* of Yugoslavia reflected the fact that people were often chained together as they were taken into slavery under Ottoman rule and could only dance together in circles.

As early as 1956, Mary worked to broaden the knowledge of character dance. She presented a lecture in April in a series for the Federation of Russian Classical Ballet well before she published her series of articles for the *Dancing Times* on the national dances of Europe, and before she developed her lecture demonstration, "Dancing Through Europe". In her lecture for the federation, she spoke on "The Dances of Yugoslavia" (with some of her students demonstrating the steps), noting the importance of the people and the country, as well as the origin of the steps. She spoke again on national dances in the following spring. In the first of her articles for the *Dancing Times*, published in June 1963, Mary describes the basic steps used in character and sets out some of the exercises at the *barre* and in the centre. (Paddy Ann Holman, the daughter of one of Mary's pianists, Muriel Holman, and then an art student, drew the sketches for these articles and for which my classmate Cheryl Mudele and I were very happy to have been chosen to pose for some of the positions.) The exercises, Mary writes, were used by Pavel Gerdt in St Petersburg in the second half of the nineteenth century and were handed down to her by Eduardova. Alexander Shiryaev taught the first formal character classes at the Theatre School, starting in 1891, working with Alfred Bekefi to develop the exercises. He describes his interest in character dance in his memoir given in "Alexander Shiryaev Master of Dance" and how he was able to convince Petipa to support his efforts to have a character class included in the curriculum of the school. Although Mary does not mention Shiryaev in her article, Eduardova must have spoken about him since they danced together on the tours organised by Fazer in 1908 and 1909, less than twenty years before Mary attended her school in Berlin. The documentary film on Shiryaev's work, "A Belated Premiere", includes Shiryaev and his wife Natalia Matveeva performing several character dances on an outdoor stage.

Shiryaev went on to publish "Osnovy kharakternogo tantsa" ("The Fundamentals of Character Dance"), co-authored with Andrei Lopoukhov (younger brother of Fedor and Lydia) and Alexander Bocharov in 1939. It includes exercises at the *barre* and a series of studies on Russian, Hungarian, Polish, Gypsy and Spanish dances, illustrated with line drawings. Joan Lawson's translation was published as "Character Dance" by Dance Books in 1986. Jürgen Pagels, who trained at the Legat School, and with Ana and Oskar at Kaštel Kambelovac, wrote his own "Character Dance", published in 1984 when he was at the dance department at Indiana University. Like Mary, he sees that training in character gives a ballet dancer freedom of movement and he regrets that, in general, little character dance is included in modern ballets. He also sets out exercises at the *barre*, followed by a series of dances, mostly based on variations from "Coppélia", but he includes "Tatovac", with choreography attributed to Oskar Harmoš and the manuscript for traditional music, which in fact is Zajc and Baranović's music for "Svatovac". His description of the steps is not easy to follow, but certainly has enough elements that are recognisable in Mary's version of "Svatovac" for it to be the same dance. While, generally, character dances have become very stylised, some notable exceptions include the Royal Danish Ballet's production of "Napoli" and the Bolshoi's "Raymonda", which have an exhilarating *tarantella* and *czárdás* in their respective final acts.

Mary's character classes started with a character *révérence* to right and left, essentially a full bow starting with a step to the side with the same arm stretched open as the working leg, the arm then taken across to the opposite shoulder as the feet are brought together, the arm stretched above the head and, finally, the bow with the arm taken to the feet. As for ballet classes, each exercise started with the preparation of the arm – stretched to the front with the hand at shoulder level, moved to the side, back to the front and then placed on the hip, and the head turned away from the *barre*. Exercises were similar to ballet exercises in that they started with full *pliés* and progressed through work with the feet and ankles to the thighs and upper body. The exercises themselves are difficult to describe without illustration or demonstration, although the first article in Mary's series for the *Dancing Times* attempts to do so, and there are more detailed descriptions in both Lawson's and Pagel's books. Most of the exercises are done with the knees in *demi plié* and involve lifting the heel of the supporting leg off the floor (with the knee still bent) for one count and bringing it down sharply on the next count. Having the knees bent in *demi plié*, means that exercises, both at the *barre* and in the centre, are done without the head bobbing up and down. I was happy to recognise Mary's exercises in the figures in Lawson's "Character Dance" and believe this confirms that Eduardova passed on the exercises which were codified by Shiryaev, Lopoukhov and Bocharov. The structure of Mary's classes was the same as that used by Anatoly Borzov from the Moiseyev Ensemble when he taught Mary's students on a visit in 1966, and is well established, at least where Russian teaching methods were and are used. Work in the centre included short *enchaînements*, as in a ballet class, but made up of combinations of steps typical of Russian, European and Yugoslav dances. Again, on her trip to Russia, Mary must have watched at least one character class, possibly part of the Moiseyev Ensemble rehearsal, because the change in style that she brought back to her character classes amounted to a modification of how the upper body was carried in centre work, with a much more stylised upright stance and open shoulders. The last fifteen minutes or so of Mary's character classes were often devoted to mime, sometimes based on the classical gestures used in ballet, sometimes an improvisation based on a theme that she proposed. Eduardova may well have taught mime this way, again based on Gerdt's teaching, which Karsavina recalls in "Theatre Street". Each class ended with the character *révérence*.

Mary's series of articles gives a sense of her love and interest in character dance and briefly shares her knowledge of the historical setting for the dances which she first learned from Eduardova and Legat. But she was also aware of how original folk dances have to be adapted for stage production since, in the theatre, they can otherwise appear simple and even dull. She drew on her own experience as a dancer and choreographer when presenting character dance every time her students or the Lewisham Club performed. Her articles in the *Dancing Times* present a simple Russian dance, "Under the Apple Tree" (July 1963), a *gopak* from the Ukraine (August), a *lesghinka* from Georgia (September and October), a Polish *mazurka* (January 1964), a Czech *polka* (February), a *czárdás* from Hungary (June), an Italian *tarantella* (October) and, finally, "Svatovac", a *kolo* from Yugoslavia (November). Mary describes the principal steps for each dance and gives references for the music for each of them, with the exception of the *kolo*. An arrangement by Swerkoff was available in "Favourite Russian Folk Dances" issued by Novello for the Russian dance, and for the Ukrainian and Georgian dances but without an attribution; the "Polish Dance Op 3, No. 1" by Z. Scharwenka; the "Czech Polka" by Jaromir Weinberger; "Hungarian Dance No. 5" by Johannes Brahms; "Tarantella" by Glinka. The music for "Svatovac" was transcribed by Mary's accompanist Michael Finnissy and his manuscript is included with the article. For each of these pieces, Mary writes from her own experience. She does not reference the three articles that Legat had written for the *Dancing Times* in 1927 and 1928, or the series which Nicolaeva published in 1938, and may not even have known about them. In 1964, Mary gave a series of eight classes based on the "new" character syllabus which she developed for the Society of Russian Style Ballet Schools. These were held on Wednesdays at 2.00pm at 60 Paddington Street starting on 7 October. She would have been particularly aware that knowledge of character dance in England, and other countries in Western Europe, was being lost as the original exponents, like Eduardova and others, were no longer able to pass on their experience. Mary's articles and lectures were a serious effort, shared by Lawson and a little later by Pagels, to bring some of this knowledge to a wider audience.

❦

The pianists for Mary's school and for the Lewisham Club were, of course, very important not only for ballet and character classes but also because they played for almost all the performances as well. Muriel Holman played for Mary at least as early as 1955 since she is credited in one of the programmes, and she continued until 1970, if not a little longer. She may well have trained as a concert pianist and then played for Mary and taught music (two of my sisters took lessons with her for a while), but we have very little knowledge of her other than as our accompanist. Michael Finnissy appeared around 1961, inevitably to some excitement, when he was still at Beckenham Grammar School for Boys. He went on to the Royal College of Music and is an internationally well-regarded composer of contemporary music. While Mrs Holman's style of playing was traditional, Michael enjoyed experimenting and his playing was often loud and percussive. He introduced us to the concept of silent beats for our *barre* exercises and sometimes rapped the piano for extra effect. They were both gifted pianists, well able to play Mussorgsky's "Pictures at an Exhibition" which is something of a virtuoso piece, and Michael transcribed and arranged the music for the *kolo* from "Ero the Joker", as well as for "Svatovac" and other Yugoslav dances which were not composed for the piano. They both understood how to accompany regular ballet and character classes, so that their playing gave the all-important encouragement and lift to the dancers, and they could tackle a fiery Hungarian *czárdás* as easily as a slow passage for a classical *adage*.

As a means to earn some money and to combine it with practice in both playing and improvisation, Michael says he probably found out about Mary through his sixth-form Russian teacher Tatiana Behr, who lived nearby in Woodbastwick Road. (Both Tamara Jakasha and Katherine Mason remember her well; she taught Katherine O-level Russian and was a great friend of her grandmother.) Michael was taken to ballet, concerts and opera from a very young age by his aunt and his great-aunt, who was also his piano teacher. As a result, he grew up enjoying ballet and knowing a lot of ballet music. He was also drawn to central European dance music because his Polish godfather, Piotr Kłos, on returning to Poland after the war, left a volume of music for Polish folk dances that Michael learned and then adapted when he first started playing and composing before he was five. While he did not go through a formal programme of lessons and examinations, on the strength of receiving the William Yeates Hurlestone prize in composition at the Croydon Music Festival, his parents agreed that he should apply to the Royal College of Music where he was awarded a Foundation Scholarship. By that time, he had been playing for Mary for two years and thinks that even then he may have wanted to compose for dance rather than just play the piano. Mrs Holman was very helpful in the early days, particularly when he had to use music that was published by the Federation of Russian Classical Ballet and which he thought very dull. Mary was happy when he started to rework it and was generally pleased with the results. Playing "Svatovac" and the *kolo* from "Ero the Joker" was a different matter altogether and Mary welcomed his ability to transcribe from recordings. (The Macedonian folk tunes were particularly complex, however, and Mary used a portable tape-recorder while teaching and rehearsing with us.) Michael calls his arrangement of "Svatovac" that accompanies the article in the *Dancing Times* a "derangement", and he went on to record "an even more deranged" version on his first compact disc, "Folklore", in 1998 – the liner notes refer to it as a "souvenir from teenage years". Michael says he recognised in Mary an innate love of the physical movement of dance and what he remembers as a slightly conservative love of music – but, at the time, he was too much in awe of her to talk to her about either.

In order to support his studies, Michael continued to play for ballet classes with Mary, as well as for Kathleen Crofton and John O'Brien, and for jazz classes with Matt Mattox. After graduation, he became more closely involved with contemporary dance, particularly at the London School of Contemporary Dance where he founded the music department and worked with choreographers Jane Dudley, Anna Sokolow, Richard Alston, Siobhan Davies, Jackie Lansley and Fergus Early. In an interesting further link with Yugoslavia, Michael collaborated with the latter to produce "Incidents from the Life of Jesus of Nazareth", which was inspired by Yugoslav frescos of the Nativity and was performed by students of the London School of Contemporary Dance in April and June 1974. Michael continued to play for dance classes for the next fifteen years. He passed on to an ex-composition student his remaining "Class Book" (one of several which did not otherwise survive changes of accommodation), and which contained manuscript copies of the music he used to play for Crofton, O'Brien, Romayne Grigorova and others, although not for Mary.

Among other accomplishments, Michael was president of the International Society for Contemporary Music between 1990 and

1996, and taught at the Royal Academy of Music, Winchester College, the Katholieke Universiteit of Leuven, and at the Universities of Sussex and Southampton. Many of his compositions have been recorded internationally. After a gap of about ten years, our paths crossed in 1979 when he was the featured composer at the Bath Festival. Not knowing this before I arrived in Bath on holiday, but having seen his name in the programme, we ran into each other by chance in a bookshop and enjoyed catching up over a pub lunch. My sister, who also took classes with Mary, came to know Michael when he was working with the East London Late Starters' Orchestra, later COMA (Contemporary Music for All). She played the cello in the orchestra and went on to organise the summer schools for COMA.

Of course, many pupils passed through Mary's school over the nearly thirty years that she taught in Beckenham, and a number went on to enjoy stage careers. To her credit, at least two students were accepted into the Royal Ballet School, Cheryl Mudele and Lorna Murray, and two more into the Arts Educational School, while her daughter, Tamara, Brenda Olivieri (*née* Sanger), and Linda Neech became teachers. Tamara's professional career started in pantomime at the London Palladium where she was engaged for three years in succession to 1961, dancing in "Sunday Night at the London Palladium" at the same time as Claire Courtney, in the Christmas shows in London and touring in the summers. Tamara and Claire were not in the Tiller Girls troupe that appeared regularly in "Saturday Night at the London Palladium". Unlike them, for the pantomimes and summer tours, Tamara and Claire danced in a wide variety of styles, including classical ballet (*en pointe*) and modern. In 1961, Tamara danced in Copenhagen and appeared in the Sunshine Street series on Tyne Tees Television. An audition call in the *Stage* took her to Italy, where, with a group of English dancers, she joined the Embassy Ballet based in Milan at the Teatro Lirico under the impresario, Elio Schiavoni. The company was led by a Filipina dancer and friend of Tamara's, Elcita Villanueva, whose father was a commercial attaché in London, hence the name "Embassy Ballet". Among other adventures was an engagement in Tripoli, Libya, when they were taken to the ruins at Leptis Magna by one of the partners in Olympic Airlines and were treated to a picnic of champagne and caviar.

Tamara met Claudio Campanati in Italy and they were married in 1965 at the newly built Catholic church of the Annunciation and St Augustine in Beckenham Hill Road. Claudio's home was in Milan, where, with the opera house of La Scala and a long tradition of ballet and dance, the city provided a good location for a new ballet studio. Tamara started teaching in 1969 after their youngest child was born and in the following year founded Seregno Dance, which she directed until 2010. Her studio is now at the New Dance Centre in Seregno just outside Milan, where she is a director and teaches classical ballet, and where her daughter and daughter-in-law teach modern dance. In the early years, Tamara mistrusted the Italian medical system and it was my mother, a doctor, who gave her children their vaccinations when they came back to Beckenham to visit Mary and Germano. On one of those visits, too, Bill Hudson was in England and Tamara remembers that my parents were invited to dinner and they all enjoyed Mary's home-made borscht soup. Unfortunately, I have no recollection of my parents ever having a meal with Mary and Germano and, given my research on Hudson's exploits with SOE, I am particularly sorry that this close connection with him is lost on me.

Cheryl Mudele's professional career took her to Italy, where she danced with the Theatre Ballet of Rome, and then back to England when she joined the London Ballet Theatre and danced in the musical "The Dancing Years". But she was invited to join the company of the Zurich Opera House, where she spent the next twelve years and where Chinko Rafique (a former student of Patricia Spalding of the Federation of Russian Classical Ballet) was a soloist. Rudolf Nureyev worked with the company on several occasions. A motorcycle accident cut short Linda Neech's promising career. She went on to study for her teacher's certificate with Mary as soon as she was able, receiving it when she was only sixteen, in 1962. Earlier she had gone to Kaštel Kambelovac to study with Ana and Oskar. She started the Russian Dance Theatre Club in West Wickham with a focus on character and especially Yugoslav dancing. Not unusually in those days, there were only a few boys in Mary's school, none of whom stayed more than two or three years. Nicholas Farrant showed promise at a young age and attended at least one of the summer courses run by Andrew Hardie for the Association of Ballet Clubs. Hardie had studied with Legat and for a period was ballet master to Inglesby's International Ballet. Nicholas and his elder sister Carole joined Hardie's school in the early 1960s. Viktor Orloff was rather younger and particularly good in character. Over the years, a number of young men were members of the Lewisham Club and Mary took every opportunity to coopt them for classes in double-work, as well as for performances of the school.

While the list of Mary's students who went on to professional careers as dancers or teachers appears short in comparison to those of Ana and Oskar, it does not include several who trained with her in the early 1950s and about whom there is virtually no information. Also, Mary's school was located in an area just south of London that was well served with ballet schools, only a few of which were affiliated with the Federation of Russian Classical Ballet or the Society of Russian Style Ballet Schools. In contrast, Ana and Oskar were among just a handful of recognised teachers in Croatia and students had the benefit of performing with the company in Split and, potentially, going on to join the company in Zagreb.

CHAPTER 19
THE FEDERATION, SOCIETIES AND ASSOCIATIONS

[H]e is, unlike many others, less known to western Europe
than to his native country where the name of Legat was a
household word in artistic circles throughout the length and
breadth of the land.

Sir Paul Dukes, foreword to "The Story of the Russian School".

Mary was an examiner for the Federation of Russian Classical Ballet from its founding in May 1950 until 1960, when the Society of Russian Style Ballet Schools was formed by a break-away group of teachers from the federation, including Mary. John Gregory and his wife Barbara Vernon were instrumental in setting up the federation and, since Mary had known Vernon since the 1930s when they were both at Legat's studio, she was directly involved in its creation. The objectives of the federation, and its successor organisations, were to follow Legat's methods of teaching and to preserve the style of Russian classical ballet. Ana Roje and Barbara Vernon were technical consultants and Patricia Spalding was the secretary general. The offices were at 27 Baker Street in London. A note in the *Dancing Times* of January 1951 reported that the syllabus was developed by Patricia Spalding, Barbara Vernon and Ana Roje and Mary, and that the first examinations would be held in the spring. Mathilde Kschessinskaya was the founding patron and came from Paris to attend the first general meeting held at the De Vere Hotel.

John Gregory was an actor and painter before he became seriously interested in ballet. A conscientious objector, he spent part of the Second

World War dancing under the name Serge Ivanoff with the Anglo-Polish Ballet, which is where he met his wife. Through her, he became an enthusiastic proponent of Legat's method of teaching and in 1949 they founded the School of Russian Ballet (or British School of Russian Ballet) which had its studios at St Luke's South Hall in Chelsea. Gregory's interest in Legat extended, of course, to the publication of his books, "Heritage of a Ballet Master" with Eglevsky, and "The Legat Saga", which remain the most detailed biographical works on Legat in English (and apparently, even in Russian), as well as a number of articles in both the *Dancing Times* and *Dance and Dancers*. Importantly, he also ensured a home at the National Arts Education Archive for Legat's papers, photographs and caricatures held by the Legat Foundation.

By the mid-1950s, the executive committee of the federation consisted of John Gregory, Barbara Vernon, Anna Lendrum, Claire Linden, Patricia Spalding and Mary. Kschessinskaya remained as patron. The board of examiners then included Mary with Kschessinskaya, Karsavina, Lendrum, Spalding, Vernon, Maria Balinska and Gabrielle Davis, all of them having been students of Legat in Russia or in London. Examinations were marked out of a score of one hundred with a passing grade at sixty-five marks. An honours grade carried ninety marks, distinction eighty-five, merit eighty, and pass plus seventy-five, with commended and highly commended being given in cases of special effort or aptitude. The badge of the federation, given to students after passing their first examination, was particularly attractive. Almost certainly, if he did not design it himself, Gregory saw to the design and manufacture. It is made of pewter or similar metal, with a depiction in relief of two dancers in a style that evokes pictures from the Romantic period.

Legat would have talked about Kschessinskaya when he reminisced about Russia with Mary and Ana and Oskar, but Mary may not have had direct contact with her until they worked together as examiners with the federation. Kschessinskaya had left Petrograd in 1917, travelling south by way of Moscow to the Black Sea with her fifteen-year-old son and her lover Grand Duke Andrei Vladimirovich, a cousin of Tsar Nicolas II. It took until early 1920 before they were finally able to leave Russia, sailing from Novorissisk to Venice, travelling on their Nansen passports. A villa at Cap d'Ail in the south of France, which Kschessinskaya had bought in 1913, became their new home, while marriage to Andrei in 1921 gave her the title of Princess Marie Romanovsky-Krassinsky. While they were certainly more comfortable than some other *émigrés*, they had left Russia with very little and relied on a modest bank account in Monte Carlo and mortgaging the villa. In order to supplement their resources, in 1929 Kschessinskaya opened what became a successful and well-known studio in Paris in the Avenue Vion-Whitcomb and where Tatiana Riabouchinskaya, one of the three "baby ballerinas" of the Ballet Russe de Monte Carlo, was a student.

The schools of the federation came together for annual congresses, which, following the tradition started with Kschessinskaya's first visit in 1951, included special classes and lectures, as well as the presentation of examination certificates and performances by students. Activities were often reported in the *Dancing Times*, giving enough detail to glean what took place and to understand Mary's contribution. (Patsy Beech, a student of John Gregory and Barbara Vernon, has also provided some additional information from the archive of Gregory's papers for which she is responsible.) Generally, a programme of classes (including some given by Kschessinskya) and lectures took place at St Luke's Hall, and performances were given at various small theatres in London. Over the years, these included the theatre of the Institut français at 17 Queensberry Place in South Kensington, the Rudolf Steiner Hall near Regent's Park, the Toynbee Hall in Whitechapel, the Cripplegate Theatre in Golden Lane and the Emma Cons Hall in Westminster. Later, Karsavina describes meeting with Kschessinskaya at her hotel and recalls "the same sparkling eyes, the same engaging smile" despite her age, and how they had danced together in "Fiametta" (*Dancing Times*, February 1966). In 1954, Kschessinskaya travelled on the same boat train as the Duke of Windsor. She arrived at Victoria Station and was met by a group including Mary, the Gregorys and their five-year-old daughter, Paula, who presented a bouquet of sweet peas and roses. As in 1951, the occasion warranted press reports and photographs, and this time short articles and photographs appeared in the London evening papers. Karsavina presided over the congresses when ill health prevented Kschessinskaya from travelling to London, although she remained patron.

For the annual presentation of examination certificates in June 1956, Mary's students performed "A Winter Night" to music by Glazunov and "Studies" to Chopin and Eduard Schütt, a Russian composer who spent most of his career in Vienna. Other teachers presenting their students and their work included Claire Linden, Joan Howe, Maria Balinska, Cleo Nordi, Patricia Spalding, Gabrielle Davis and Anna Lendrum. By 1957, schools in Holland had joined the federation and, in the following year, examinations at Eeke Thomée's school in Delft were presided over by

Gregory and Vernon. On the last evening of the annual congress that year, Karsavina spoke of her teachers, Pavel Gerdt, Christian Johansson and his daughter Anna, and of her work in Diaghilev's Ballets Russes with Fokine and Nijinsky. She recalled that Johansson taught beauty of movement but gave "no ideas" to his students, while it was Anna Johansson who taught her how to understand the woman's role in ballet. Gerdt's teaching of mime was passed on in the classes that she gave at several of the congresses. Surely, Mary would have enjoyed listening to Karsavina's memories as much as any of the students. In 1958, the annual performance took place on 8 June. Although the writer does not name individual schools, a note in the July issue of the *Dancing Times* reports on central European character numbers, a *mazurka*, a *polonaise*, a Hungarian dance to music by Béla Bartók and a "Croatian Village Scene", which would have been staged by Mary and which provided the "best moments" of the evening. A similar programme was put on at the Cripplegate Theatre on 8 November, when pupils from Vernon and Gregory's school were seen to have "beautifully free backs and arms", while the dancing of Patricia Spalding's pupil Chinko Rafique was particularly noted. The "Croatian Village Scene" was described as "altogether attractive". It included variations for a Flower Girl, a Dalmatian Dance, a Croatian Dance and "Svatovac".

In the meantime, Gregory and Vernon had formed the Harlequin Ballet Company to give students of their school, and some other schools in the federation, the opportunity to perform, much as Nicolaeva and Ana and Oskar had done earlier. It was named in honour of Nijinsky's role as Harlequin in Fokine's "Le Carnaval" for the Ballets Russes. (Their school was renamed the Harlequin Ballet School in 1961.) In December 1959, the *Dancing Times* reported on a performance at the Esplanade Theatre in Bognor Regis in the previous October, for which the highlight was Karsavina's version of "Harlequin and Columbine" in which Linda Neech and Tamara Jakasha were "charming" Pierrettes. (Linda also danced with the Harlequin Ballet when the company gave its first performances at the Stables Theatre, Hastings, in September 1959.) Mary staged "Svatovac" for the Harlequin Ballet in its 1959–1960 season. The next year, however, following the rift among members of the federation, the Gregorys remounted it as "Slavonia" with additional choreography of their own. The first London performance of the company was in the Great Hall of Queen Mary College, with the college orchestra, in a programme which again included "Harlequin and Columbine" and a piece by Maria Balinska, "La

Jeunesse dorée". (Balinska had been a member of the Anglo-Polish Ballet with Vernon and Gregory.)

cℊ

Karsavina comes into Mary's story because of their involvement with the federation. Probably they did not meet in London in the 1930s since Karsavina was living in Hungary through the time when Mary was taking classes with Legat. But surely Elena Poliakova told Mary about when she and Karsavina were Lace Dolls in "The Fairy Doll" and when they danced with the Ballets Russes, and Legat must have talked about her too. Having danced "La Bayadère" at the Mariinsky for the last time in May, 1918, Karsavina left Russia in June with her second husband, Henry Bruce, an English diplomat, and their small son Nikita. In contrast to the winter journeys on foot by Mary's family and by Olga Preobrazhenskaya, Karsavina and her family travelled north by steamer on the River Neva to Petrozavodsk from where they planned to continue by train to Murmansk. At Petrozavodsk that route proved impossible, however, and they and other passengers from the steamer continued overland through the forest of Olonets to Sumskoy, where they managed to find places on the last boat to the village of Soroka on the other side of the White Sea. Finally, a train took them to Murmansk and from there they boarded a British collier, the SS *Wyvisbrook*, which took them to Middlesborough in Yorkshire. At his request, Bruce was then posted to Tangier as a quiet place for the family to recover from their last months in Russia and their journey. Karsavina writes about this period in a series of letters to Walter Welch, the father of an aspiring dancer who sought her out having just auditioned for the Sadler's Wells School. Started in 1958 and intended to form the basis of a sequel to "Theatre Street", the letters were rediscovered among papers donated by Welch's daughter, Walda Welch Cobain, in the Ballets Russes Archive and Special Collections at the University of Oklahoma School of Dance. They were published in 2018 as "Tamara Karsavina, Beyond the Ballerina, Her Unpublished, Untitled Manuscript about the First Years in England". The family clearly enjoyed their days in Tangier. In her engaging style, Karsavina describes the social activities of the legation, the wild flowers and riding her own pony. But this relaxed and amusing time was cut short when, in the middle of 1919, Diaghilev managed to send a telegram directly to the legation requesting Karsavina to join his company for its first London season following the war.

Karsavina continued to dance with the Ballets Russes in Paris and in her own engagements in London, including J.M. Barrie's "The Truth About the Russian Dancers", which was written for her, and with Laurent Novikoff in "Nursery Rhymes" at the Coliseum in 1920. (Karsavina's friend Lydia Kyasht called "The Truth About the Russian Dancers" a clever burlesque but felt that Barrie was unkind to suggest that dancers only walked on their toes, adding that it was not good for dancers to walk anyway.) Having retired from the Foreign Office and working in banking, in 1921 Bruce was asked to go to Bulgaria as secretary general to the British delegation of the Interallied Reparations Commission. He stayed there for the next five years while Karsavina toured, mostly in Germany but also in North America. She continued to perform but at the suggestion of Arnold Haskell started work on her memoir, "Theatre Street", which was published in 1930 and remains in print. In 1927, she and Flora Fairbairn set up the Karsavina-Fairbairn Academy at the International Hall in Westbourne Grove. This arrangement did not last long and she later opened a studio with Fairbairn off Baker Street. Money was always short, however, and Bruce had difficulty finding a series of unsatisfactory jobs. Things took a turn for the better in 1931, when, through a friend at the Bank of England, he was asked to go to Hungary as an adviser to the National Bank on a contract that he thought would be for a few months but extended to eight years. At first, Karsavina and Nikita remained in England but, when it became clear that her husband would be in Hungary for some time, she joined him in Budapest for the years until the outbreak of the Second World War. Her performing career is described in some depth in "Thamar Karsavina" by the critic Valerien Svetlov, published in English in 1922 and available in facsimile published by Dance Books.

By the time she became associated with the federation, Karsavina was in her sixties. "Theatre Street" and her numerous articles for the *Dancing Times* show how much she loved the world of ballet and that she was passionately interested in its history. Her series of articles written in 1964, called "Family Album", show her warmth and humour, and her love and respect for her teachers and colleagues. That was followed by a series on her partners and her tours. As well as "Theatre Street", she published "Ballet Technique: A Series of Practical Essays" as a book in 1956, based on her articles for the magazine, and "Classical Ballet: Flow and Movement" in 1962. But she was not a promoter of the Russian Imperial system that she grew up with simply for the sake of its being the Russian system, and she helped to develop the syllabus (later known as the Karsavina Syllabus) for the teacher training course of the Royal Academy of Dance, of which she was a founding member. As Russians, Mary and Karsavina were in the minority among the examiners in the early days of the federation and, while they were not close friends, they and other Russian dancers in London enjoyed meeting up after mass for the Orthodox Easter, first at the church in Buckingham Palace Road and then at the cathedral in Ennismore Gardens.

My own memory of Karsavina dates from the presentation of certificates in 1959 for my first and only examination under the federation. After the formal proceedings, I sat on the floor near her feet with the other younger students, watching her sway and move her arms to the music of a *balalaika* (or a *balalaika* group, perhaps). In those days, she was a somewhat plump, grandmotherly figure, not at all fearsome or overbearing, and clearly enjoyed the evening's festivities.

By 1960, however, the teachers of the federation had become divided and the Society of Russian Style Ballet Schools was established by Mary and some of her federation colleagues. No reason for the split was publicised but the society proved the more lasting institution while the federation continued to operate under the patronage of Karsavina for the next few years. A note in the *Dancing Times* of March 1960 announced that the society's examinations would be held in May and that, as patron, Svetlana Beriosova, ballerina with The Royal Ballet, would present examination certificates in June. In contrast to the attractive metal federation badge, the society badge was utilitarian, consisting of a small block of coloured plastic mounted on a pin with SRSBS engraved in plain letters and the colour representing the most recent successful examination. As well as Mary, the examining board included Nina Hubbard, Patricia Spalding, Anna Lendrum, Claire Linden and Anna Northcote. Eeke Thomée also moved to the society and other member teachers in Holland were Alice Hutton of The Hague and Dordrecht, Claire Renée of The Hague and Nel Roos of Amsterdam. Gool Hogben, based near London, joined the society around 1962. Beriosova remained patron, although, according to Lendrum, she had little personal involvement. Ana Roje became honorary president in 1973. In later years, the society expanded into Canada and the United States, with branches established in Toronto, Boston and Lubbock, the latter operating as the American Society of Russian Style Ballet. Patricia Deane-Gray in Bermuda represented the American society from 1976 and is a past president. Mary visited Bermuda at least twice as an examiner, as well as visiting the schools in the Netherlands. In Canada, the Society of Russian Ballet, founded by Marijan Bayer, Nesta Toumine and Ann Vanderheyden, operated as a branch of the society with schools in Toronto and Ottawa from 1975, but became independent in 1980, and continues to operate as the Society of Russian Ballet. Toumine knew both Ana and Oskar, not only from Legat's studio in London, where she studied in the mid-1930s, but also from when all three of them danced with the Russischen Ballets aus London in Germany in 1936. She and Mary may well have met originally at Legat's studio. It is interesting to note as well that Beriosova's professional debut in 1947 was with Toumine's Ottawa Classical Ballet Company when she was only fifteen and appeared courtesy of the Vilzak Schollar School of Ballet in New York.

In September 1961, the *Dancing Times* reported on the annual meeting and prize-giving held in London in July. Anna Wooster, a student of Nina Hubbard and recently returned from three years at the Leningrad Choreographic Institute, was the guest of honour. As well as presenting certificates, she described her time in Russia and danced a variation from "The Little Humpbacked Horse" in a costume originally owned by Pavlova. (A little younger than Wooster, Chinko Rafique had also gone to study in Leningrad, where he was a contemporary of Mikhail Baryshnikov and, later, a friend of Rudolf Nureyev. He returned to England in 1967 to join the Royal Ballet.) The following year, the annual meeting was held at St James's Hall, Gloucester Terrace, when Irina Baronova was the guest of honour and gave one of her entertaining talks on her experiences as a "baby ballerina" with the Ballets Russes de Monte Carlo. She was both graceful and glamorous and wore a dark cocktail dress with a full skirt and a wide-brimmed black hat, which was notable, for those of us who had never seen one before, because it had no crown.

The record of the society's activities over the next few years is sparse since they were not reported on regularly in the *Dancing Times*. In 1965, 1966 and 1967, the annual certificate-giving took place at the YMCA Hall (King George's Hall, Great Russell Street). Belinda Wright was to have presented the certificates in 1965 but was indisposed and her place was taken by Pamela Marten. In 1967, Baronova again presented the certificates and, for the performance, Mary choreographed "Phase d'amour" to music by Josef Suk. It portrayed a group of young girls in Grecian costume who come upon a young man; one of the girls is much taken by the boy but, although they dance together, it comes to nothing as he goes on his way. A young man was brought in from the Lewisham Club to dance the Boy and I was the Girl. Claire Courtney danced the same or a very similar piece in 1952 or 1953 and Mary may well have seen that it would be especially memorable for me. I had spent ten years training with her and latterly had also been attending professional level classes with teachers in London. But at the age of seventeen I had come to realise that I would not go on to have a professional career as a dancer and that this would be my last performance before an audience on a stage.

In 1972, Mary was invited to Switzerland to teach character at a summer school held by the Ballet Academy of Maria Gorkin in Basle, and she also taught some ballet classes. As a result, Gorkin, as well as Vera Paztor and Erno Vashegyi in Zurich, requested that society examinations be held at their schools in the following year. From 1973, Tamara Jakasha's school near Milan also held examinations under the society, and schools in Holland continued to be part of it. By 1980, the name had been shortened to the Society of Russian Style Ballet. Overseas representatives in the 1980s were Tamara Jakasha in Italy, Henny Meerloo in Holland, Marijan Bayer in Canada and Gerda von Arb in Switzerland. Until 1984, Mary taught occasionally as a guest teacher at Paztor's school and possibly also for von Arb in Zurich, who Mary had examined for her teacher's certificate in 1978. Anna Lendrum took over as honorary chairman in 1986 and Mary remained an examiner for the society until her death the same year.

Anna Lendrum fills in some of the gaps on the later activities of the society in her memoir, "My Life in Ballet – A Russian Heritage". In the early 1980s, she encouraged Beriosova to participate more actively and by the early 1990s brought in Hans Meister from Switzerland as a second patron to work alongside Beriosova and invited Gabriela Komleva to become president in 1994. Having been a soloist with the National Ballet of Canada and with European companies, Meister went to Leningrad to train with Alexander Pushkin and returned to Switzerland to direct the ballet company of the Zurich Opera. He regularly partnered Komleva, who danced with the Kirov company and then taught at the Vaganova Academy/Leningrad Choreographic Institute. Shortly afterwards, in 1996, and after nearly forty years of the society's existence, personal differences caused another a rift and the schools in Italy and Switzerland withdrew. Tamara Jakasha recalls that she and others felt that the approach of some teachers in the society was too rigid and inappropriate for students who attended class perhaps only twice a week. The Russian Ballet Association was formed in 1997 by the Italian and Swiss teachers of the society and with Meister as founding president. Headquartered in Switzerland, the association is led by Meister and von Arb, with member schools located in Italy, Spain and Japan. An international dance competition for dancers from the schools was set up in Mary's name and ran from around 2002 to 2006. It now takes place within an annual Festival of Dance in Milan and the prizes support dance training. Other members of the society, led by Gypsy Booth and Claire Linden, formed the Association of Russian Ballet and Theatre Arts (ARBTA) at the same time.

The Legat School, founded by Legat's widow Nicolaeva was not a member of the federation or the society, although she did work closely with John and Barbara Gregory in the 1950s, but all of the schools fostered and upheld the traditions of the Russian Imperial style and system of teaching. Despite the differences between the members of the societies, their experience was rooted in Legat's studio in Colet Gardens and they were determined to pass on his approach. As such, however, they were outside what had become the mainstream institutions in British ballet, the Royal Academy of Dance and Imperial Society of Teachers of Dancing. Legat, himself, was of an older generation than most of the dancers who arrived before him, and he seems to have had neither the inclination nor the energy to become closely involved in the development of England's own system of teaching, unlike Karsavina. But, as Oskar Harmoš pointed out as far back as 1960 (*Dancing Times*, July 1960), Legat's influence had been somewhat neglected, while perhaps too much emphasis had been placed on Cecchetti's methods. Writing in the *Dancing Times* of November 1981 at the time of the announcement of a scholarship set up in Nicolaeva's name, Jelko Yuresha notes that the work of both Legat and Nicolaeva was largely unrecognised. He goes on to say that it was not until he and Belinda Wright were touring extensively that they appreciated the reach of Legat's and Nicolaeva's influence in many parts of the world. Today, Legat's system is maintained by the Legat Foundation of Russian Classical Ballet and the Russian Ballet Society in syllabi, examinations and teacher certification. Other societies like the Russian Ballet Association, ARBTA and the Society of Russian Ballet, have their origins in the society with its direct links to Legat, but use the Vaganova method or a blend of the Vaganova and Legat methods. Mary herself was not rigidly opposed to other influences. Her training and experience were solidly grounded in the Russian Imperial style but she was open to the influences of modern dance and, as we have seen, often incorporated character dances into her theatrical productions.

⁓

The Association of Ballet Clubs, of which the Lewisham Club was a member, played a valuable role in fostering interest in dance from its founding in 1947 by G.B.L. Wilson, a regular contributor to the *Dancing Times*. Member clubs were quite widely distributed geographically through England, Northern Ireland and Ireland. The programme for a performance in May, 1964 lists the participating clubs dating from 1958 as the Belfast Ballet Club, Janet Cranmore Ballet Theatre (Birmingham), the Bournemouth Ballet Club, Bristol Ballet Club, Nina Hubbard Ballet Club (Cambridge), Dublin Ballet Production Group, Eastbourne Ballet Group, Enfield Ballet Theatre Club, Harlow Ballet Club, Irish Ballet Society, the Masque Ballet Club, Phoenix Ballet Group (Newcastle-upon-Tyne), the RAD Production Club, Sheffield Ballet Club, University College (London) Ballet Group, Willesden Jazz Ballet Group and Wimbledon Ballet and Arts Society, as well as the Lewisham Ballet Theatre Club, although not all were functioning in 1964. Wilson was chairman, and Beryl Grey and John Field were president and vice president. The latter were well known as principal dancers with the Sadler's Wells and Royal Ballet companies. Grey saw the association as an important support for visiting ballet companies since its members helped to encourage an interest in ballet outside the major centres. She was active in visiting as many of them as possible, and in arranging presentations by outside speakers. As founder, Wilson would have made sure that the association had adequate publicity and notices of performances, and reviews appeared regularly in the *Dancing Times*, at least until the mid-1980s. Summer schools were inaugurated in 1955. A number were held at Headington School, Oxford, and Lydia Kyasht was one of the first teachers. Around 1970, Mary gave a lecture, or series of lectures, on character in Oxford – her son-in-law remembers clearly that it was at a college on the river, which could have been Magdalen, or possibly Magdalen College School, and may well have been arranged by the association.

Lydia Kyasht, Karsavina's great friend and classmate at the Imperial Theatre School, was one of the first teachers at the association's summer schools although by the time of its founding she had moved her own school to Cirencester and it was not a member of the federation. Mary must have known her and, because of her connections with Legat as well as the association, it is worth giving a brief account of her activities in England. She appeared in London at the Empire Theatre in Leicester Square with Adolf Bolm in 1908 and was the first Russian to appear in England as a *"première ballerina"*. She went on to enjoy a five-year engagement at the Empire followed by a tour in America. She was in Russia at the time of the 1917 Revolution when she and her husband lost all their possessions. Shortly afterwards, they left Russia for the last time. Kyasht does not describe her month-long journey back to England but she seems to have arrived in London ahead of her husband. Her journey must have been at least as harrowing as other *émigrés'* journeys since she says she arrived in a state "bordering on collapse". Between the wars, she lived in St John's Wood, where she opened her own school and continued to perform in theatre and cabaret. She founded Ballet de Jeunesse Anglaise or Russian Ballet de la Jeunesse Anglaise in 1939, later named the Lydia Kyasht Ballet. (Mona Inglesby choreographed "Endymion" for the company which gave the first performance at the Cambridge Theatre in 1938.) Kyasht also taught at a number of other schools, among them the London Academy of Music and, from 1953, the Legat School and Sadler's Wells School.

CHAPTER 20
PERFORMANCES BY MARY'S SCHOOL AND THE LEWISHAM BALLET THEATRE CLUB

"Pictures at an Exhibition", the kolo from "Ero the Joker" and "Dancing through Europe".

Like her own teachers, Mary regularly staged performances to showcase the school, and her students were often coopted to dance with the Lewisham Ballet Theatre Club, which took part in performances of the Association of Ballet Clubs and the Children's Ballet Theatre Club. "Pictures at an Exhibition" and Mary's lecture demonstration on character dance, "Dancing through Europe", were particularly memorable and enjoyable to perform because of the opportunities to dance in a variety of pieces and to learn how to manage quick changes of costume. The *kolo* from "Ero the Joker", with its exhilarating *finale*, was always great fun. Incomplete though it is, the information on performances by the school and the club spans about fifteen years from 1955 to 1971 and shows Mary's ability to present her dancers to best advantage. Her choreography for a wide variety of works was informed by her experiences, going back even to her early training with Evgenia Eduardova in Berlin. This she did with energy and creativity, while at the centre of all the activity, she was calm and unflustered. Backstage or in the wings, she always found time to spit three times behind the ears of her younger students for good luck in the Russian custom.

One of Mary's great gifts was not only to bring out the best in her dancers from both her school and the club but to take advantage of the differences between them given the great range of ages, shapes and sizes, and levels of proficiency. There were a few memorable characters at the club who must have presented some challenges in casting. "June and George", a married couple, were June Patrice and Austyn Georges, who thoroughly enjoyed both classes and performances. These enthusiastic stalwarts seemed, to our young eyes at least, not only rather old but also a little grotesque. Even allowing for the perception of age being exaggerated, they must have been in their sixties because their faces were quite lined. June, with her obviously dyed, rather dishevelled and straw-like platinum blonde hair pulled into a rough *chignon*, wore lots of mascara and red lipstick, both of which were a little haphazardly applied. Her figure was trim and she was happy to show it off wearing a black leotard with pink tights, enhancing the effect with a generous "falsies" bra. Georges (he was known by his surname, but we thought of him as "George") was stooped, almost to the point of being hunchbacked, and he may well also have dyed his hair – black in his case, to hide the grey, or even the white. Ross, Ian Ross, must have been in his sixties as well, although he seemed a little younger than June and Georges. He was not tall, was somewhat round in the figure, and had a full head of white hair. Walter Gent may only have been in his forties and was tall and imposing – and he was always Walter rather than Gent. He had had polio and had been advised to take up ballet to strengthen his legs and feet, although his feet remained somewhat stiff and crooked. Mary managed not only to find roles for these people but used their physical attributes so that some of her choreography really was created especially for them. They all brought a real understanding of drama and mime to the stage and were very friendly to Mary's young students. Often for performances of both the school and the club, Linda's father, Ivan Neech, was responsible for the scenery, while costumes were designed by her mother, Daphne, and lighting and sound were looked after by John Fagg. Students' mothers were often enlisted to help with wardrobe and to sew costumes.

Mrs Bromley, a leading light for the League of Pity children's charity hosted an annual fundraising fête in the garden of her home at Oaklands, 42 Oakwood Avenue in Beckenham. The family owned the Russell and Bromley chain of up-market shoe shops so the house was large and the gardens extensive with a lake at the far end. Mary provided a dance performance at around five of the fêtes from the late 1950s. As well as a chance to dance, they were good fun because there were amusements like old-fashioned painted swing boats and a bran tub, music played by a brass band, and opportunities for games among the shrubberies. We changed in a ground-floor room which opened onto a stone terrace from which steps led down onto the main lawn for our dances. In 1959, Cheryl Mudele and Nicholas Farrant danced a *pas de deux* and there must have been at least four or five other pieces. Among them was a solo to one of Mendelssohn's "Songs without Words", the "Spinnerlied", also nicknamed the "Bee's Wedding", probably choreographed especially for me because my parents had given me a real *tutu* as a birthday present. (It was a treasure because it was properly constructed with a satin bodice and V-shaped seaming at the hips and had multiple graduated layers of net. But it was not new and could not hold its own against *tutus* made by Daphne Neech, or by Cheryl's mother, for which the net was much whiter and stiffer.) Another time, Mary choreographed a solo for me of the "Little Match Girl" in Hans Christian Andersen's story to a shortened version of Chopin's "Raindrop" prelude (opus 28, number 15). The piece was in mime only as the Little Match Girl, shivering with cold, strikes all her matches to give a moment of warmth, and then simply lies down to sleep and then to die. Mary may have seen the opportunity to use my costume for the Masha, the orphan girl in "Easter Magic", before it became too small. Over the years, dances from "The Land of Toys" and "Easter Magic", the Russian court dance and "Svatovac" were included in these performances, as were solos and *pas de deux* for some of the older students like Linda Neech and Marijke van Doorp who visited from Eeke Thomée's school in Holland.

"Listen to the Wind" in 1960 was the first of the Beckenham Amateur Dramatic Society pantomimes for which Mary choreographed the dance numbers. A children's musical based on a book by Angela Ainsley Jeans with music and lyrics by Vivian Ellis, the storyline includes children kidnapped by gypsies, a magical musical box, a mermaid-witch and a creature called the Gale Bird. Mary choreographed a dance number, "The Tides", for Tides, a Shell and a Boy. Our costumes were designed by Mrs Neech. The Tides' costumes were asymmetrical tunics in blue and green shades of diaphanous silky fabric garlanded with seaweed made out of coloured cellophane. The Shell costume was spectacular with alternating panels of pink and white satin to look like a scallop shell. It was particularly exciting to be made up by Tamara Jakasha and some of her friends in a basement room of the Beckenham Public Hall (the use of mascara was debated, and then applied from one of those little oblong boxes in which the pigment was worked with water – or even spit – and a tiny brush), and to dance in two evening performances as well as the Saturday matinée (8 and 9 January). Bernard Daly was the Gypsy Man and Joan Daly assisted the property mistress. We all knew Mrs Daly, a little plump, slightly breathless and good fun, because she ran Daly's Shoes in Beckenham High Street.

The following year, Mary's students took part in "The Glass Slipper" when they danced as dolls. It has proved impossible to find any information on this pantomime, except that it may be based on the story of Cinderella. "The Enchanted Walz" was produced in 1962 when Mary's students performed as elves and fairies in a dream sequence. Mrs Daly had an important, if not a leading part in one of these productions, along with Pamela Bennett and Hilary Mann from the Lewisham Club and who both worked at Gamba's shop in Soho (which seemed a perfect job to the rest of us). Mrs Daly, Pamela and Hilary all wore white romantic *tutus* and my clear memory is of Mrs Daly singing something about "to help me when dancing the swan", possibly while trying on a ballet shoe. "The Enchanted Walz: A Fairy Pantomime" is by Frederick Davis, loosely based on "A Midsummer Night's Dream". (One of the characters is Petunia Periwinkle, a Charwoman at the Court, which, possibly, was the part played by Mrs Daly.)

The earliest programme my former classmates and I have among our personal collections of materials is for a school performance on 3 December 1955 when matinée and evening performances were held at the Azelia Hall in Beckenham in aid of the King George's Fund for Sailors. "Winter" to Glazunov's music was followed by a series of variations and European national dances, but, certainly, there were other regular performances, including "Pictures at an Exhibition" in 1958, when Mariangela Polich was the Mother Hen. (Her father and Germano were old friends from Croatia. Claire Faraci remembers that Mariangela's ambition had always been to open a ballet school in Italy and she lived with Mary for about a year while completing her teacher's training.) The first performance of "Easter Magic" was presented on 6 May 1961, with "Pictures at an Exhibition" in An Evening of Ballet by the Lewisham Club at the Dick Sheppard School in Tulse Hill. The programme also included the *kolo* from "Ero the Joker" and the full version of "Svatovac". "Easter Magic" is based on a Russian folk tale about Masha, a little orphan girl, who goes to the Easter midnight mass but is ignored by everyone and cannot enter the crowded church. Feeling sad and lonely after the service, Masha's fairy godmother appears to her and gives her a magical egg and a golden plate, telling her that if she rolls the egg on the plate she will see wonderful visions – but she must be careful not to break the egg or the magic will come to an end. Masha rolls the egg around the golden plate and sees many beautiful visions but, later, the villagers are curious to see what she is holding so carefully and, in their excitement, the egg is knocked off the plate and is broken. Masha is inconsolable and the villagers try to comfort her by giving her coloured eggs, the symbol of Russian Orthodox Easter. They realise that they should not treat her so unkindly and the story ends happily with Masha joining in the village dances. At least part of Mary's inspiration for "Easter Magic" must have come from a round copper tray (almost certainly from Yugoslavia) on which the stage lights were reflected up into Masha's face as she tilted the tray to roll the egg. In that first performance, Masha was danced by Margaret Childs, with June as the Fairy Godmother ("Juin Patrice" in the programme and, if it was a misprint, she might have been delighted). The dream variations were "Eastern Princesses", "Roses" and "Dragonflies".

May, 1961 was a particularly busy month. With scarcely a pause for breath, on 19 May, Mary staged "Land of Toys" and "Easter Magic" at the Azelia Hall to mark the tenth anniversary of the opening of her school. Costumes for "Land of Toys" were designed by Mrs Neech and, as always, Mrs Holman played the piano. A review in the *Beckenham Journal* fills in some details. Over fifty of Mary's pupils took part and were joined by Linda Neech and Walter Gent from the Lewisham Club, who performed a Croatian dance, perhaps the *pas de deux* version of "Svatovac". In "Land of Toys", the Fairy Queen introduces a new doll to the other toys. Toy soldiers and a Drummer led the toys to Leon Jessel's "The Parade of the Tin Soldiers". The music for other variations in the ballet may not have been composed by Jessel, and Mary may have used a selection, including parts of the score for the Legat brothers' original production of "The Fairy Doll", which almost certainly inspired "Land of Toys". Possibly, Mary used part of Vladimir Launitz's ballet suite "The Toy Shop", which dates from around 1924. A dance of the little white ponies was performed by ten of the youngest members of the school and a dance of painted dolls by those somewhat older. Then, a succession of dolls in national costume danced their variations – a trio of Chinese dolls, a Cossack doll and Italian, Polish and Spanish dolls, and a doll in Russian court costume who danced to Tchaikovsky's music for a variation from "Swan Lake". Costumes for the little ponies were white leotards with white net tails and red ribbons across the chest and headdresses of stiff pleated white net and red ribbons with bells; the painted dolls had dresses with multi-coloured flounced skirts and matching rosettes on their heads. A dance for mice and the Pied Piper was later included in one of the League of Pity fêtes. Linda and Walter would have danced in "Easter Magic" as well –

probably as the Fairy Godmother and the Boyar or Merchant. In the school performance, I was given the part of Masha and my costume was made by my mother from lengths of parachute silk dyed brown, yellow and orange, with the skirt and sleeves in layers to look like rags. (The review notes that there was music by Mendelssohn and Chopin as well as traditional tunes.) Then, just a few days later, the Lewisham Club took part in the Association of Ballet Clubs' performance on at the Rudolf Steiner Hall, where, according to a report in the *Stage* of 25 May, Mary presented "The Devil in the Village" and "The Gingerbread Heart". Oskar Harmoš assisted with the choreography and staging of these ballets on one of his visits to England. While Tamara Jakasha remembers him rehearsing some of the younger students for a performance at Her Majesty's Theatre in London, in the event they were not permitted to appear because they were too young.

On 12 May 1962, the Lewisham Club presented An Evening of Ballet with "Easter Magic", "Pictures at Exhibition" and "Svatovac" at Hayes School in support of the school's swimming pool fund. The father of four young students at Mary's school, Trevor Parnacott, was not a regular member of the club but he was an imposing and convincing Mussorgsky in many of the performances of "Pictures at an Exhibition". He also appeared as the Khan in the Georgian dance in "Dancing Through Europe" on at least one occasion.

Nineteen sixty-three saw the first performance of Mary's lecture, demonstration, "Dancing through Europe", on 14 June by the Lewisham Club at the Whitfield Hall of Bromley Congregational Church. She spoke from a podium on one side of the stage to present the dances which had been developed in conjunction with her series of articles for the *Dancing Times*. This work gave Mary the opportunity to formally present the results of her many years of research into the various dances and dancing styles across Europe from Russia to Italy and Yugoslavia. It opened with the demonstration of character *barre* work followed by dances from Russia, the court dance and a group piece; a *gopak* from Ukraine; a dance from Georgia with characters including the Khan, slave girls, Tatars and a Tatar boy; a *mazurka* from Poland for which the choreography made use of fans; a *polka* from Czechoslovakia; a *czárdás* from Hungary; a *tarantella* from Italy; and, from Yugoslavia, a Dalmatian dance, "Svatovac" and, finally, the *kolo* from "Ero the Joker". (Possibly, the Dalmatian dance was similar to "Dalmatinka", which, much later, in 1992, was taught by John and Barbara Gregory's daughter Paula at a summer course in Ardpatrick, Scotland; some of Mary's dances were taught to the pupils there and recorded to video. But "Dalmatinka" may also have originated with Ana Roje's early solo, "Dalmatian Girl".) The Ukrainian *gopak* was arranged as a *solo* and the *czárdás* was danced as a *pas de deux*. "Pictures at an Exhibition" was also on the programme. Cheryl Mudele and Linda Neech were Adolescence and Womanhood, respectively, in "The Catacombs", in which a man searches for the ghost of his wife. It was an example of how Mary tailored her choreography to suit the dancers she had to work with since, usually, "The Catacombs" had only one female dancer. The reviewer in a local newspaper commented particularly on the change in mood between the playful children in the gardens of "Les Tuileries" and the journeying refugees of "Bydlo", and the article was accompanied by a photograph of "The Catacombes".

Mary presented "Dancing through Europe" at the Beckenham and Penge Boys' Grammar School on 14 January 1964. A review and photograph appeared on the front page of the *Beckenham and Penge Advertiser* reporting that the lecture opened the school's arts and music season. Michael Finnissy must have helped to get the lecture into the programme. The *Beckenham Journal* also covered the performance with a photograph of a rehearsal in the studio the week before and another photograph, almost certainly from "Ero the Joker", appeared the week after. Without a complete series of the programmes, it is difficult to know how many times Mary presented "Dancing through Europe" but it joined "Pictures at an Exhibition" as a staple of the Lewisham Club.

Over the years, Mary collected costumes from Yugoslavia, particularly the woven and embroidered aprons and waistcoats that could be worn with white cotton skirts, blouses and trousers. In order to replicate the gold coins, often British sovereigns, that are characteristic of authentic costumes, the Lewisham Club acquired a machine which, somewhat laboriously, flattened hundreds of metal bottle caps and punched a small hole as well. These were sewn in rows to the bodices of the women's costumes and added wonderful jingling to the dances. Around this time, Mary brought back two particularly elaborate women's costumes and headdresses, heavy with beadwork and embroidery, but which were wonderful to wear. Mary also found us some of the traditional leather shoes, or *opanci*, sewn like moccasins and with turned up toes. It would have been when she was planning "Dancing through Europe" that she gave each member of her senior class a traditional silver Yugoslav button with our names and the date, 1962, engraved on them – treasured possessions still.

In May 1964, the Lewisham Club presented "Legend", the Macedonian *oro* and the *kolo* from "Ero the Joker" at the Rudolph Steiner Theatre as part of an Evening of Ballet put on by the Association of Ballet Clubs. Rudolph Steiner House, with its theatre, is an architectural gem dating from the mid-1920s. For "Legend", Mary used music by Carl Maria von Weber and costumes were designed by Paddy Holman. The ballet is set in a village during a plague and offered ample opportunity for mime and choreography in a contemporary style. The performance was reviewed in the *Dancing Times* in July when the writer noted "most noble-looking partnering" – but which almost certainly should have referred to a young man, Owen Mortimer, rather than Georges. He warmed to Mary's choreography as it proceeded and called it "rewarding". The other clubs presenting that evening were the Nina Hubbard Ballet Club, the Masque Ballet Club and the Wimbledon Ballet and Arts Society.

The Macedonian *oro* resulted from Mary's visits to Macedonia specifically to learn the dances of that region, perhaps consciously emulating the researches of Anatoli Zhukovski thirty years earlier. She came back with a wealth of new and complicated steps which she used in this dance. It was always referred to as an *oro*, in keeping with Macedonian terminology, while the final dance from "Ero the Joker" was always referred to as the *kolo*. Both words mean "circle" or "round"; other variations in spelling, *horo* or *hora*, for example, reflect the different languages of the Balkans where these dances are typical. The music had more complex rhythms and melodies than we were used to in "Svatovac" and the *kolo* from "Ero the Joker", and the footwork was much more intricate. It took us longer to learn the choreography and to get the steps right but the dance quickly became another favourite and audiences enjoyed it. The *oro* was performed within "Dancing through Europe" as well as a separate number in other programmes. Using one of her inspired pieces of casting, Ross from the Lewisham Club appeared as the accompanying musician, miming the traditional Macedonian high-pitched wind instrument and looking every bit an elderly Macedonian peasant. Sadly, sometime later in 1964 or in 1965, he died suddenly while waiting for a bus; we were shocked, but relieved that he did not suffer a long illness.

Later in the year, in October, under the auspices of the Children's Ballet Theatre Club, Mary staged the Macedonian *oro* and the *kolo* from "Ero the Joker", followed by "Pictures at an Exhibition", at King George's Hall in Great Russell Street. An almost identical progamme followed on 19 January 1965 at the City Temple Hall, Holburn Viaduct. While there must have been at least one other performance in 1965, the next record is for a Performance of Russian Ballet, by "Lewisham Ballet" also under the auspices of the Children's Ballet Theatre Club in December, although the location is not given in the programme. It included a selection of national dances including "Svatovac", another *kolo*, "Opšaj diri", and the Russian court dance, followed by "Pictures at an Exhibition".

In 1966, the Lewisham Club took part in the Evening of Ballet put on by the Association of Ballet Clubs in May, again at the Rudolph Steiner Theatre. A notice appeared in the *Dancing Times*, but there is no information on the programme. At the end of the year, Mary was able to demonstrate her expertise as a presenter of character dances more widely when the Macedonian *oro* was included in the Northern ABC Network production of the talent show "Opportunity Knocks", hosted by the television personality Hughie Green. According to a short article (with an accompanying photograph of three dancers with the "musician") in the January 1967 edition of the *Dancing Times*, the producers were particularly interested in good dance pieces.

School performances would have continued in the following years, but there are no available programmes and few notices. The last record is from January 1971, when the *Dancing Times* carried an announcement for a performance at Fulham Town Hall on 6 March in which the programme consisted of Russian and Yugoslav dances, variations from "Coppélia" arranged by June Sandbrook, a member of the Lewisham Club and former dancer with Ballet Rambert, and "Pictures at an Exhibition". (Sandbrook's school, the Sydenham School of Ballet, was a member of the Society of Russian Style Ballet Schools at least in the late 1970s and early 1980s.)

✎

Despite the fact that we performed them often, three dances were particular favourites, both at the school and at Lewisham: the Russian court dance, the short *kolo* from "Svatovac" and the *kolo* from the *finale* of "Ero the Joker"; and we always enjoyed "Pictures at an Exhibition". The Russian court dance from the second act of "Swan Lake" can be seen online in various stylised versions performed *en pointe*, but the choreography in most of them is very similar to the one that Mary taught, as is the traditional Russian court costume with a diadem-like headdress, or *kokoshnik*, and the use of a handkerchief in one hand. In the early photograph shown in Chapter 3, Mary's costume is particularly elaborate and would have been worn for a performance of the same dance while she was at Eduardova's school in

Berlin. The court dance was included in numerous performances, as a *solo* or *pas de deux*, danced in either ballet shoes or character shoes, and it was also incorporated into "Easter Magic". In early performances, Mary may have used a peasant costume but certainly in later versions costumes were based on the court style – and danced in soft ballet shoes rather than character shoes. There is just enough material to suggest that 'our' Russian court dance, to Tchaikovsky's music, is part of Legat's heritage passed on by Mary to her pupils, and that he could have choreographed it to assist Petipa. Now, however, this is impossible to substantiate from English language sources. Alastair Macaulay, writing in *The New York Times* (13 October 2015) notes that originally the solo was performed by Odile as she seduces Siegfried in Act III. When it is included in modern productions, particularly in Russia, it is used for one of the princesses introduced to Siegfried. In "Dancing in Petersburg", Mathilde Kschessinskaya refers to what may well be the same piece, a favourite of hers, as "Tchaikovsky's Russian dance". One of the last times she danced it may have been at Covent Garden in July 1936, when it was billed as the "Boyar Dance". In her memoir, Anna Lendrum, who was also a student of Legat in London, includes a picture of herself in a Russian dance with a note that the choreography was by Legat. Her pose is a position which appears in Mary's version, although her costume is peasant style with headscarf and apron. Jill Lhotka learned a dance at the Legat School that must have been similar to the dance Nicolaeva describes in her article on the "Boyar Dance" for the *Dancing Times* in February 1938, and which, in turn, would have been based on the dance described very generally in Legat's article of November 1927. Nicolaeva gives some detail on the general structure of the dance, with the first half having a slow tempo and the second much livelier, the use of a handkerchief towards the end, and the final bars with a series of turns on the spot, finishing with a low bow. It does seem to have been quite similar to the Russian court dance performed so often by Mary's students. The biography of Ana Roje lists a "Russian Dance", a *pas de deux*, to music by Tchaikovsky, but with choreography by Ana and Oskar – among a number of other pieces that specifically credit Legat. However, they could easily have choreographed a *pas de deux* to the same music based on his choreography. Of course, there is also a dance for the Russian Doll in "The Fairy Doll"; in "Ballet's Magic Kingdom", Volynsky describes Evgenia Biber's performance but gives no indication of the steps.

In many of the performances for the school and Lewisham, Mary used "Svatovac", both as a ballet based on a Croatian wedding celebration and the *kolo* as a single dance. The *kolo* was performed more often on its own by two or four dancers and, a little later, it was incorporated into "Dancing through Europe". As students, we may have thought of "Svatovac" as ours alone, although we did understand that the *kolo* from "Ero the Joker" came from an opera. The choreography for the *kolo* from "Ero the Joker" was originally Margarita Froman's, as was "Svatovac", although both have later been attributed to Oskar Harmoš. Mary may well have danced "Svatovac" with Ana and Oskar in Split. It was intriguing to discover that "Svatovac" had been performed in Bermuda in 1959, until the links between Ana in Yugoslavia and Patricia Deane-Gray in Bermuda cleared up the apparent mystery.

Mary would have danced in "Ero the Joker" many times when she was in Belgrade, as well as on the tour to Frankfurt where she was able to conceal her British identity. The final *kolo* was often the last piece in performances of both the school and the Lewisham Club. Gotovac's music starts slowly with the dancers holding hands in a circle. As Mary told us, this is the traditional reference in *kolos* to villagers being led into slavery in Ottoman times, although the story for the opera has nothing to do with that aspect of the region's history. As the tempo quickens, the circle breaks up and single dancers or couples perform increasingly spirited steps in front of the main body of dancers (or the chorus in the opera), moving with small steps or on the spot. In the final bars, the dancers move in several lines backwards and forwards across the stage in an exuberant and exciting *coda*. The dance as performed by the Croatian National Theatre is almost identical to the version Mary taught her students.

"Pictures at Exhibition", was another great favourite. Composed after Mussorgsky viewed an exhibition of pictures by his friend Viktor Hartmann, who had recently died, "Pictures at an Exhibition – A Remembrance of Viktor Hartmann" is a series of musical "pictures" linked by passages which suggest the composer walking sadly through the gallery. It was perfect for the Lewisham Club in many ways because the variety of the pictures allowed Mary to use the range of age and skills among her dancers, both amateurs from the club and students from the school. The people at Lewisham all brought a real understanding of drama and mime to the ballet. Georges and Ross, as two gnomes in the first picture, played with a star. "The Gnome" is in the singular in Mussorgsky's composition, but Mary choreographed it for two gnomes and these two even looked a bit like gnomes in real life – Georges with his stooped shoulders and deeply lined face, and Ross with his round figure and white hair. Walter and Ross were the two Jews in Samuel Goldenberg and Schmuÿle – Walter, as the wealthy Goldenberg, towered over Ross as the poor and subservient, Schmuÿle. (One can also imagine Oskar Harmoš relishing the opportunities for dramatic mime in portraying these figures.) June was equally memorable as the witch, Baba Yaga, in "The Hut on Fowls' Legs". Her peroxide hair prevented her from being too crone-like in real life. In Mussorgsky's score, "Bydlo" depicts a lumbering ox cart but Mary interpreted the music to denote a group of refugees on their long journey, an image informed by her own knowledge of emigration. While the choreography consists almost entirely of the group simply walking slowly across the stage, she used their posture and gestures in mime to show their suffering. At one point, a child lags behind and there is a moment of panic until it is found and brought back into the group. A more light-hearted picture is "The Ballet of Unhatched Chicks in Their Shells", though in Mary's version the chicks were already hatched and hopping around the Mother Hen. Older students sometimes did this dance *en pointe*. Mary must have staged "Pictures at an Exhibition" every two to three years starting from the early 1950s, when Claire Courtney studied for a *pas de deux* for "The Old Castle" with a boy from Yugoslavia, who may have been Jelko Yuresha. (But the two of them fought so much during rehearsals that Mary had to abandon Claire.) This was around the time when Ana and Oskar first staged it and, given Claire's recollection, it seems likely that Ana, Oskar and Mary developed their ideas for the ballet together.

CHAPTER 21
LAST WORDS

Ah? We must die once.

Marius Petipa on hearing of the death of Christian Johansson, in "The Story of the Russian School".

Sadly, in 1976, Germano had become ill with cancer. He was treated in London but the family went to Split and Milna in the summer and also visited a cousin in Zagreb who was a doctor. Mary decided against letting Germano know of his cousin's prognosis. He died on 1 December, about a year before I ran into Mary at our chance meeting in London in 1977. Later, his ashes were taken from Beckenham Crematorium to the cemetery in Split where his parents are buried.

Mary's regular advertisement in the "Where to Learn" pages of the *Dancing Times* ceased to appear after May 1976 and running of the school in Beckenham was taken over by Christine Del-Roy during that year. Christine and her husband, John Del-Roy, a noted ballroom dancer and teacher, lived at number 7 Copers Cope Road from about 1977, just after they were married. They planned to bring ballroom dancing into the school curriculum (a clip of them together in a *paso doble* in 1978 can be seen online), but not long afterwards, Christine also became ill and had to give up teaching. She owned Julienne, a dancewear shop, at 163 High Street in Beckenham, the same premises where Mrs Daly, who performed in the pantomimes of the Beckenham Amateur Dramatic Society, had had her shoe shop.

Although she had given up the school in Beckenham, Mary continued to travel to teach both ballet and character and to examine for the society and then its successor, the Russian Ballet Association. She taught regularly at her daughter's school near Milan, which gave welcome opportunities to see Tamara and her grandchildren. Mary visited Ana and Oskar and taught at Primošten in the summers and, sometimes, in Switzerland when she was the examiner for Gerda von Arb's students. She was also able to see her sister Kitty and brother-in-law Viktor when the family holidayed together in Milna. For a short time in 1980–1981, Mary was the director of the Teatro Reggio Torino in Turin and also taught at the Teatro San Carlo di Napoli on the invitation of her predecessor in Turin.

Discussions with the BBC must have brought Bill Hudson to London before and after the filming of the documentary on SOE, "The Sword and the Shield", and, surely, he and Mary met up then, especially if his visits to England were less frequent than in the past. But by the early 1980s Mary went to Primošten less often. Ana and Oskar's last years were marked by the gradual loss of Ana's sight and the onset of dementia, while Oskar's health also deteriorated. Mary spent the Christmas holiday in 1985 with Tamara's family at their home outside Milan and was looking forward to the coming year's activities. Within a few days of her return, however, John Del-Roy found her at home after she suffered a stroke. She died very shortly afterwards on 11 January 1986 and was buried in the Russian part of Beckenham Crematorium on 17 January.

Mary was spared learning of the deaths of Ana, Oskar and Bill Hudson. Unable to live with each other, Ana and Oskar separated for the last time. She moved to a nursing home in Šibenik, not far from Primošten, and died there on 17 March 1991. She is buried at the Lovrinac cemetery in Split. Oskar moved back to Zagreb and was remarried, in 1989, to a woman named Nevenka who was twenty years his junior. Tragically, he lost his life in a fire in his apartment on 6 April 1992. A newspaper report suggests that it was caused when the candle that he would light every night to Ana's memory overturned and, as he opened a window, the rush of air set the apartment ablaze. He is buried at the Mirogoj cemetery in Zagreb. Although he suffered from Parkinson's Disease in the last years of his life, Bill Hudson outlived them all and died in Durban, South Africa, on 1 November 1995.

⌒〇⌒

In bringing together the strands of Mary's story, I have been struck by the contrast between the gentle and soft-spoken "Madame" that we all knew, and the dramatic events of her life, starting with the revolution in 1917 and leaving Russia with her family. Reading of how Legat lived through the revolution and how he, Eduardova, Poliakova and Preobrazhenskaya made their own ways out of Russia illuminated the experience of the Zybins. In learning about Legat, Eduardova, Poliakova, Preobrazhenskaya and Karsavina, my appreciation of ballet performance, the history of ballet and how teachers pass on their own knowledge and experience has deepened immeasurably. Finding out that Mary knew at first hand about the first performances of the *kolo* from "Ero the Joker" and "Svatovac" and, above all, how she came to study with Legat in London as a result of her friendship with Ana was enthralling. The war diaries of her first husband's regiment in the Great War brought almost forgotten history lessons into sharp focus. The diaries informed my own family history too since we know little of either of my grandfathers' wartime experiences. My knowledge of the Second World War was also scanty, although I remember the partisans being talked about as we holidayed in Yugoslavia – in the 1960s, memories of the war were still fresh for the people we visited in Ljubljana and Zagreb. Researching Bill Hudson's experiences and those of his colleagues in SOE opened a window on another aspect of twentieth-century European history and informed my understanding of Mary and Germano's experiences and the experiences of their good friends, the Morgans and the Parsons. Learning Mary's story and the stories of so many of the people around her I gained insight into

| *Mary teaching a character class at Primošten, ca. 1980, courtesy of Patricia Deane-Gray.*

the effects of revolution and war, and displacement and loss on so many lives. I found new appreciation for the resilience and determination of the dancers who worked so hard to convey their artistry to new audiences and a generation of students far from the Imperial Theatres of St Petersburg and Moscow.

Finally, though, in making my way on this journey to tell Mary's story, I discovered that my debt to her is much greater than I thought. She influenced my personal development subtly and more deeply than any of my academic teachers and she stands alongside my parents who supported my early ambitions and gave me the opportunity to learn ballet with her in the first place.

APPENDIX I
THE RUSSIAN BALLET IN CARICATURES

The album contained ninety-four cartoons of the most
famous people of the day in the ballet world.

Nicolai Legat, "The Story of the Russian School".

Towards the end of the nineteenth century, Nicolai and Sergei Legat
developed their joint interest in caricature. They were encouraged by
Fyodor Stravinsky, who promised to be the first subscriber for a published
collection. Their album, "*Русскій балетъ въ каррикатурахъ*", or "The
Russian Ballet in Caricatures", was published in 1902–1905. It contained
ninety-four coloured lithographs in a white leather binding lettered in gold
and one copy was presented to Tsar Nicolas II. Legat says in his memoir that
the "original" caricatures are held at the theatrical museum established by
the art collector Alexei Bakhrushin, now the Bakhrushin Theatre Museum
in Moscow.

The caricatures capture almost all of the soloists, principal dancers
and ballet masters in the Mariinsky company in the first few years of the
twentieth century, together with some well-known guest artists, and the
more important conductors, musicians and backstage artists. As Legat says,
they were the "most famous people of the day in the ballet world" and the
caricatures capture some of the grace and spirit of the years when Petipa,
Johansson and Cecchetti led the company before the upheavals of the first
decade of the twentieth century. (Nijinsky had not graduated from the
Theatre School by then and was just too young to be included.) In terms of
draftsmanship, they are technically accomplished, and colour and shading
are both subtle and meticulous. Contemporary photographs are black

and white, so the colours and detail of the caricatures bring the Mariinsky costumes to life. Each is a single figure and probably even the simplest makes reference to a particular role, event or character trait through the costume or the inclusion of a key accessory. The brothers' witty observations and visual comments certainly would not have been lost on the subjects and their friends and colleagues.

Well over a century later, the Legats' caricatures continue to appear as single images to accompany articles, on book covers and as illustrations, although not always in colour. If opportunity allows, they are best appreciated as the brothers intended, as a folio of coloured portrayals to celebrate the Mariinsky ballet at the turn of the nineteenth century.

The frontispiece to the album shows the two brothers working together on the caricature of their good friend Alfred Bekefi. Nicolai wields pen and ink (and smokes a cigarette, in spite of Johansson's abhorrence of the habit), while Sergei paints in the colours with a double-ended brush. As was the custom, Nicolai wore wigs for performances but by drawing attention to his already-thinning hair he was making a joke at his own expense, while emphasising Sergei's youthful good looks. The two images of Nicolai and Sergei individually show them in their costumes for "Raymonda" in which Sergei was well known in the lead role of Jean de Brienne and Nicolai as the troubadour, Béranger.

As for most caricatures, the faces and hair are more finely drawn and finished than the bodies although most of the clothes and costumes are also very detailed. For some of the ballerinas, they are merciless in showing facial hair, exaggerated noses and chins, and weighty bosoms and thighs. Other faces, Johansson's for example, are close to being true portraits, and only out-of-proportion heads and unnatural poses make them caricatures. Armpit hair is also in evidence, conspicuous in Pavlova's case, although by the early 1900s it was generally removed for performances. It is possible that the Legats were poking fun at an occasion when Pavlova failed to do so. Many of the men who are not in costume appear to be heavy smokers.

At the time, several families had more than one member in the company. As well as Nicolai and Sergei, their sister Evgenia and her husband, the musician Ivan de Lazari, were also in the Mariinsky. (Vera Legat had already married and left the stage.) Christian Johansson is accompanied in the collection by his daughter Anna, as is Marius Petipa by his daughter, Maria. Enrico Cecchetti appears with his wife, Giuseppina de Maria. Mathilde Kschessinskaya is joined by her father Felix and her brother Joseph, and Lydia

Kyasht by her brother Georgiy. Natalia Matveeva was the wife of Alexander Shiryaev and Ekaterina Geltzer was married to Vasiliy Tikhomirov.

The dancers who come directly into Mary's story – Olga Preobrazhenskaya, Evgenia Eduardova, Elena Poliakova and Tamara Karsavina, as well as Legat himself – are all included in the collection. Preobrazhenskaya is drawn in her costume for the Butterfly in "Les Caprices du papillon". She first danced the title role in 1893, replacing Varvara Nikitina. Although Johansson took much persuading that she, only a *coryphée*, was capable of replacing an established ballerina, it was a breakthrough for Preobrazhenskaya, whom Johansson unkindly called a "hunchbacked devil" because of her less than perfect physique. Her costume can be seen in a photograph with Legat in the 1939 edition of his memoir and the Butterfly was one of her favourite roles. Karsavina, Eduardova and Poliakova were relatively junior members of the company and may not have achieved recognition for a particular role. The caricature of Karsavina shows her in a simple white tutu with her hair in a simple low bun that may be rehearsal dress. Eduardova has no headdress but the bodice of her *tutu* has coloured shoulder straps and she has a ribbon tied in a bow around her upper arm. Her expression is coquettish or teasing, and the Legats seem to have picked up on the aspect of her dancing described by Franz Kafka and documented by Johanna Laakkonen. Poliakova has distinctive gold ribbons in her hair and the fabric of her bodice, which has stars on it, extends as an overskirt to her pink *tutu*.

Although it is not possible to identify more than a few of the costumes, the roles and the ballets would have been those the dancers were particularly well known for and which were popular with audiences. Pavlova's references her recent success in the role of Nikiya in "La Bayadère" since she wears a simple *tutu* and carries a flowing white scarf that characterises the *pas de deux* in the "Kingdom of the Shades" scene in Act III. Her first performance in 1902 surprised and delighted the audience with its dramatic interpretation. Kschessinskaya reluctantly had to pass on the role due to her pregnancy, but wrongly assumed that Pavlova was too weak a dancer to enjoy great praise. Vassily Stoukolkin is the drummer in the Hindu dance in the temple scene in Act II of the same ballet. As well as Nicolai and Sergei in their costumes for "Raymonda", both Alexander Gorsky and Georgiy Kyasht are shown wearing the same costume for Béranger. "The Pharaoh's Daughter" is represented by Nikolai Aistov as the Pharaoh and Stanislav Gillert is Father Nile from the same ballet (complete with trident in one hand and in the other a crocodile on a leash which has a ibis perched on its head). Almost certainly, Evgenia Lopoukhova is in her costume for the Lace Doll in "The Fairy Doll". (Like Nijinsky, her siblings Lydia and Fedor were too young to have graduated into the company.) Many of the images show dancers in character costume – Alfred Bekefi and Felix and Joseph Kschessinsky were all famous character dancers – and they also show how important character dances and character roles were within the *répertoire*. Joseph Kschessinsky is in the role of Birbanto in Petipa's 1899 revival of "Le Corsair".

Some of the vignettes associated with the caricatures do stand out, however. Kschessinskaya is portrayed in the costume for "La Esmeralda", her favourite role in the ballet of the same name, with her own pet goat, named for the heroine's pet goat Djali, prancing beside her. A live goat continues to appear in performances of the ballet by the Bolshoi and other companies, while a goat is shown in a lithograph from around 1844 of Fanny Cerrito as Esmeralda. Kschessinskaya wears outsize diamonds in her ears, a reference to her habit of wearing her own jewellery on stage, including diamonds and emeralds as large as "walnuts" according to Bronislava Nijinska, the lavish gifts of her lover the Tsarevitch Nicholas and others of the Imperial family. In an article for the *Dancing Times* (February 1966) to mark the fiftieth anniversary of Kschessinskaya's debut as Aurora, Karsavina describes her dramatic and moving performance as Esmeralda, saying that she danced as much for her "own delight" as for the audience.

The Italian ballerina Pierina Legnani is in her costume for Odette in "Swan Lake" in which she received acclaim from critics and audiences alike. She sent a wreath to the choreographer Lev Ivanov on the occasion of his fiftieth anniversary benefit performance in 1899 inscribed "*de la part d'Odette*". Legnani retired from the stage in 1901 and her inclusion in the collection indicates the high regard in which she was held as a guest artist. Another Italian ballerina, Henrietta Grimaldi, is drawn as Giselle in the mad scene in the ballet. She holds a sword by its point, dragging it behind her, and her hair is loose, although perhaps her expression is a little more mischievous than deranged. While the sword with which Giselle kills herself is an obvious clue to the ballet, a photograph of Preobrazhenskaya with Legat in the ballet's flower scene shows her wearing a similar *tutu* with broad horizontal stripes. Again, Grimaldi's caricature shows the esteem in which she was held as a guest artist.

Maria Petipa is portrayed in Spanish costume and with castanets, befitting her fame as character dancer. Her body is in a deep sideways tilt, and she appears more buxom than most of her photographs suggest. As her common-law husband, Sergei may have enjoyed the exaggeration of her bosom but Shiryaev does observe in his memoir (in "Alexander Shiryaev: Master of Movement") that she had "thin legs and a heavy torso", adding that she did not have good technique and constantly muddled her steps. She was celebrated for a number of Spanish dance roles, including *divertissements* in "Carmen" and the Chocolate variation in "The Nutcracker". Olga Tchumakova, Nicolai's common-law wife, is shown wearing a gold laurel wreath on her head, big gold hoop earrings and a Roman-inspired *tutu*. Possibly, the costume is from Petipa's "The Vestal". She would have been in her twenties and is rather plain-looking. Alfred Bekefi is in costume for a character role. He specialised in Hungarian dances and regularly partnered Maria Petipa. The flowers decorating his black hat, the wide fringed trousers and short waistcoat, reference costumes from the Transdanubia region.

Shiryaev, the noted teacher and choreographer of character dance, was just two years older than Nicolai. His caricature shows him in a sailor costume which Shiryaev himself says was for his *matelote*, based partly on an earlier version of the dance by Bekefi (see "Alexander Shiryaev: Master of Movement"). In contrast to all the other caricatures, however, Shiryaev's legs are impossibly twisted together. In the *matelote*, a sailor's hornpipe, the dancer's legs twist and untwist while the upper body does not move, so the Legats' caricature clearly captures the essence of Shiryaev's performance. In 1900, he danced the *matelote* with Bekefi in the revival of "Graziella", and later, with both Bekefi and Preobrazhenskaya, as a *pas de trois*. (Preobrazhenskaya based her celebrated solo, the "French Sea Cadet", on this *matelote*.)

Lev Ivanov died in 1901, before the album was published, but the brothers would hardly have thought that he should not be included. He is captured in a camel overcoat over pinstriped trousers looking calm and pensive, his head wreathed in cigarette smoke. His shoes are in need of repair and turn up at the toes, a reference to his perennial shortage of money; Johansson's wry comment on his death, recalled by Legat in his memoir, was "it must have been his debts strangled him".

Cecchetti is all in green, holding a violin, but instead of a formal tailcoat, the tails are insect wings. In his memoir, Cecchetti recounts how, in "Les Caprices du papillon", he appeared as the Grasshopper in green make up (carefully mixed from blue and yellow to avoid the poisonous arsenic in green make up) and a tight green cap with antennae. During a performance, one of the antennae caught on his wing and pulled off the cap to reveal his hair and the outline of his green face. He says that an "excellent" caricature appeared in one of the papers and, although this may not have been by the Legats, theirs must have been inspired by the same event. The libretto for the ballet was based on Yakov Polonsky's poem, "The Grasshopper Musician" and Cecchetti appeared as the Grasshopper in Petipa's revival of his ballet in October 1895. This short work has not been revived since but was popular in the late 1800s and early 1900s.

Petipa's caricature is more serious. It shows him as the old man he was in the early 1900s, in evening dress complete with the chain of miniature medals used for evening dress on his lapel, a watch chain across his waistcoat and pince-nez. He is leaping in a near *grand jeté* and carries a banner which reads "Петербургскій Балетъ", or "St Petersburg Ballet", signifying his life-long devotion and commitment to the Mariinsky Theatre. The caricature may have been completed during, or shortly after, the time when Petipa was being forced by the then director Vladimir Teliakovsky to retire from his position. The Legats may have taken the opportunity to make a pointed comment to the authorities on Petipa's stature and to ensure that his legacy was not forgotten.

Unlike most of the others, Johansson's caricature is reverential. Like Petipa, he is in evening dress, but weating the old-fashioned knickerbockers, black stockings and patent leather shoes that he must have worn for class. He carries his violin and is gesticulating with his bow, as he did when teaching. His face in profile shows him with a serious, if not downright severe, expression looking towards the recipient of his gesture. Like Petipa, he would have been in his late eighties, with a full head of white hair, bushy white eyebrows and a moustache. As can just be seen, his eyes are light blue. Where Petipa is slightly hunched in his shoulders and has a genial half-smile, Johansson carries himself erect and commanding. Although several memoirs describe him as stooped towards the end of his life, here the brothers are also referring to his impeccable style and elegance. The caricatures of Johansson, Petipa and Cecchetti are grouped on one page in Gregory's "The Legat Saga" over the caption "The Holy Trinity", a phrase which must have been used by Legat. (Later, and also reproduced in "The Legat Saga", Legat drew what he called "The Unholy Trinity of the Camargo Society", P.J.S. Richardson, editor of the *Dancing Times*, Edwin Evans, music critic of *The Times*, and Arnold Haskell, critic and writer.)

Around the same time, Nicolai and Sergei must have done a number of caricatures that do not appear in the folio – one of Petipa is reproduced as the endpiece in Nadine Meisner's biography, "Marius Petipa", for example. After his brother's death, Nicolai continued to draw the people around him, and himself, making light of the troubled times that followed publication of the album. Later, in England, his style became sparer and more graphic, with a bold use of colour, as shown, among others, in the caricature of Anton Dolin in the collection of the Legat Foundation at the National Arts Education Archive. His caricatures of animals and of round faces drawn on the lids of cheese boxes are reproduced in "The Legat Saga" and are also held at the National Arts Education Archive.

ACKNOWLEDGEMENTS

The following have kindly provided permission to quote passages or to reproduce photographs or illustrations:

Patricia Deane-Gray MBE for passages from an interview with Maria Zybina tape-recorded around 1980, and for a photograph of Zybina teaching at Primošten.
Tamara Jakasha for photographs of Maria Zybina.
Katherine Mason for the self-caricature of Oskar Harmoš.
The Legat Foundation for passages from the memoirs of Nicolai Legat and caricatures by Nicolai Legat; for illustrations from "The Legat Saga"; for passages from "Heritage of A Ballet Master: Nicolas Legat"; and for a photograph of Legat.
Davor Schopf, co-author, with Mladen Mordej Vučković, of "Ana Roje", for a passage from this biography.
The Royal Ballet School Special Collections for the photograph of Legat and Zybina.
Steve Fuller for passages from the war diaries of the Bedfordshire Regiment available on www.bedfordregiment.org.uk (copyright under the Open Government Licence for public sector information is acknowledged, see www.nationalarchives.gov.uk/doc/open-government-licence/version3/).
The Wellington College Archive for the passage from the College Yearbook, 1923.

Every effort has been made to trace copyright holders and to obtain their permission for the use of copyright material. The author and publisher apologise for any omissions and would appreciate being notified of any corrections that should be incorporated in future reprints or editions of this book.

BIBLIOGRAPHY

A.B. [Briger, Andrew]. "Nicolas Legat." *Ballet*, January 1952.

Albert, Gennady and Bouis, Antonina W., transl. *Alexander Pushkin: Master Teacher of Dance*. The New York Public Library, 2001.

Amery, Julian. *Approach March; a Venture in Autobiography*. Hutchinson, 1973.

Anderson, Jack. *The One and Only: The Ballet Russe de Monte Carlo*. Dance Books Ltd., facsim. 2010. Dance Horizons, 1981.

Anon. "A Chapter in the History of Russian Ballet. The Life Story of Maestro Nicolas Legat." *The Dancing Times*, June 1926.

———. "An Evening of Ballet." *The Dancing Times*, July 1958.

———. "Colet House – the 9th Studio." 4 May 2009. https://rememberthewindow. wordpress.com

———. "Colonel D.T. Hudson" [Obituary]. *The Times*, 10 November 1995.

———. "Death of Monsieur Nicolas Legat." *The Dancing Times*, February 1937.

———. "Distinguished Visitor" [Anatoly Borzov]. *The Beckenham Journal*, December 1965.

———. "Elena Poliakova" [Obituary]. *The Dancing Times*, February 1973.

———. "Enrico Cecchetti." *The Dancing Times*, June 1959.

———. "Enrico Cecchetti. 1850–1928." *The Dancing Times*, December 1928.

———. "Federation of Russian Classical Ballet." *The Dancing Times*, January 1951.

———. "Federation of Russian Classical Ballet." *The Dancing Times*, December 1958.

———. "Harlequin Ballet." *The Dancing Times*, December 1959.

———. "John Gregory" [Obituary]. *The Independent*, 31 October 1996.

———. "M. Nicolas Legat, The School of Classical Ballet" [Obituary]. *The Times*, 25 January 1937.

———. "Maga Magazinović a Pioneer of Modern Dance in Serbia." *The Information Service of the Serbian Orthodox Church*, 1 December 2011.

———. "Margarita Froman Dies: Famed Prima Ballerina." *Willamantic Daily Chronicle*, 25 March 1970.

———. "Maria Zybina." *The Dancing Times*, September 1958.

———. "N. Nicolaeva Legat" [Obituary]. *The Dancing Times*, January 1971.

———. "Nicolas Legat, The Life Story of a Great Artiste." *The Dancing Times*, April 1937.

———. "Off Stage!" [Anna Northcote]. *The Dancing Times*, October 1980.

———. "Off Stage!" [Oskar Harmoš]. *The Dancing Times*, July 1960.

———. "Olga Preobrajenska" [Obituary]. *The Dancing Times*, February 1963.

———. "Paul Dukes February 10, 1889–August 27, 1967." *The Times*, 28 August 1967.

———. "Russian Ballet Association." *The Dancing Times*, August 1938.

———. "The Russian Ballet – Revival of 'Petrouchka.'" *The Times*, 25 October 1930.

———. "Two New Companies" [Ballet Legat]. *The Dancing Times*, November 1951.

Anthony, Gordon. *Ballerina, Further Studies of Margot Fonteyn*. Home & Van Thal Ltd., 1945.

Antze, Rosemary Jeanes. "Nesta Toumine's Legacy: From the Ballets Russes to the Ottawa Ballet." In *Canadian Dance, Visions and Stories*. Dance Collection Danse Press/es, 2004.

Argyle, Pearl. "Nicolas Legat, An Appreciation." *The Dancing Times*, March 1937.

Atkin, Malcolm. *Section D for Destruction: Forerunner of SOE*. Pen and Sword Books, 2018.

Attlee, C.R. *As It Happened*. W. Heinemann, 1954.

Auty, Phyllis. *Tito: A Biography*. Penguin Books Ltd., 1974.

Auty, Phyllis, ed. and Glogg, Richard ed. *British Policy towards Wartime Resistance in Yugoslavia and Greece*. The Macmillan Press Ltd., 1975.

Baer, Nancy Van Norman, ed. and Garafola, Lynn, ed. *The Ballets Russes and Its World*. Yale University Press, 1999.

Bailey, Roderick. *Forgotten Voices of the Secret War: An Inside History of Special Operations During the Second World War*. Ebury Press, 2008.

Bargarić, Marina. "Pavel Froman's Stage Designs for the Hrvatsko Narodno Kazaliste in Zagreb." *Music in Art: International Journal for Music Iconography* 30 no.1/2, 2005.

Baronova, Irina. *Irina: Ballet, Life and Love*. University Press of Florida, 2005.

Beaton, Cecil. *Ballet*. Allan Wingate (Publishers) Ltd., 1951.

Beaumont, Cyril. *Ballets of Today*. Putnam, 1954.

Beaumont, Cyril W. *Complete Book of Ballets*. Putnam, 1937.

———. *Michel Fokine and His Ballets*. Dance Books Ltd., 1996. C.W. Beaumont, 1935.

———. *Supplement to Complete Book of Ballets*. Putnam, 1942.

———. *The Diaghilev Ballet in London*. The Noverre Press, 2017. Putnam, 1940.

———. *The Romantic Ballet as Seen by Théophile Gautier*. C.W. Beaumont, 1932.

Benois, Alexandre and Britnieva, Mary, transl. *Reminiscences of the Russian Ballet*. Putnam, 1941.

Beumers, Birgit, ed., Bocharov, Victor, ed., and Robinson, David, ed. *Alexander Shiryaev: Master of Movement*. Le Giornate del Cinema Muto, 2009.

Binney, Marcus. *Secret War Heroes*. Hodder & Stoughton, 2005.

Borzov, Anatoly. "The Russian Rope That Tied Them in Knots." *The Dancing Times*, January 1966.

Bourman, Anatole, and Lyman, D., col. *The Tragedy of Nijinsky*. Greenwood Press, 1970. McGraw-Hill, New York, 1936.

Bowlt, John E. *Moscow & St. Petersburg 1900–1920: Art, Life & Culture of the Russian Silver Age*. The Vendome Press, 2008.

Bowlt, John E., ed., Tregulova, Zelfira, ed., and Giordano, Nathalie Rosticher, ed. *A Feast of Wonders: Sergei Diaghilev and the Ballets Russes*. Skira Editore S.p.A., 2009.

Brahms, Caryl. *Footnotes to the Ballet*. Peter Davies Ltd., 1936.

Brillarelli, Livia, and Oslansky, Deborah, transl. *Cecchetti. A Ballet Dynasty*. Arts Inter-Media Canada/Dance Collection Danse Educational Publications, 1995.

Brod, Max, ed. *The Diaries of Franz Kafka, 1910–1913*. Schocken Books, 1948.

Brown, Ismene. "Black-Out Ballet: The Invisible Woman of British Ballet," 11 December 2012. theartsdesk.com.

Bruce, H.J. *Thirty Dozen Moons*. Constable & Company Ltd., 1949.

Buckle, Richard. *Buckle at the Ballet. Selected Criticism by Richard Buckle*. Dance Books Ltd., 1980.

———. *Nijinsky*. Simon and Schuster, 1971.

Celi, Claudia. "Cecchetti, Enrico." In *International Encyclopedia of Dance: A Project of Dance Perspectives Foundation, Inc.* Oxford University Press, online edition 2005.

Clarke, Mary. "Karsavina, Tamara." In *International Encyclopedia of Dance: A Project of Dance Perspectives Foundation, Inc.* Oxford University Press, online edition 2005.

———. "Kathleen Crofton" [Obituary]. *The Dancing Times*, January 1980.

———. "Moira Shearer" [Obituary]. *The Guardian*, 2 February 2006.

———. "Mona Inglesby" [Obituary]. *The Guardian*, 10 October 2006.

Clarke, Mary, ed. and Vaughan, David, ed. *The Encyclopedia of Dance and Ballet*. Peerage Books, 1977.

Cohen, Selma Jeanne, ed., and Dance Perspectives Foundation, ed. *The International Encyclopedia of Dance: A Project of Dance Perspectives Foundation, Inc.* Oxford University Press, 2005.

Commire, Anne, ed. and Klezmer, Deborah, ed. *Dictionary of Women Worldwide: 25,000 Women Through the Ages*. Gale/Yorkin Publications, 2006.

Cooper, Artemis. *Cairo in the War 1939–1945*. John Murray, 1989.

Coton, A.V. "Ballet in Opera." *The Spectator*, 11 February 1955.

Craine, Debra and Mackrell, Judith. *The Oxford Dictionary of Dance*. Oxford University Press, 2010.

Crofton, Kathleen. "Madame Olga Preobrajenska: Some Impressions of Her Teaching." *The Dancing Times*, January 1951.

———. "Some Early Ballet Films, Kathleen Crofton on Pavlova." *The Dancing Times*, July 1954.

———. "Unqualified Success!" *The Dancing Times*, January 1966.

Crosland, Margaret. *Ballet Lovers' Dictionary*. Arco Publications, 1962.

Currie, Jean. "Nine Days in Russia." *The Dancing Times*, March 1965.

———. "Nine Days in Russia, Part 2." *The Dancing Times*, April 1965.

Danilov, A.A., ed. and Hammond, Vincent E., ed. *The History of Russia: The Twentieth-Century*. Herron Press, 1996.

Danilova, Alexandra. *Choura: The Memoirs of Alexandra Danilova*. Dance Books Ltd., 1987.

Davidson, Basil. *Partisan Picture*. Bedford Books Ltd., 1946.

Davidson, Gladys. *Ballet Biographies*. Warner Laurie, 1952.

Deakin, F.W. *The Embattled Mountain*. Oxford University Press, 1971.

Deane-Gray, Patricia MBE. *The Legacy of Legat*. Hilarion, 2017.

Djilas, Milovan. *Wartime*. Harcourt Brace Jovanovich, Inc., 1977.

Dolin, Anton. *Alicia Markova: Her Life and Art*. Allen, 1953.

———. *An Autobiography*. Oldbourne Book Co. Ltd., 1960.

Dukes, Sir Paul KBE. *An Epic of the Gestapo: The Story of a Strange Search*. Cassell and Company Ltd., 1940.

Duncan, Isadora. *My Life*. Liveright Publishing Corporation, 2013. Boni and Liveright, 1927.

Dunjohn, Kenneth. "Colet House." *Hammersmith and Fulham Historic Buildings Group Newsletter*, no. 30, 2014.

Durrell, Lawrence. *White Eagles Over Serbia*. Faber and Faber Limited, 1957.

Eglevsky, André and Gregory, John. *Heritage of a Ballet Master: Nicolas Legat*. Dance Books Ltd., 1978.

Eliot, Karen. *Albion's Dance: British ballet during the Second World War*. Oxford University Press, 2016.

Fisher, Hugh. *The Story of the Sadler's Wells Ballet*. Adam and Charles Black, 1954.

Fokine, Vitale, transl. *Fokine, Memoirs of a Ballet Master*. Constable & Company Limited, 1961.

Fonteyn, Margot. *Margot Fonteyn: Autobiography*. W.H. Allen, 1989.

Foot, M.R.D. "Obituary: Colonel D.T. Hudson." *The Independent Online*, 13 November 1995.

———. *SOE An Outline History of the Special Operations Executive 1940–46*. Arrow Books, 1984.

Forrester, F.S. *Ballet in England: A Bibliography and Survey*. The Library Association, 1968.

Foster, Andrew R. *Tamara Karsavina: Diaghilev's Ballerina*. Andrew Foster, 2010.

Frame, Murray. *The St. Petersburg Imperial Theaters: Stage and State in Revolutionary Russia 1900–1920*. McFarland & Company, Inc., 2000.

Gadan, Francis ed. and Maillard, Robert ed. *A Dictionary of Modern Ballet*. Methuen and Co. Ltd., 1959.

Garafola, Lynn. *Diaghilev's Ballets Russes*. Oxford University Press, 1989.

———. *Legacies of Twentieth-Century Dance*. Wesleyan University Press, 2005.

Gottlieb Robert, ed. *Reading Dance: A Gathering of Memoirs, Reportage, Criticism, Profiles, Interviews and Some Uncategorizable Extras*. Pantheon Books, 2008.

Gray, Richard T., Gross, Ruth, V., Goebel, Rolf, J., and Koelb, Clayton. *A Franz Kafka Encyclopedia*. Greenwood Publishing Group, 2005.

Gregory, John. "A Visit to the Bolshoi School." *The Dancing Times*, May 1965.

———. "A Visit to the Kirov School." *The Dancing Times*, March 1965.

———. "Christian Johansson." *The Dancing Times*, February 1986.

———. "Legendary Dancers, Nicolai Legat." *The Dancing Times*, October 1987.

———. "Legendary Dancers, Pavel Gerdt." *The Dancing Times*, November 1987.

———. "Legendary Dancers, Pierina Legnani 1865–1923." *The Dancing Times*, December 1987.

———. "Letters from Johansson [Part 1]." *The Dancing Times*, March 1986.

———. "Letters from Johansson [Part 2]." *The Dancing Times*, April 1986.

———. "Letters from Johansson [Part 3]." *The Dancing Times*, May 1986.

———. "Letters from Johansson [Part 4]." *The Dancing Times*, June 1986.

———. "Letters from Johansson to Bournonville." *The Dancing Times*, July 1986.

———. *The Legat Saga*. Javog Publishing Associates, 1992.

———. "Why I Started a Ballet Company." *The Dancing Times*, February 1963.

Grey, Dame Beryl. *For the Love of Dance: My Autobiography*. Oberon Books Ltd., 2017.

Grigoriev, S.L. and Bowen, Vera, transl. *The Diaghilev Ballet 1909–1929*. Constable and Company Ltd., 1953.

Guest, Ivor. "Christian Johansson." In *Britannica Online Encyclopedia*, 21 December 2020.

———. *The Dancer's Heritage. A Short History of Ballet*. Penguin Books Ltd., 1960.

Hall, Coryne. *Imperial Dancer, Mathilde Kschessinska and the Romanovs*. Sutton Publishing Limited, 2005.

Haskell, Arnold and Clarke, Mary. *World Ballet*. Hulton Press Ltd., 1958.

Haskell, Arnold, L. *Ballet*. Penguin Books Limited, 1938.

Haskell, Arnold and Nouvel, Walter, collab. *Diaghileff. His Artistic and Private Life*. Victor Gollancz Ltd., 1947.

Haskell, Arnold and Richardson, P.J.S. *Who's Who in Dancing 1932*. The Noverre Press, facsim., 2010. The Dancing Times Ltd., 1932.

Hawkesworth, Celia. *Zagreb. A Cultural History*. Oxford University Press, 2008.

Henry, Robert. *A Village in Piccadilly*. J.M. Dent & Sons Limited, 1942.

Homans, Jennifer. *Apollo's Angels. A History of Ballet*. Random House Inc., 2010.

Hrbud, Višnja. "Froman, Margarita." In *Hrvatski biografski leksikon*. Leksikografski Zavod Miroslav Krleža, 1998.

———. "Harmoš, Oskar." In *Hrvatski biografski leksikon*. Leksikografski Zavod Miroslav Krleža, 2002.

Inglesby, Mona and Hunter, Kay. *Ballet in the Blitz, The History of a Ballet Company*. Groundnut Publishing, 2008.

Janković, Ivančica. "The Quest for Preserving and Representing National Identity." In *Dance in a World of Change: Reflections on Globalization and Cultural Difference*. Human Kinetics, 2008.

Jovanović, Milica. "Mlakar, Pia and Pino." In *International Encyclopedia of Dance: A*

Project of Dance Perspectives Foundation, Inc. Oxford University Press, online edition 2005.

Jovanović, Milica, Mlakar, Pia, and Mlakar, Pino. "Yugoslavia – Ballet." In *International Encyclopedia of Dance: A Project of Dance Perspectives Foundation, Inc.* Oxford University Press, online edition 2005.

Kafka, Franz. *Letters to Felice*. Schocken Books, 1973.

Kant, Marion. "Joseph Lewitan and the Nazification of Dance in Germany." In *The Art of Being Jewish in Modern Times*. University of Pennsylvania Press, 2008.

Karina, Lilian and Kant, Marion. *Hitler's Dancers: German Modern Dance and the Third Reich*. Berghahn Books, 2003.

Karsavina, Tamara. *Ballet Technique. A Series of Practical Essays*. Adam and Charles Black, 1956.

———. *Classical Ballet: The Flow of Movement*. Adam and Charles Black, 1962.

———. "Family Album – Carissima Maestra, A Memoir of Signora Beretta." *The Dancing Times*, November 1964.

———. "Family Album – Cavaliere Enrico Cecchetti." *The Dancing Times*, December 1964.

———. "Family Album – Platon Karsavin." *The Dancing Times*, October 1964.

———. "Family Album: 1 Pavel Andreevitch Gerdt." *The Dancing Times*, June 1964.

———. "Family Album: 2 Christian Petrovich Johansson." *The Dancing Times*, July 1964.

———. "Family Album: 4 Eugenia Sokolova." *The Dancing Times*, September 1964.

———. "Imperial Schooldays." *The Dancing Times*, December 1927.

———. "My Partners at the Maryinsky." *The Dancing Times*, December 1966.

———. "Nikolai Legat." *The Dancing Times*, August 1964.

———. "Origins of the Russian Ballet." *The Dancing Times*, September 1966.

———. "Planning the Practice." *The Dancing Times*, January 1957.

———. "The First Russian Aurora – Kschessinska." *The Dancing Times*, February 1966.

———. "The Supreme Teacher, Anna Christianovna Johannson." *The Dancing Times*, January 1965.

———. *Theatre Street*. Dance Books Ltd., 1981. W. Heinemann, 1930.

———. "Touring in Europe." *The Dancing Times*, November 1967.

Kavanagh, Julie. *Nureyev*. Pantheon Books, 2007.

Keeney, Jean Ashburn. "Dancing in the Grand Tradition." *The Day*, 29 September 1979.

Kemp, Peter. *No Colours or Crest: The Secret Struggle for Europe*. Cassell & Co. Ltd., 1958.

Kidd, C.A. *Trepča, A History of the Trepča Mines in Yugoslavia*. Unpublished corporate history of Trepča Mines Ltd., 1982.

Kingscote, Flavia. *Balkan Exit*. Geoffrey Bles, 1942.

Kosik, Viktor I. "Russian Ballet Dancers and Choreographers at the Belgrade Stage in the XX and Early XXI Centuries." *Accelerando: Belgrade Journal of Music and Dance* 2 no. 8, 2017.

Krasovskaya, Vera M. "Ivanov, Lev." In *International Encyclopedia of Dance: A Project of Dance Perspectives Foundation, Inc.* Oxford University Press, online edition 2005.

———. "Petipa, Marius." In *International Encyclopedia of Dance: A Project of Dance Perspectives Foundation, Inc.* Oxford University Press, online edition 2005.

Kulakov, Valery A. "Johansson, Christian." In *International Encyclopedia of Dance: A Project of Dance Perspectives Foundation, Inc.* Oxford University Press, online edition 2005.

Kyasht, Lydia and Beale, Erica, ed. *Romantic Recollections.* The Noverre Press, facsim., 2010. Brentano, 1929.

Laakkonen, Johanna. *Canon and Beyond. Edvard Fazer and the Imperial Russian Ballet 1908–1910.* Academia Scientiarum Fennica, 2009.

Large, David Clay. *Berlin.* Basic Books, 2000.

Lawson, Joan. "The Yugoslav Opera and Ballet." *The Dancing Times,* March 1955.

Lazzarini, Roberta. "Pavlova, Anna." In *International Encyclopedia of Dance: A Project of Dance Perspectives Foundation, Inc.* Oxford University Press, online edition 2005.

Leeper, Janet. *English Ballet.* Penguin Books Ltd., 1945.

Legat, Nicolas. "Anna Pavlova, Some Memories." *The Dancing Times,* March 1931.

———. "Folk Dancing in Russia." *The Dancing Times,* December 1927.

———. "Polanaise and Mazurka." *The Dancing Times,* April 1928.

———. "Russian Boyar Dance." *The Dancing Times,* November 1927.

———. "What Is 'Élan' in Dancing?" *The Dancing Times,* February 1937.

———. "Whence Came the 'Russian' School." *The Dancing Times,* February 1931.

Legat, Nicolas and Dukes, Sir Paul, transl. *Ballet Russe. Memoirs of Nicolas Legat.* Methuen & Co. Ltd., 1939.

———. "Twenty Years with Marius Petipa and Christian Johannsen. Pages from the Memoir of Nicolas Legat." *The Dancing Times,* April 1931.

———. "Famous Dancers I Have Known, I. Pages from the Memoirs of Nicolas Legat." *The Dancing Times,* May 1931.

———. "Famous Dancers I Have Known, II. Pages from the Memoirs of Nicolas Legat." *The Dancing Times,* June 1931.

———. "Limbering the Limbs for Practice." *The Dancing Times,* December 1932.

———. "The Making of a Dancer and Ballet Master, Pages from the Memoirs of Nicolas Legat." *The Dancing Times,* March 1931.

———. "The Secret of the Pirouette." *The Dancing Times,* August 1932.

———. "The Secret of the Pirouette, II." *The Dancing Times,* September 1932.

———. "The Secret of the Pirouette, III." *The Dancing Times,* November 1932.

Legat, Nicolas and Dukes, Sir Paul, transl. *The Story of the Russian School.* British Continental Press, Ltd., 1932.

Legat, Nicolas and Legat, Sergei. *The Russian Ballet in Caricatures (Русскій Балетъ Въ Каррикатурахъ),* 1903.

Legat, Nicolas and Legat, Sergei. *The Russian Ballet in Caricatures.* The Noverre Press, 2021.

Lendrum, Anna. *My Life in Ballet – A Russian Heritage*. Zeebra Publishing Ltd., 2004.

Leonard, Maurice. *Markova, The Legend*. Hodder & Stoughton, 1995.

Leshkov, D.I. *Marius Petipa*. C.W. Beaumont, 1971.

Lhotka, Jill. *Dance to the Challenge*. Jill Lhotka, 2013.

Lieven, Prince Peter and Zarine, L., transl. *The Birth of the Ballets-Russes*. The Noverre Press facsim., 2010. George Allen & Unwin, 1936.

Lifar, Serge. *A L'aube de mon destin chez Diaghilew. Sept ans aux Ballets Russes*. Editions Albin Michel, 1949.

Lockhart, R.H., Bruce. *Memoirs of a British Agent*. Pan Books, 2002. Putnam, 1932.

Lopoukov, Andrei, Shirayev, Alexander, Bocharov, Alexander, and Lawson, Joan, transl. *Character Dance*. Dance Books Ltd., 1986.

Lopukhov, Fedor. *Writings on Ballet and Music*. University of Wisconsin Press, 2002.

Macaulay, Alastair. "'Swan Lake' Discoveries Allow for a Deeper Dive Into Its History." *The New York Times*, 13 October 2015.

Macdonald, Nesta. *Diaghilev Observed by Critics in England and the United States 1911–1929*. Dance Horizons and Dance Books Ltd., 1975.

MacDonough, Giles. *Berlin: A Portrait of Its History, Politics, Architecture, and Society*. St. Martin's Press, 1998.

Mackrell, Judith. *Bloomsbury Ballerina. Lydia Lopokova, Imperial Dancer and Mrs John Maynard Keynes*. Weidenfeld & Nicholson, 2008.

Maclean, Fitzroy. *Disputed Barricade. The Life and Times of Josip Broz-Tito, Marshal of Jugoslavia*. Jonathan Cape, 1957.

———. *Eastern Approaches*. The Reprint Society Ltd., 1949.

Markand, Anna. *Kurt Jooss, The Green Table*. Routledge, 2003.

Markova, Dame Alicia DBE. *Markova Remembers*. Hamish Hamilton Ltd., 1986.

Marks, Leo. *Between Silk and Cyanide: A Codemaker's War 1941–1945*. HarperCollins Publishers, 1998.

Mason, E.C. "So You Want to Dance? A Teacher of Character Dancing" [Maria Zybina]. *Dance and Dancers*, October 1957.

———. "So You Want to Dance? Kyasht at the Empire" [Lydia Kyasht]. *Dance and Dancers*, April 1957.

———. "So You Want to Dance?" [Patricia Spalding]. *Dance and Dancers*, February 1957.

———. "So You Want to Dance? Teaching in a Great Tradition" [Anna Lendrum]. *Dance and Dancers*, January 1957.

———. "So You Want to Dance? The Influence of Pavlova" [Kathleen Crofton]. *Dance and Dancers*, November 1956.

Matthews, Peter. *House of Spies. St Ermin's Hotel, The London Base of British Espionage*. The History Press, 2016.

McCarthy, Kathy. "Ballet Is Air Fromans Breathe – Refugee Camp Taught Them What 'Matters.'" *The Day*, 28 June 1969.

McConville, Michael. *A Small War in the Balkans: British Involvement in Wartime Yugoslavia, 1941–1945*. Macmillan, 1986.

Meinertz, Alexander. *Vera Volkova, A Biography*. Dance Books Ltd., 2007.

Meisner, Nadine. *Marius Petipa, The Emperor's Ballet Master.* Oxford University Press, 2019.

Messerer, Asaf and Briansky, Oleg, transl. *Classes in Classical Ballet.* Dance Books Ltd., 1976.

Meylac, Michael, and Kelly, Rosanna, transl. *Behind the Scenes at the Ballets Russes. Stories from a Silver Age.* I.B. Taurus & Co. Ltd., 2018.

Milin, Melita. "The Russian Musical Emigration in Yugoslavia after 1917." In *17th IMS Congress.* Leuven, 2002.

Milton, Giles. *Russian Roulette: How British Spies Thwarted Lenin's Plot for Global Revolution.* Bloomsbury Press, 2013.

Moberg, Pamela, transl. "Pehr Christian Johansson: Portrait of the Master as a Young Dancer." *DanceView*, 1999.

Moore, Lillian. "Marius Petipa in America." *The Dancing Times*, December 1937.

Morris, Jan. *Oxford.* Oxford University Press, 1978.

———. *Trieste and the Meaning of Nowhere.* Da Capo Press, 2001.

Mosusova, Nadežda. "Are Folkloric Ballets an Anachronism Today?" In *16th International Congress on Dance Research.* Corfu, Greece, 2002.

———. "The Heritage of the Ballet Russe in Yugoslavia Between the Two World Wars." In *Proceedings of the Eleventh Annual Conference Society of Dance History Scholars.* North Carolina School of the Arts: Society of Dance History Scholars, 1988.

Mulley, Clare. *The Spy Who Loved: The Secrets and Lives of Christine Granville.* St. Martin's Press, 2012.

Nicholas, Larraine. *Dancing in Utopia. Dartington Hall and Its Dancers.* Dance Books Ltd., 2007.

Nicolaeva Legat, Nadine. *The Legat Story.* Cadmus Publishing, 2021.

Nicolaeva-Legat, N. "Dances of Russia, I. Mainly Geographical and Historical." *The Dancing Times*, January 1938.

———. "Dances of Russia, II. The Boyar Dance." *The Dancing Times*, February 1938.

———. "Dances of Russia, III. The Varlets' Dances." *The Dancing Times*, March 1938.

———. "Dances of Russia, IV. Dance of the Serving Maids." *The Dancing Times*, March 1938.

———. "Dances of Russia, IV [sic]. Village Dances – 'Derevenskia Pliasky.'" *The Dancing Times*, May 1938.

———. "Dances of Russia, V. Costumes." *The Dancing Times*, June 1938.

———. "Dances of Russia, VI. Tchastoushky." *The Dancing Times*, August 1938.

Nicolaeva-Legat, Nadine. *Ballet Education.* Geoffrey Bles, 1947.

———. "Dances of Russia, VII. 'Ukraine or Little Russia.'" *The Dancing Times*, September 1938.

———. "How I Came to England (i)." *Ballet*, February 1951.

———. "How I Came to England (ii)." *Ballet*, March 1951.

Nijinska, Irina and Rawlinson, Jean. *Bronislava Nijinska: Early Memoirs.* Holt, Rinehart and Winston, 1981.

Nijinsky, Romola. *Nijinsky.* Simon and Schuster Inc., 1934.

Norris, David A. *Belgrade. A Cultural History*. Oxford University Press, 2009.

Norton, Leslie. *Frederic Franklin: A Biography of the Ballet Star*. McFarland & Company, Inc., 2007.

Odom, Selma Landen, ed., and Warner, Mary Jane, ed. *Canadian Dance: Visions and Stories*. Dance Collection Danse Press/es, 2004.

Pagels, Jürgen. *Character Dance*. Indiana University Press, 1984.

P.D. [Dukes, Paul]. "Nicolas Legat and the Class of Perfection." *The Dancing Times*, February 1930.

Peručić Nadarević, Jasna. "Yugslavia – Modern Dance." In *International Encyclopedia of Dance: A Project of Dance Perspectives Foundation, Inc.* Oxford University Press, online edition 2005.

Petipa, Marius, Moore, Lillian, ed., and Whittaker, Helen, transl. *Russian Ballet Master, The Memoirs of Marius Petipa*. A. & C. Black Ltd., 1958.

Phelan, Andrew L. annot. *Tamara Karsavina, Beyond the Ballerina, Her Unpublished, Untitled Manuscript about the First Years in England*. Quail Creek Editions, 2018.

Pimlott, Ben, ed. *The Second World War Diary of Hugh Dalton 1940–45*. Cape, in association with the London School of Economics and Political Science, 1986.

Pintar, Marijana. "Roje, Ana." In *Hrvatski biografski leksikon*. Leksikografski Zavod Miroslav Krleža, 2015.

Pritchard, Jane, ed. *Diaghilev and the Ballets Russes, 1909–1929*. Victoria and Albert Museum, London in association with National Gallery of Art, Washington, 2013.

Pritchard, Jane and Hamilton, Caroline. *Anna Pavlova: Twentieth Century Ballerina*. Booth-Clibborn Editions, 2012.

Racster, Olga. *Master of the Russian Ballet: The Memoirs of Cav. Enrico Cecchetti*. The Noverre Press, facsim., 2013. Hutchinson & Co., 1923.

Rambert, Marie. "Marius Petipas – Choreographer." *The Dancing Times*, April 1926.

Rankin, Nicholas. *Ian Fleming's Commandos: The Story of 30 Assault Unit in WWII*. Faber and Faber Limited, 2011.

Roje, Ana. "Ana Roje and the Kirov Ballet." *The Dancing Times*, May 1958.

———. "The Art and Science of Teaching Ballet." *Dance Magazine*, December 1954.

Romanovsky-Krassinsky, HSH The Princess and Haskell, Arnold, transl. *Dancing in Petersburg. The Memoirs of Mathilde Kschessinska*. Dance Books Ltd., 2005.

Roné, Elvira and Hall, Fernau, transl. *Olga Preobrazhenskaya, A Portrait*. Marcell Dekker, Inc., 1978.

Rootham, Jasper. *Miss Fire: The Chronicle of a British Mission to Mihailovich, 1943–1944*. Chatto & Windus, 1946.

Roslavleva, Natalia. *Era of the Russian Ballet*. Victor Gollancz Ltd., 1966.

Ruvigny et Raineval, Marquis de. *The Plantagenet Roll of the Blood Royal: Being a Complete Table of All of the Descendants Now Living of Edward III, King of England*. 1994 Genealogical Publishing Co. Inc. T.C. & E.C. Jack Publisher, 1905.

Ruyter, Nancy Lee Chalfa and Ruyter, Hans C. "Pietro Coronelli: Dance Master of

Zagreb." *Dance Research* 7, no.1 April 1989.

Scheuer, L. Franc. "Two Celebrated Nurseries of Russian Ballet." *The Dancing Times*, December 1933.

Schopf, Davor and Vučković, Mladen Mordej. *Ana Roje*. Zaposlena d.o.o., 2009.

———. *Yuresha: Visions and Dreams*. Hilarion, 2011.

Schouvaloff, Alexander. *The Art of Ballets Russes: The Serge Lifar Collection of Theatre Designs, Costumes, and Paintings at the Wadsworth Atheneum, Hartford, Connecticut*. Yale University Press in association with the Wadsworth Atheneum, 1997.

Seitz, Albert, B. *Mihailovic, Hoax or Hero?* Leigh House, Publishers, 1953.

Sepahbody, Farhad. "Will Anyone Miss Us?" *The Iranian, Online*, 25 April 2003.

Serge, Wolkonsky, Prince, and Chamot, A.E., transl. *My Reminiscences. Volume 2*. 2012 The Noverre Press, fascim., 1924.

Serguéeff, Nicolas. "Memories of Marius Petipa." *The Dancing Times*, July 1939.

Simkin, John. "Paul Dukes." Spartacus Educational, September 1997. www.spartacus-educational.com.

"Sitter Out". "[Madame Nicolaeva's Class of Perfection]." *The Dancing Times*, November 1936.

———. "[Yugoslav National Opera and Ballet Company]." *The Dancing Times*, January 1955.

Sitwell, Sacheverell. *The Romantic Ballet from Contemporary Prints*. B.T. Batsford Ltd, 1948.

Smakov, Gennady. *The Great Russian Dancers*. Alfred A. Knopf, Inc., 1984.

Snodgrass, Mary Ellen, ed. "Christian Johansson 1817–1903." In *Encyclopedia of World Ballet*. Rowman & Littlefield, 2015.

Sokolova, Lydia, and Buckle, Richard, ed. *Dancing for Diaghilev*. John Murray, 1960.

Solly-Flood, P. "Pilgrimage to Poland." *Blackwood's Magazine*, May 1951.

Solway, Diane. *Nureyev: His Life*. Weidenfeld & Nicholson, 1998.

Starič, Jerca Vodušek. "The Concurrence of Allied and Yugoslav Intelligence Aims and Activities." *Journal of Intelligence History*. 5, no.1, Summer 2005.

Struchkova, Raisa S. "Gerdt Family." In *International Encyclopedia of Dance: A Project of Dance Perspectives Foundation, Inc.* Oxford University Press, online edition 2005.

Svetlov, Valerien, de Vere Beauclerc, H., Evrenov, Nadia, transl., and Beaumont, Cyril W., ed. *Thamar Karsavina*. The Noverre Press, facsim., 2019. C.W. Beaumont, 1922.

Sweet-Escott, Bickham. *Baker Street Irregular*. Methuen & Co. Ltd., 1965.

Taylor, Paul Beekman. "Gurdjieff and Prince Ozay," 2004. www.gurdjieff-bibliography.com.

Telyakovsky, V.A., and Dimitrievitch, Nina. "Memoirs." *Dance Research* 8, No.1, spring 1990.

———. "Memoirs: Part 2." *Dance Research* 9, no.1, spring 1991.

Tudor, Dawn, ed. and Armeanu, Hilary Hunt, ed. "Recollections of Legat." The Legat School, 1998.

Tugal, Pierre. "A Witness of a Glorious Past – Olga Preobrajenska." *The Dancing Times*, April 1952.

———. "A Witness of a Glorious Past, II – Lubov Egorova." *The Dancing Times*, June 1952.

———. "A Witness of a Glorious Past, III – Mathilde Kschessinska." *The Dancing Times*, January 1953.

Turner, W.J. *The English Ballet*. William Collins of London, 1944.

Volynsky, Akim and Rabinowitz, Stanley, J., transl. *Ballet's Magic Kingdom. Selected Writings on Dance in Russia, 1911–1925*. Yale University Press, 2008.

Walker, Kathrine Sorley. *De Basil's Ballets Russes*. Atheneum, 1983.

Wearing, J.P. *The London Stage 1920–1929: A Calendar of Productions, Performers, and Personnel*. Rowman & Littlefield, 2014.

Webb, Sam. "The Glorious Dead: Students Re-Enact Horror of Somme in Tribute to Former Pupils Killed in the Trenches of the First World War." *Online Daily Mail*, 9 November 2012.

Wharton-Tigar, Edward, and Wilson, A.J. *Burning Bright, The Autobiography of Edward Wharton-Tigar*. Metal Bulletin Books Limited, 1987.

Wicks, Wendy Roxin. *Tim Draper – From Eastman Theatre's Muses to the Founding of Rochester City Ballet*. Boydell & Brewer Ltd., 2014.

Wiley, Roland John. *A Century of Russian Ballet. Documents and Eyewitness Accounts, 1810–1910*. Dance Books Ltd., facsim., 2007. Clarendon Press, 1990.

———. *The Life and Ballets of Lev Ivanov: Choreographer of The Nutcracker and Swan Lake*. Clarendon Press, 1997.

Windreich, Leland, ed. *Dancing for de Basil – Letters to Her Parents from Rosemary Deveson, 1938–1940*. Dance Collection Danse Press/es, 1996.

Wingrave, Helen and Harrold, Robert. *Aspects of Folk Dance in Europe*. Dance Books Ltd., 1984.

Wolkonsky, Prince Serge. "A Memory of Petipa." *The Dancing Times*, March 1928.

Wolkonsky, Prince Serge, and Chamot, A.E., transl. *My Reminiscences. Volume 2*. The Noverre Press, fascim., 2012. Hutchinson & Co., 1924.

Zabina [sic], Maria. "The National Dances of Europe." *The Dancing Times*, June 1963.

Zozulina, Natalia. "Christian Johansson: Petipa's Great Associate." *Sovietsky Ballet*, no. 1, 1988.

Zybina, Maria. "A Dance from Georgia." *The Dancing Times*, September 1963.

———. "A Dance from Georgia (2)." *The Dancing Times*, October 1963.

———. "A Dance from Hungary." *The Dancing Times*, June 1964.

———. "A Dance from the Ukraine." *The Dancing Times*, August 1963.

———. "A Kolo from Yugoslavia." *The Dancing Times*, November 1964.

———. "A Simple Russian Dance." *The Dancing Times*, July 1963.

———. "Italian Tarantella." *The Dancing Times*, October 1964.

———. "The Czech Polka." *The Dancing Times*, February 1964.

———. "The Polish Mazurka." *The Dancing Times*, January 1964.

INDEX

Maria (Mary) Zybina is represented by the initials "MZ."